SOLD
by
OWNER!
Secrets of Selling Your House
without a Broker's Fee

Dedication

To my wife Barbara, who read the manuscript many times and gave much advice.

To my children, John and Olga, who put up with my countless hours in front of the computer.

To my parents, Colonel J.M. Dubois and Olga G. de Dubois, for their continuous encouragement.

My thanks to David Conti of Liberty House for his many ideas and suggestions.

SOLD by OWNER!

Secrets of Selling Your House without a Broker's Fee

Maurice Dubois

LIBERTY HALL
PRESS™

LIBERTY HALL PRESS books are published by LIBERTY HALL PRESS, an imprint of TAB BOOKS. Its trademark, consisting of the words "LIBERTY HALL PRESS" and the portrayal of Benjamin Franklin, is registered in the United States Patent and Trademark Office.

First Edition
Third Printing

Copyright © 1988 by TAB BOOKS
Printed in the United States of America

Library of Congress Cataloging-in-Publication Data

Dubois, Maurice.
Sold by owner!

Includes index.
1. House selling. I. Title.
HD1379.D78 1988   333.33′8   88-6762
ISBN 0-8306-9316-5 (pbk.)

TAB BOOKS offers software for sale.
For information and a catalog, please contact:

TAB Software Department
Blue Ridge Summit, PA 17294-0850

Questions regarding the content of this book
should be addressed to:

Reader Inquiry Branch
TAB BOOKS
Blue Ridge Summit, PA 17294-0214

Contents

Introduction

Welcome to the world of real estate selling. Handling the sale of your own property can be rewarding not just in dollars, but in the joy you get any time you accomplish a rather complex task.

THE ADVANTAGES OF SELLING YOUR OWN HOME

There are several advantages to selling your own home. The first and foremost, of course, is the savings of a rather hefty real estate brokerage commission. A 5% commission on a $250,000 house is $12,500. How about at 7%? That's a larger chunk, amounting to $17,500.

Another advantage is that, if you're handling your own selling, you don't get half of the real estate agents in town walking through your home with—or without—their clients. By talking directly to buyers, you can weed out the lookers from the serious prospects, and work only with the legitimate ones.

You do your own advertising. You advertise as much or as little as you wish. In a strong sellers' market, it means getting a sale faster than if you had listed with an agent.

You work at your own pace. If you need to be out of town, you stop advertising, and no stranger will set foot on your property. Also, you only set appointments to show the home when it's convenient for you. You'll have no calls from agents who are sitting in an office with their clients, ready to come peek at your house.

You know the property intimately. You see it everyday; you live it year-in and year-out. You are the one who is most interested in selling it, the most able to talk about it intelligently and with complete confidence: what its utility bills run; what its best amenities are, especially those hidden to the first-time looker; and where the schools, churches, and shops are located.

THE DISADVANTAGES OF BEING YOUR OWN SALESPERSON

Along with the advantages come the disadvantages. The biggest one is, naturally, the amount of time and effort it takes to truly merchandise the property correctly. It takes time. So, to those folks for whom time is truly golden, a good real estate agency can be a real boon.

The cost of advertising is another disadvantage. Some ads can be rather expensive. And if you get little or no response from an ad, what have you accomplished? Nothing besides learning not to run that ad again.

In a normal market it usually takes a while longer to sell your own home than if you have a strong agency with a lot of top-notch agents trying to sell it for you. Most people don't have the time it takes to do a perfect job of merchandising their house. But as a whole, I believe the advantages far outweigh the disadvantages.

Consider this. Even a 5% commission on your $250,000 house is 25% of your equity, if your equity in the house is $50,000. And a 7% commission would be 35% of your equity. What if your equity were only $25,000? The 7% commission would be a whopping 70% of your equity.

BECOME A GOOD FSBO

As an active real estate broker, I often deal with folks attempting to sell their own homes. In the business we call them *"fisbos"* (For Sale By Owners or FSBOs).

Too often FSBOs assume that by placing an ad in the classified section of their local paper and standing a For Sale By Owner sign in the front yard, they'll quickly sell their home. This only happens in a hot *sellers' market*. More often than not, the market is fairly well balanced, or it may be a *buyers' market*— when there are more homes for sale than there are buyers. Selling a home usually takes a long and discouraging time in those circumstances.

A COURSE IN SALESMANSHIP

This book is a course in real estate salesmanship for the individual working on selling his own property. My aim is not to teach you to be a professional real estate salesman, but to guide you in merchandising your home knowledgeably.

The book will take you from step one, which is getting your mind set for the challenge, to showing you how to advertise, write the contract, and close the deal.

In the Appendices of this book are many forms that will help you with the selling process. If you need to copy any of the legal forms I've included, I suggest using an enlarging copier set for the percentage indicated at the upper right-hand corner of the forms. This will result in full legal-size copies.

I've also included a glossary of many real estate terms that you may come across in this book, as well as when dealing with agents, lenders, and title and escrow companies.

Not everyone wants to sell his or her own home. But those who do so deserve a guide written by someone who has been a FSBO—many of the homes I built when I was a young builder I sold myself—as well as a professional broker. I've been on both sides of the fence, and I understand the needs and feelings of both sellers and agents.

Keep in mind that anyone can do anything—within reason. You *can* sell your own home. If you understand the problem, and know the formula, you can arrive at the solution. This book will help you understand the problem, and it will give you the formula. With a little effort you'll find the solution.

1

Expectations & Attitudes

YOUR OBJECTIVE IN SELLING YOUR OWN HOME IS TO GET THE TRUE WORTH OF the property, with the least cost to you. Ideally, that means receiving top dollar with no expenditure on your part for either broker fees or advertising expenses. That's a rare occurrence. It could happen if you kept the property on the market a year or two—an impractical situation for most folks.

Real estate is generally a family's least-liquid asset. *Liquidity* means, of course, the degree of ease or difficulty in converting an item into cash. An item has liquidity if it can be sold for cash in a very short time. If you had a "Widget" that sold for $1.50, and everyone needed and wanted one, you would have a very liquid asset. At that price, anyone could afford it, so it would be easy to sell.

BE PATIENT

Houses are not easy to sell, even for the real estate professional. Unless you're in an extremely hot market—a sellers' market—you must expect the house to be on the market a number of weeks or months before it sells. To a great extent, this is true even if you place your property with a broker. So patience is one of the important ingredients in the successful selling of a property.

While price is probably the single most important item affecting the sale of real estate—anything will sell if it is cheap enough—there are two other factors that are more important if you're not willing to sell dirt-cheap. Those factors are location and condition. I'll go into these elements, as well as price, in later chapters of this book.

BE REALISTIC

If you look at the whole picture before you attempt to sell your home, you'll be able to make an intelligent decision about the marketability of your property—what to expect, and what can only be a dream. Too many home sellers are in a fantasyland. Be realistic. If you determine how difficult your particular property will be to sell—considering size, condition, location, price, and terms—you will have the right attitude towards your intended task. Your attitude—you might call it your mental holding power—can be as much a part of your success as is your knowledge. Without the right attitude, you won't persevere long enough to give success a chance.

Once you've assimilated the techniques of this book, you must be honest with yourself. You have to compare what's for sale in your area with what you have to offer. If yours is better than average, you'll either sell it quickly at a modest price, or you'll take the normal amount of time to sell it, but get more money for it. If your property is below average in condition or location, then accept that fact, and sell it for less—or perhaps sell with better terms (such as owner financing). Or you might be able to do something about the condition: clean it up, fix it up.

I must stress again that price can make anything very saleable, or extremely hard to sell. If you have a $100,000 house and price it at $70,000, you have a very marketable property, a very liquid asset. If you price it at $120,000, then you have a tough object to merchandise. You can distort liquidity with price. So keep in mind that you're trying to get the highest *reasonable* value for your property, and that it will take *time* to do so.

The Marketplace

WHEN YOU GET READY TO PUT YOUR HOME ON THE MARKET, YOU MUST FIRST determine the status of the marketplace to learn how long it might take to sell. If you keep up with the business news of your local newspaper, you'll get a good idea of the real estate market conditions in your local, as well as regional, area.

TALK WITH LENDERS

Talk to your banker. He'll give you a good idea from his point of view. If he doesn't sound convincing about his knowledge of the local real estate market, talk to lenders who specialize in home mortgages. Loan officers with savings and loan associations, mortgage bankers, and loan officers with mortgage companies will be glad to give you information concerning the marketplace.

THE KNOWLEDGEABLE TITLE AND ESCROW COMPANIES

Other good sources of information are *title and escrow companies*. Title companies (some states don't have title companies) insure the title of your home against possible legal clouds on ownership. Often, title companies perform another important function: they "close" real estate transactions, acting as escrow agents. In other words, they are the disinterested third parties who make sure the terms of the real estate contracts between sellers and buyers are carried out, and that the loan papers are signed according to the lenders' instructions.

Title company people know how real estate is moving in their area, what type of loans are the most prevalent at any given time, and what rates and terms are associated with those loans. They can give you a very close estimate of the cost of closing any number of possible financing transactions that may work with your property. They want your business, so they'll be very happy to answer questions.

Call several title companies to see how each one feels about current market conditions in your area. It's possible that one will give you an optimistic view, while another will be somewhat pessimistic. By talking to several, you'll have a good handle on your marketplace.

In some states, escrow companies handle the closing transactions, instead of title companies. They can be as good a source of information as the title companies, since they know what properties are selling with what type of loans.

Real estate trade journals are another good source of information. If you haven't acquired a good enough "feel" for the marketplace from the above sources, then visit a public library. You'll find magazines on home sales, real estate investing, and home building that can give you further insight into market conditions.

YOUR OWN MARKET—HOT OR COLD?

Keep in mind that even though home sales may be great nationwide, you may be in an area that is suffering from a glut of homes or an outflow of people. Conversely, the country can be an economic basketcase, and you could be sitting in a hot spot for home sales due to one or more reasons; therefore, your most reliable information will come from local people and local news.

Once you have a good general idea of the local home market, you'll know what to expect in the following two important areas:

- TIME: The stronger the market, the sooner you'll sell your house. Under ideal circumstances, two to four weeks will be enough to find a buyer. If the market is slow, it may take four to six months. And if things are drastically poor—in other words, high interest rates, weak local economy, and high unemployment—it could take you a year to sell it.

- PRICE: As with time, the strength of the market will cause price to fluctuate 10–15% or even more, one way or the other. As a rough example, a home worth $100,000 in normal times could bring $115,000 under ideal times and only $85,000 during a housing slump—perhaps only $70,000 in a severe recession.

Armed with enough knowledge of the marketplace, you'll know how to price your property and how long to expect to wait for a buyer.

HELP FROM REAL ESTATE BROKERS

One final source of marketplace information is real estate brokers. In fact—without attempting to patronize my profession—they are the best source. Call several and get their opinion. Tell them that you'll be selling your house in a few months, and that you want to start getting an idea of what you can expect.

Don't get discouraged if you've read this far, have checked your marketplace, and found that it will take you a year to sell your home. There are alternative ways of selling that can drastically cut the time required to sell under almost any economic condition. You'll find the answers in the financing chapters.

The House: Making It Presentable

BEFORE YOU GET YOUR FANCY SIGN FOR THE FRONT LAWN, GET YOUR HOME IN the best shape possible. Don't do anything in the way of merchandising it until you take a careful look at the house.

Determine what needs to be done, then get those items taken care of. Economically speaking, *you must be realistic* about what you can and can't do, and what you should and should not do, to get the property in its best shape.

THE THINGS TO DO

Start by looking at the house as if you were the buyer. The first thing he or she sees is the outside of the property. The yard must be neat and the exterior of the house in good repair. You won't get any appointment calls off your lawn sign if the lawn needs mowing, or the shrubs are overgrown, or there's rubbish in the flower beds. If you advertise heavily in the newspapers, you might make many appointments to show the property, but few prospects will get out of their cars if the outside doesn't look inviting.

If it's summer, make sure the lawn is watered, reasonably weed-free, and *always* neatly cut and trimmed. If it's winter, depending on your location and winter's severity, there's much less to do to the lawn, except to have any trash picked up. If you live in a snow area, the more snow the better—except on walks and drives. Keep them clean.

If paint is peeling or highly faded, repaint the siding and trim. Paint will do more for a house than almost anything else. It's the best improvement for the money.

It's hard to place a critical eye on something you see day-in and day-out, year after year. But force yourself. If you were buying this home, are there any items that are in absolute need of repair: a loose board, a broken shutter, peeling paint?

On the inside, if it's been a few years since you painted, now is the time to do it. As on the outside, interior paint is the best improvement for the money.

Inspect the walls, doors, trim, and ceilings. Patch any holes, dents, and especially cracks, then paint or refinish as necessary.

Rent a carpet cleaner, and do a thorough job on your rugs. Work out all spots and stains as much as possible. Repair any loose carpet or vinyl tile. Clean and wax all hard floors.

Eliminate all clutter. Clutter makes a house look smaller, older, and inefficient. Put away any items that don't look right or that add to the clutter. Don't stuff the items in closets. Closets need to look spacious, and they don't when full of junk. Either get rid of your excess items, or put them in boxes and stack them neatly in the garage. But remember, the garage won't look right either if it's stuffed with junk or too many boxes. If you've got too much clutter, store the excess in a public storage building.

REPAIR ANYTHING INEXPENSIVE TO FIX

Inside the house, repair anything that is an eyesore but is inexpensive to fix. In this category, I would include torn screens, broken doorknobs, broken light fixtures, missing or burnt-out light bulbs, electric switch and outlet plates heavily laden with paint, leaky or broken faucets, and other items you've put off fixing because they don't bother *you* much in their present condition. A missing doorknob or a broken door hinge will bother the potential buyer much more than it does you.

Cleanliness, especially in the baths and kitchen, goes without saying. The house *must* be clean, and it should be as odor-free as possible. Be careful with pets. They *do* hurt the value of a house. You must realize that your sense of smell dulls to familiar odors. But to someone coming in for the first time, even a mild odor can be a real turn-off.

When you're done with the facelift, you must consider the major items. If your roof *looks* old, that's one thing. If it leaks all over the house, that's an entirely different matter. You have no choice but to replace it, even if it takes borrowing money to do it. The buyer will discount *considerably* for structural or water-leakage problems. This type of problem can also be a sticky legal problem if it is not fixed and the fault is hidden from the buyer.

If you're in a hot climate in the middle of summer and your cooling unit doesn't work, then you *must* fix or replace it. You can't sell a house if the prospective buyers are sweltering while trying to make a favorable decision on your home.

If your carpets have a few minor stains and some repairable breaks or tears, then fix the tears and work as much as possible on removing the stains. You can use carpets from closets for repairs in open areas, then put tile in the closet. But if the carpets are worn and soiled beyond help, replace them. If you have a small home, be careful not to replace only the worst areas. Small homes need one color of carpet throughout to make them look larger. Flooring is second in importance to paint in showing off a neat home. Fresh carpet and tile could be a real selling feature to your prospective buyer.

You get the idea of the do's. Get the home in as neat, fresh, and clean condition as possible with a minimum outlay of money. Don't leave anything obvious undone.

THE THINGS NOT TO DO

What you do must be cost-effective. Four hundred dollars worth of paint and $500 worth of attractive landscaping on the front yard could bring you an additional $3000 for the home. But don't change the heating unit just because it looks old and has a few minor items that need fixing. Have it serviced, and ask the serviceman to clean it and make it look as neat as possible. A thousand dollars spent on a new heater won't get you $1000 more for the house. But the *lack* of a $1000 heater could drop the value of the property by $2000.

Don't waste an excessive amount of money trying to get the house to look like a model home. If a few hundred dollars will do it, that's fine. But if it would take a few thousand dollars, it's not worth it. Keep in mind that you are selling a used product, and unless you have been an immaculate homeowner throughout your years in the house, there's no way you'll get it to look like-new unless you spend a fortune updating it.

Don't install storm windows or more insulation just to have a more saleable property. Four thousand dollars spent for storms and extra ceiling insulation, if you can find it that cheap, might get you an additional $500 when you sell the house—a mighty poor investment at that late a time in your ownership of the home.

Don't paint and redecorate to your taste if your taste leans to the wild or unusual. Stay with standard, soft colors, preferably off-whites for walls, earth tones for floors. Anything that will appeal to the masses.

If your house is a basketcase and most of the houses in the neighborhood are the same, don't spend much money on it. Fix the most blatant flaws, and hope for the best. There are the few rare times when no work expended and no money spent is the best alternative. In other words, if your $50,000 home could be worth $65,000 if you spent $12,000 to fix it, let an enterprising buyer get a good deal. Gambling $12,000 to gain $3,000 is not smart economics.

THE DIAMOND-IN-THE-ROUGH

There's one particular situation that I'd like you to be aware of. If you're in a neighborhood that has appreciated considerably, and all of the homes around you are worth substantially more than yours, but are not much larger than yours, then you may have a diamond-in-the-rough, and you need to take advantage of it.

Let's assume you bought your home 20 years ago for $20,000. Your area is now an extremely desirable location. Your neighbors' homes are all worth (and are actually selling for) $250,000, but you can't find anyone who will give you even $180,000 for yours. Then it's worth spending some money to improve; $5,000 worth of landscaping and $20,000 worth of fix-up and improvements would certainly be money well spent:

VALUE	$180,000
SHRUBS	5,000
FIX-UP	20,000
COST	$205,000
SELL	250,000
GAIN	$ 45,000

If you're in this situation, hire professional help: a landscaper, a decorator, a builder, and a real estate broker. Pay them a fee to suggest ways to improve. Get bids on the improvements. You may be thousands ahead in the long run.

THE HOME IMPROVEMENT CHECKLIST

If you make a list of the items that need attention, you can determine which will help the sale, which you have time and money to work on, and which aren't going to be a good investment. If you'll photocopy and complete the checklists in Appendix A, you can then sit down with paper, pencil, and calculator, and figure out a game plan for getting maximum return for your effort. The list will walk you about the house through the eyes of a buyer; an extremely picky buyer.

If an item is fine as it is, then check OK and go on to the next item. If it needs work, make a short note of the work needed in the space provided. When you've gone through the entire house inside and out, make your calculations to see what's worth doing and what you need to pass up on.

4

Setting the Price

SETTING PRICE IS NO MYSTERY. THE MARKET WILL ACTUALLY HAVE ALREADY SET it for you, because your house will sell for an amount between the top price and the bottom price of all property in your neighborhood. Rarely will you beat the best price—very rarely. Rarely, also, will you not be able to get at least what the least expensive house in your area has sold for. So when you discover what the top price is, and have a good idea of the size, location, and condition of that top property, then you'll know what more than likely is the very top limit of what you could get for your house.

The price of existing for-sale property will give you a good idea of what the competition in your neighborhood will be. If you deduct between 2–8% from the asking price of each property, you'll have a close estimate of what the final selling price will be under most normal market conditions. A house listed for $100,000 will generally sell for $92,000 to $98,000. If the terms are good, such as an assumable low-interest first lien and a low down payment coupled with low-interest seller financing, the selling price will probably be the same as the asking price, and could even go higher.

A SELLERS' MARKET CAN BE A BONANZA

If you're in a sellers' market, you may find that all homes are consistently selling at or above the listed price. This is where knowing the market is so vital.

In a true sellers' market, it is not unusual for buyers to line up at your door to place bids. But even if that's the case, you still must know where to start.

Drive around your neighborhood and jot down the address and general outside appearance of every house that has a for-sale sign. Write down the name of the agent and phone number listed on each sign. When you get back to your house, sort them out so you don't call the same person more than once, in case an agent has more than one listing.

Photocopy the Property Information Sheet (Appendix B) and fill out a copy for each property. When you're done, compare the houses on those sheets to your house. This will give you a good idea of what price to ask for the house. When you use this method, keep some items in mind.

First: Many people will have overpriced their property.

Second: The houses that are for sale by owner are often the least accurately priced.

Finally: Sellers don't set price; buyers set price.

SOLD COMPARABLES

A good indication of what to expect for your house will come from *sold comparables*, houses that have sold within the past one to six months.

Because real estate agents handle the great majority of home sales, they have the best record of sold comparables, through their *Multiple Listing Service (MLS)*. When you call agents to find out about the price of some of the houses you're wanting information on, also ask for prices on houses that have already sold in your area. They will generally be happy to give you the information. Most will offer to do a free *market analysis*—a comparison of your house to houses that have sold and are for sale. You may or may not want to have a real estate agent give you a free market analysis. A good agent will be able to give you a very good idea of price on the phone; that will save both of you time.

In some states, the sale price of the property is a matter of record. Check with the County Clerk or County Recorder to see if this is the case in your state.

Call the tax offices of your city, school district, or county to see if they have information that will show what recent sales have been like in your area. Local lenders will also have a good idea of values in your area.

Tax offices always have an appraisal on all the properties in their jurisdiction. Some have appraisals that reflect market value quite accurately. Ask the people at the tax office if that's the case. The tax offices will usually have information about the number of square feet of living area in each property they tax. That's very useful information.

SQUARE FOOTAGE

Most home builders offer information about their houses which can show you how to price your house according to its size. Let's say you have a property that is as desirable as a certain group of new homes: excellent condition, good location, attractive exterior appearance. Visit the new homes and get information about amenities, financing, square footage, and price. Use the information on the houses that are close to yours in size and amenities. Figure out the price per square foot for those new houses, and multiply the average price per square foot by the size of your house to come up with a value for your property.

Here are some examples:

Let's say you find the average price per square foot for a house like yours at Victorian Estates is $85. Their houses range from 3,000–4,000 square feet (heated living space). Your house is 35' × 100' excluding the garage. That's 3,500 square feet. You simply multiply 3,500 by $85 to get a value of $297,500.

If the average price per square foot for a three-bedroom, two-bath home with no garage in Cozy Corners is $40, and your house is similar, with no garage, and it is 24' × 42', then you multiply $40 by 1,008 to come up with $40,320. But if yours has a garage, you're not looking at the right properties to get a good comparison.

CO-OPS AND CONDOS

With condominiums and co-op units you could have a more complex situation if you have an unusual location with unique buildings and features. Comparables will be hard to find. But it will be easy if yours is one of countless other units that are basically equal in size, location, and amenities.

You may have to do more research to get an accurate idea of price. Make sure you document your findings. Here's an example: you have a 1,500 square-foot dwelling, on the first floor, in a complex with a large, well-maintained pool and recreational area, with a superb security system. You look around and find many other units of similar size, with equal amenities, but none have as complex a recreational area. The other units are selling for $100 per square foot. You're asking the same price per square foot for yours. You would demonstrate what a bargain yours is by showing prospective buyers the data on the comparables, including details on the competition's shortcomings and your property's strengths.

When doing a market analysis, you'll first check the *actual* sales price of units that have sold within the last six months or so in your own complex, or in similar complexes located very close to yours. If you don't find enough comparable sales this way, then you'll check units in other parts of town, keeping in mind the following:

- Amenities
- Location
- Number of units in building
- Density of buildings, and types of buildings
- Size of all units in buildings, with respect to number of rooms per unit
- Size of units in square feet
- Age of development

With co-ops you won't be able to come up with comparables by looking into public records that list recent sales in your area. Private corporations or partnerships do not have to disclose financial transactions, so you will have to rely more on what is available for sale, and not what has actually sold. That's not very accurate, but it might be your only choice.

OBTAIN AN APPRAISAL IF NECESSARY

If you do your best to determine the correct price for your home, but you still don't feel you have a handle on true value, then you need to obtain a professional *appraisal*. You can look in the yellow pages for real estate appraisers, but you may do better to work through a loan company. They should be able to have it done quicker, and by someone very familiar with your type of property.

FHA Appraisal

If your home is worth $100,000 or less, then an *FHA appraisal* is the best route. It will cost you about $175, and the expense is worth it.

To begin with, if you sell your house with an FHA-insured loan, you'll already have the appraisal and you'll know what maximum the house will sell for under that type of loan. The appraisals are good for six months, so you have plenty of time to get the house sold and still use your appraisal.

Also, you'll have an unbiased value. An appraiser's only business is to determine home values, not to get you to list your property with his firm, as might be the case with a real estate agent.

Conventional Appraisal

For more expensive homes, you'll need a *conventional appraisal*. The cost will be higher—$100–$200 more—but the more expensive the home, the more desirable it is to have a professional appraisal.

When you're showing your property to a prospective buyer, the appraisal is a *very* convincing sales tool. That's because most buyers don't want to take the seller's word on value; they want to hear it from a third party. Look at the pricing system used in other selling situations, starting with "normal" real estate, when an agent is involved. The agent is the third party. He wins the buyer's trust; he convinces the buyer that the seller's price is fair, even though in most states the agent is working for the seller and has a legal duty to represent the seller's interests.

When buying a new car, the buyer looks at the sticker price. That's a third party—the factory—telling him the price the dealer is requesting is fair and correct. By setting it high enough, the buyer feels he got a "deal" when there's a discount, even though the buyer might be aware the pricing system is a bit distorted.

When buying clothes, the price label is on the garments. The third party, the store, is verifying price to the buyer. The store is telling the buyer that the salesclerk's price is correct and fair.

So the price of almost everything we buy is confirmed to us by a third party. And no matter what type of market you're selling your home in, if you're doing the selling yourself, you will do *much better* if you have the opinion of a third party to confirm your price.

INTELLIGENT PRICING

Let's assume you don't have an appraisal. Once you know what houses have sold for, and what they are currently selling for in your neighborhood, then you must price your home intelligently. Be realistic. Look at the price from the buyer's point of view—from what other buyers have been willing to pay for houses in your neighborhood.

Let's look at what happens when the competition—your neighbor—sells his house. Assume he has priced his house right, say at $100,000, allowing himself some negotiating room. In this case, because it's well priced, assume his negotiating margin is 2%. He accepts an offer for $98,000. Then there's the brokerage fee, commonly around 6%. We won't take into account any points or closing costs. So $98,000 less 6% is a net of $92,120. That's what your neighbor will *receive* for his property.

If you've done your homework, you'll know that your house could be very competitive at that same $100,000. So you set your price at $98,900. Then you negotiate the same 2% reduction. You'll net $96,922, almost $5,000 better than your neighbor. That's your profit for handling the sale of your own home.

DEPRECIABLE AMENITIES

When you look at the above example, bear in mind that buyers rarely pay for frills or relatively minor amenities. If you had the exact same floor plan as your neighbor, but you had a trash compactor and an intercom system, it's doubtful you'd get another few hundred dollars for your home over what your neighbor received. And if you did, I would attribute it more to slightly different market conditions, or better buyer acceptance by the particular buyer of your home, than to the amenities. Even builders have a hard time receiving total value for some of the amenities they build into their homes.

Large amenities, such as pools, have a poor and disappointing track record for returning a substantial share of the money invested in them. A good example again is the automobile industry. If you purchase a fairly basic new car for $15,000, in a year it might be worth $12,000. If you pay $18,000 for that same model, but with leather interior and all the goodies, at the end of a year it probably won't be worth much more than $13,000. The *car* didn't depreciate any more. It depreciated the same $3,000 as the basic model did. But the frills depreciated an additional $2,000.

The frills, or amenities as we call them in the housing industry, depreciate at an exceedingly fast rate. While a house may go up in price in relation to a car, amenities will depreciate almost immediately, and your house will be worth not much more than comparable houses without amenities.

As an example, assume your 2,000 square-foot house is worth exactly $100,000. That's $50 per square foot. You install a $15,000 pool and a $5,000 patio cover. You now have $120,000 invested in a house in a homogeneous neighborhood of $100,000 houses. Your cost in the house is now $60 per square foot.

It's unlikely you'll sell the house for $120,000 in a normal market. In a hot market, perhaps you can. In a slow market, you'll give the pool and patio cover away. In the normal market, you might get $55 per square foot. That's $110,000. You must assume you had $10,000 worth of fun out of your amenities.

Now let's say that, instead of the pool, you had added a fourth bedroom to your house for the same $20,000. The bedroom and one closet are 14' × 16'. You've added 224 square feet to your house in addition to making it a most desirable house for a large family. Because there are not many four-bedroom houses built in the 2,000 square-foot range, there would probably not be too many four-bedroom houses in your neighborhood. Your house would be one of a few, and it would be very desirable for a large family. People will often pay full price for a *need*, while they generally won't pay full price for an amenity. In a normal market a family with three children would be more likely to pay your price of $120,000 for your four-bedroom home, even though they're paying $53.95 per square foot, than they would be to pay the $110,000 for the 2,000 square-foot home with a pool and patio cover.

PUSH THE MAJOR AMENITIES

If, because of large amenities, you have to price your house higher than the neighborhood warrants, you need to do a good sales job supporting the amenities. Write down, and have handy, the wonderful things that the beautiful pool and patio cover will do for the new owner: refreshing dips in the pool for the parents on hot summer evenings; wonderful exercise for the children; merry parties with friends and relatives by the pool, under the cool patio cover. One old fellow justified his pool to me by swearing that his three now-grown children had never been tempted to try drugs because they were always busy around the pool all summer. No one will ever know if that's the reason he raised healthy kids. But who cares? What a good sales tool he showed me. How about asking your prospect this question: "Aren't your kids worth an extra $10,000?"

5

Advertising

KNOWING THAT YOUR PROPERTY LOOKS GOOD AND THAT YOU'VE PRICED IT COR-
rectly gives you a big psychological push when advertising it. You can talk it up
forcefully, knowing quite confidently that what you say about it is true.

THE IMPORTANCE OF CURB APPEAL

I must reiterate that the outside appearance of the property is your greatest
advertising tool. If it looks great, just a simple for-sale sign will often be enough
to get you a buyer. We call this *curb appeal* in the real estate business.

We'll be looking at some great forms of free advertising, but I'd like you
to keep in mind that not all advertising is free. When a real estate broker sells
a house, his commission is not all profit. He will have spent good money for
advertising.

You also must accept the fact that you'll have to spend a certain amount
of money for advertising. After studying the media available, and deciding how
long it will take to sell, set a realistic advertising budget.

THE YARD SIGN

Here's the first and best advertising tool: the *yard sign*. Many, many sales
that brokers make are a direct result of yard signs. The most successful real

estate professionals know what a good yard sign means. They spend a lot of money for large, fancy ones. *You* don't need a very expensive, fancy one. But you do need a *good* one.

What I mean by a good one is a *professionally-painted* one that tells the buyer you're serious about the sale of your property.

Here's an example:

```
FOR SALE
BY OWNER

3-2-2 with formals
POOL

555-5555
Shown by appointment
BROKERS WELCOME
```

Let's dissect this most important piece of advertising:

- The size of the sign—the metal area—should be exactly the same size as the largest residential yard sign in use by brokers in your town. Stop and measure a couple to be sure. That way you won't be violating any city ordinances, and you'll have one as large as the competition's.

- Make the background white and the lettering red. This will give it the greatest visibility.

- Place it in the center of your yard, as much towards the street as possible.

- Place it firmly in the ground. Nothing looks worse than a leaning sign.

- Always keep the sign neat, clean, straight, and new-looking. Wax it with car wax if you need to. If it gets damaged, replace it. An old-looking or damaged sign will hint that the property has been on the market too long, and that there might be something wrong with the house.

- The words "For Sale" and the phone number should be large.

- If you have a very special amenity, such as a pool, that should also be prominent.

The sample sign above tells the buyer that the house has three bedrooms, two baths, and a two-car garage. It has a formal living room and dining room.

It gives important, basic information. If you give people basic information from the start, you won't be bothered by callers who are looking for something other than what you have. Of course, you don't want to overdo it and make the sign too busy.

The last two items on the sign we'll discuss in future chapters. For now, suffice it to say that they should *never* be left off the sign.

THE BROCHURE BOX

A *brochure box* is a small mailbox on a metal stake set in the ground as close to the street as possible. It will hold a supply of Property Information Sheets (Appendix B) filled out for your home—I'll discuss this form later in this chapter. Letter a sign on the front of it that says: "Free, take one." This is optional, but the *very good* real estate brokers use one on each of their properties. Haven't seen one? Are there any *very good* real estate brokers in your area?

BULLETIN BOARDS

Bulletin boards are a great source of *free* advertising that is not available to real estate agents. Many supermarkets and public buildings have bulletin boards so people can advertise free. Take advantage of them. Make up neat, well-written signs in red ink on index cards, or on cards that the store supplies, and place them on as many free bulletin boards as you can find in an area five or six miles around your house. Talk up the house on the card as you would if you were advertising in a long newspaper ad. Make the important features stand out.

Every week or two, go back to where you placed the cards. Replace those that are damaged or missing. Some may have been buried by new cards. This is free advertising, so keep up with it. Often the person that buys your house is your neighbor.

WORD OF MOUTH

Word of mouth advertising is also free. Talk about your house with everyone you meet. Think of "10 up, 10 down, and 10 across." That means your first task should be to talk to your neighbors within 10 doors down, 10 doors up, and 10 doors across the street. Ask them if they know anyone who might be interested in buying your house. Leave them your brochure.

Talk to your doctor, his secretary, the grocery store cashier, your neighbors, friends, and family. Don't be shy. This is easy and free advertising that often leads to a sale.

Even to a perfect stranger, such as a store clerk, you can say something like, "I have a lovely home for sale. Do you know anyone who is looking for a three bedroom home in south Rocky City?"

You'll be surprised how many will tell you that they have an acquaintance, friend, or relative who has been talking about buying a house in Rocky City. Get a name and telephone number, as well as the name of the person giving you the referral. When you call the interested party, tell him Mr. Jones at the supermarket told you that he knew he was interested in purchasing a home and you'd like to show him yours, or maybe send him some information. If he sounds interested but only wants information, you'll send him one of your Property Information Sheets.

Top-notch real estate brokers work up Property Information Sheets on all their listings. Most real estate firms, though, only include plain facts on each property. *You* must do better than that. You must market your real estate on features and benefits.

My example of a Property Information Sheet (Appendix B) asks only for facts. You need to add features and benefits. For example, "A large fireplace for cozy winter evenings." Or how about, "On a cul-de-sac street for the utmost safety of your youngsters." People don't buy a house because it has a 20' × 30' living room; they buy it because the living room will hold their grand piano and they can enjoy great parties with a large group of friends in it.

You don't have to go to a great deal of expense to work one up. Here's what you do:

If you don't have an instant camera, borrow one. Take a picture of your house with the best possible light—whenever the sun is behind you and you can get the most contrast and the clearest picture. Try to use a camera with an adjustable or self-adjusting lens so you can get as much detail in the picture as possible. Paste the picture on a copy of the Property Information Sheet. Type in as many details and benefits as possible, and take the sheet to a jiffy printer. You should be able to have him make you 100–200 copies for five to ten dollars.

Don't worry about a halftone for the picture. If you took a reasonably good picture, the printer's copier will make sufficiently clear copies. They'll show plenty of detail. Remember, a picture is worth a thousand words. Does your home have a great pool? Then include a picture of it as well.

You might want to try placing the brochures at the free bulletin boards mentioned earlier, along with, or in lieu of, the index cards. You'll be able to use them in some places, but not in others. The brochure is totally superior to the card, though.

PLACEMENT OFFICES AND COMPANY NEWSLETTERS

Large companies and military bases offer housing assistance to their new people. Your brochure should go to each reasonably large company or military base, along with a letter explaining financing options. You'll learn to work up financing for your buyer in later chapters. These placement offices are *free* advertising. Make the most of their services.

Company newsletters are another form of *free* advertising. You may find newsletters, other than from your company, which are mailed to you free and would accept your house ad. Make full use of every opportunity to advertise your house.

NEWSPAPERS AND MAGAZINES

There are two types of newspapers: those that carry the news, and those that carry only advertising. Both are useful for advertising your property, but you must discover which one will do you the most good.

Study your local papers carefully. See which ones carry the most advertising from real estate brokers. Remember, they're the professionals; they know what works best for the price-range house that you are selling. I'm not talking about display advertising, but small classified ads. Display advertising is generally prohibitive in cost. Brokers use display ads not only to attract buyers, but also to show themselves off and attract listings.

If you check the papers carefully and find that several local brokers are advertising heavily in the local "Shopper's Special"—a simple little paper that carries only advertising—and that the homes they're advertising are in the same price range as yours, then you will want to give a lot of attention to that paper, because it's obviously working for the brokers who advertise in it.

You'll want to use other newspapers as well, but perhaps not with as much emphasis. If you keep track of your calls, as I'll discuss in the chapter on telephone answering, you'll know where your advertising is doing the most good. I've found that the least expensive papers with free distribution are the most effective for medium- and lower-priced homes.

There are a few specialty magazines that might be useful in advertising your property. Local home magazines are an example. But look at them very carefully. Many are either too expensive or too generalized to do the FSBO much good.

There are some magazines specifically for FSBOs. As with the newspapers, you'll have to experiment to see if one can do you any good.

RADIO AND TELEVISION

If you have a local cable television station that has a free (or relatively inexpensive) bulletin board, you could snag a buyer through this medium. And in a small town a radio station might work for you. The ads would probably be quite inexpensive. But, generally, both radio and television are prohibitive in cost and not recommended.

THE ADS

There's a great difference between the advertising that brokers do and the advertising that *you* must do. Brokers, as a general rule, aren't really pushing a particular property with each ad. If you read their ads, you'll see that they are fishing ads, or call-getter ads. They advertise the most interesting properties to get the most calls. Once they have a captive and qualified buyer, they find out his needs and switch him to a property that will suit him better than the one advertised. They use the shotgun approach to advertising.

Because you are selling only one property, the ad has to be more specific—a rifle-with-a-scope approach to advertising. While you don't want to give it all away in the ad (you may not get the prospect to come look at the property if you overdescribe it), do give the buyer some of the following information:

- Indicate the fact that the property is for sale by owner—buyers love to call owners.

- Give information on the number of bedrooms, baths, and whether it has a garage.

- Use an introduction that stops them and makes them curious to find out more about the house.

- Mention any special amenities, such as a pool or a large lot.

- Give an idea of the location, such as The Country Club Addition.

- Mention price and terms only if you offer particularly good ones. In fact, if you have good terms, this is the *most important, most useful* information you can give the buyer.

Go through the ads in your local papers to get the feel of the way brokers write their ads. Use their ideas, but give a bit more information, as yours is a custom ad designed to sell only one house. Don't get carried away. Keep it short. Here's an example:

BY OWNER. Like living in the country. ½ acre lot in Country Club Estates. 3-2-2, formals, huge game room. Best in the neighborhood. Low $90s. 555-5555.

If you use your imagination, you'll find more ways to advertise inexpensively and efficiently. The more free or inexpensive advertising you can do, the better your chance of success.

The following examples will give you ideas on classified ads that work with different properties and different situations:

Ads for a Home with Good Terms

Let's say you are selling a house under the following circumstances: you purchased it 10 years ago for $40,000 with an FHA loan of $38,000 at 9% fixed. You now owe about $34,000, and your payments are $400 per month. You have enough money to purchase another home without getting the equity out of this house, so you'll do a *wraparound* sale. The market is slow. The house would bring $100,000 in a normal market, but you'll probably only net $85,000 after you discount it and pay many of the seller's points and closing costs for a new loan at 11%, which we'll assume is the going rate. With easy owner financing, you'll sell it at full price with $2,500 down, 9⅝% fixed rate. Even in a weak market you'll probably find a good buyer in two to three weeks with this type of ad:

> **9⅝% FIXED-RATE OWNER FINANCING.** Just $2,500 total cost to move in. Gorgeous 3-2-2 brick home with fireplace, large fenced yard with mature trees. Great southside location. Only $99,990. 555-5555.

While this is a good ad, you'll find that it isn't a cheap ad to run. When you've got something the competition doesn't have, you don't need to make your ads long and costly. The great financing in this ad will stand out bright as a five-carat diamond ring on a poor maiden's hand. So let's take out some of the non-essential items, making sure we leave plenty of meat on the bones:

> **9⅝% FIXED OWNER FINANCING.** $2,500 total move-in. 3-2-2 brick, fireplace, fenced yard, trees, great location and condition. 555-5555.

This one's better. It gets right to the point yet doesn't waste words with embellishments that just cost money. Here's another ad for the same house:

> **$2,500 TOTAL DOWN.** 9⅝% owner financing. Beautiful 3-2-2 brick. 555-5555.

This one's shorter and cheaper to run. It's very lean, and it's almost as effective. You can probably run this ad in three papers for the same cost as you'd run the first one in only one paper. That should get a lot more calls. The most important items in any one of these ads are:

- Small down payment
- Owner financing (easy and quick qualifying)
- 3-2-2 (3 bedrooms, 2 baths, 2-car garage)
- The fact that the home is in good condition
- Your telephone number

You can get as carried away with too much information as you can with an ad that's too thin. Out of the three ads above, the middle one is the best all around compromise. As I stated, it leaves plenty of lean meat on the bones.

Ads for a Home with Unusual Amenities

The above ads emphasized the easy terms with owner financing. Even if the property had had exciting and unusual amenities, the most important fact was the financing, so we concentrated on that. But let's say you have a home that has two amenities that are exciting *for your price range or location*, but you have no special financing terms. Then you must emphasize the amenities and give only basic information on other details.

Assume your home sells for $150,000, which is the going rate for most of the homes in your neighborhood. It's a 4-3-2 brick with stucco, on an unusually large lot with plenty of trees. If it's located in Birmingham, Alabama, you won't emphasize the trees. Most houses there have trees. But if you live in Fort Worth, Texas, you'll emphasize the trees because not that many homes there have trees. The ad for the Fort Worth house would be thus:

> **½ ACRE LOT WITH A FOREST OF TREES**. Gracious 4-3-2 brick and stucco custom home in Nottingham Estates. Large kitchen, formal areas. Beautiful condition. Only $149,990. By owner. 555-5555.

This ad gives good, basic information. Many more words than this will not get any more calls. It will just help the newspaper publisher's budget.

The most important item here is the size of the lot. You start with that. Even if you're writing an ad for a publication that allows 100 words, you start with the punch line.

A shorter version would be thus:

> ½ **ACRE LOT**. Trees. Gorgeous 4-3-2 brick. Formals. In Nottingham. By owner. $149,990. 555-5555.

You could leave out the price, but you might end up with a lot of calls from people looking for a $70,000 house. You might as well weed those out from the start.

On the ads with owner financing, I left out the words "by owner." On those it was understood that the home was being sold by the owner. On all other ads, be sure to add "by owner." Many people need to be reminded that they'll be dealing directly with the owner. They like that.

Ads with Rock-Bottom Price

Let's say you have a house you bought in 1970 for $25,000 that's now worth $100,000 in a somewhat slow market. You were just offered a fantastic job 1,000 miles away. You determine it will take you six months to get full price, but you need to move it in 30 days. So you drop the price 15% for a quick sale. You'll still have plenty of equity at $85,000. Now the most important item is price; $85,000 is the punch line. So you start with that first:

> **ONLY $85,000 IN PRESIDENTIAL MEADOWS**. Neat 3-2-2 split level in prestigious area at $15,000 discount. Investors, bargain hunters: *MUST* sell in 30 days. By owner. 555-5555.

Here's another one:

> **HELP!** Must move quick. $15,000 discount. Pretty 3-2-2 split level in Presidential Meadows. Only $85,000. By owner. 555-5555.

You notice I'm not showing you how to write graceful, flowing, wordy ads. You don't need help on those. Just pick up any newspaper, and copy some of the ads many real estate brokers and FSBOs use. Here's an example:

6767 RICHMEADOW CIRCLE

BY OWNER

GOTHIC GABLED ELEGANT!
Executive living in Lakewood Heights.
Formals, gourmet kitchen, breakfast
room, library, 2 master-sized bedrooms,
sunporch, patio, double garage with storage room, full attic. All amenities
including wet bar, chandeliers, security
system, marble dressing vanity, plaster
moldings, rock fireplace, domed 12'
living room ceiling, arched doorways,
central heat/air, leaded windows,
professional landscaping w/fish pond.
$169,500. Open Sun. 4-6PM. 555-5555
or 666-6666.

This mess is from a major Dallas paper. Most of the amenities mentioned
are taken for granted in that area, for that price. This is a needlessly expensive
ad. I dare you to find a house in Dallas for $169,500 without "central heat/air,"
so why waste the effort including it in the ad? Save your money when you're
paying for an ad by the column line. Keep it short and to the point. Let's rewrite
this one to save money, keep it less boring, and give it more punch:

BY OWNER. Elegant Gothic at 6767
Richmeadow Circle in Lakewood
Heights! Only $169,500. Formals, li-
brary, huge double gar., all executive
amenities, and landscaping. Open Sun.
4-6. 555-5555 or 666-6666.

Here's another lengthy, expensive one by a broker:

CUTE ONE BEDROOM

2222 ANYWHERE ST.

$29,500

OWNER FINANCE

New central heat/air & carpet on
beautiful treed lot just off Lake June.
$1500 down.

JACK JACKSON

Realtor   **555-5555**

It appears that this broker is committed to running a certain size ad every day. Or perhaps he likes to waste money on advertising. Let's shrink the ad and start off with the punch line:

OWNER FINANCE, $1500 DOWN.
Cute 1 BR. 2222 Anywhere St., off Lake
June. Trees. New central A/C, carpet.
Jack Jackson, Realtor. 555-5555.

When buyers are looking through the ads in the classifieds, they'll look at *all* the ads. They don't just look at the big and pretty ones. So the vital information is *all that matters*. Save yourself money; keep it short and to the point. You don't need a lot of blank space, headlines, or bold letters. Advertise in as many publications as you can. You can only do so economically if you keep your ads trim and packed only with essential facts.

REAL ESTATE AGENTS

One type of advertising I haven't mentioned yet is advertising your property to real estate agents. I'll cover that in the chapter on dealing with brokers.

6

Answering the Phone

KEEPING THE PHONE COVERED AT ALL TIMES IS A THOUGHT UTMOST IN THE minds of any professional real estate office manager. Walk-in traffic is a very small part of a real estate business. The telephone is where most listings and sales originate.

A well-run office will divert its phones—that is, forward all incoming calls—to an agent on duty after business hours. Telephones are answered 24 hours a day, 7 days a week. If *they* do it, so must you.

I've often called FSBOs—called them repeatedly—only to have the phone ring and ring without an answer. Or how about this: somebody answers and tells you to call back at 11:30 that evening, when the owner will be home. Or a child answers and leaves you holding for 10 minutes. That's an impossible way to sell a house.

Many times, a buyer will call once and not call again. The reason he won't call again is that if he's a genuine, interested buyer, he'll call on several ads at the same time that he calls on yours. One of those calls will go to a top-notch real estate salesman. Once that salesman gets ahold of him, he'll have the buyer sold—and it won't be your house.

Once your ads start running—and that includes the moment you place your sign out in front of the house—you must do everything possible to answer the phone at all times. If the husband or wife happens to be at home during the day, that's great. But there will be times when everyone must be away from the phone.

When no one's at home, there are two methods you can use to answer the phone: an electronic answering machine or the telephone company's call-forwarding service.

THE ANSWERING MACHINE

An answering machine is the least satisfactory of the two methods, but it's much better than to leave the phone unanswered, even though many people will simply hang up when they get an automatic answer. If your message is catchy, it holds the caller's attention; you have a chance of keeping him interested enough to leave his name and phone number.

Make your message soft and smooth and somewhat as follows:

> Hi, I'm Sally. I'm sorry I can't answer the phone. We have a beautiful home for sale. There are three bedrooms, two baths, a huge double garage, and a gorgeous pool with a large covered patio. The price is great. We'd love to give you more information or perhaps show it to you. Please leave your name and number when you hear the tone. We'll call you back soon. Thank you.

Answering machines are relatively inexpensive. One of them could pay off handsomely in helping you sell your property.

CALL FORWARDING

For something like a couple of dollars a month and a nominal hookup charge, most phone companies offer call forwarding. When the house will be left alone you can transfer the calls to wherever you're going to be. If you won't be at a phone, you can transfer them to a relative, a friend, even your secretary. Of course, whoever answers the phone should already have one of your information sheets, so they can give out all the pertinent facts. This is very important. People want to get the information on the property the first time they call.

HANDLING THE CALL

When the phone is being answered at home, teach young children how to answer the phone, and make sure teenagers and young adults do a good job of answering it, too. Handling the phone call takes good technique. Not only must you answer the caller's questions, but you must have him answer your own questions. For example, your first question should be where he saw your ad, or is he calling off your yard sign. If most calls come from the ad in the *Daily News,* then you'll want to concentrate on that one publication for your advertising.

Keep a record of each call next to the phone, and ask the caller other questions, such as:

- Name. Take the time to have him spell it correctly for you.

- Phone number. Get his home number as well as work number.

- Family size. If he has three children and your home only has three bedrooms, you can give him some features yours has that a four-bedroom home doesn't have.

- Whether he owns or rents. If he currently owns, he may not be a buyer, but still only a seller like yourself.

- What part of town he lives and works in.

- His address.

- His approximate monthly or yearly income. You have to know if he can afford your house.

Answers to these questions tell you the type of person you're talking to— whether he's a serious buyer or just a "tire kicker." The more you know about your buyer, the better you can determine whether you should show your home to the prospect, or whether to do so would be a waste of time for both of you.

Don't just sit there and answer all of his questions. Have handy a list of all the questions you'll ask each caller. For each and every question he asks of you, you *must* finish your statement with a question for him to answer.

If it sounds like you've got a qualified buyer, but he doesn't make an appointment to see the property, then you have his name, phone number, and address. You should mail him one of your information sheets. You can also give him a call in a week or two to find out if he's ready to come out and see your house. People sometimes take months to buy a house. They get hot, then cool down on the idea, until finally they'll see one they fall in love with and buy. The only way you can get someone to fall in love with yours is to show it, and show it often.

THINK SAFETY

Don't show the house to anyone who does not give you his name and phone number. There are two reasons for this: salesmanship and safety. If you have their name and number, you can call them back to try to push a sale. That's salesmanship.

As for safety, you're going to be showing your house, as a general rule, to perfect strangers. If they give you their name and phone number, you should be able to look them up in the phone book. You can check that you're dealing with legitimate lookers.

If you get a call from someone in a phone booth, and he tells you he's just coming into town, you want to make sure that, if you're a woman, your husband or a friend or neighbor is with you when you show the property.

I don't recommend showing the house to anyone who just pops at the door and wants to see it without an appointment, unless the husband and wife are both at home.

If you do get some Sunday drivers who just drop in, ask them for their name and phone number before they come in. I can't overemphasize how important follow-up is to the success of a selling campaign. I've often called people back two or three weeks after showing them property, rekindled their interest in buying a home with just a little bit of prodding and many times have convinced them to go on contract.

7

Showing the Property

I'VE SHOWN HOUSES TO CUSTOMERS WHILE THE OWNERS WERE HOME, AND SOME of those owners later complained to me because I didn't push the house enough to the prospective buyers. In other words, I didn't talk enough. I explained to my clients that there are many times when it's better to say nothing when showing a property.

The house usually sells itself. If it's priced right, is in the neighborhood the buyers are interested in, and the house shows well, you don't have to do much more than let the buyers walk through it and have a contract ready for them to sign.

I don't mean to imply that you shouldn't say anything. The very good points or amenities that may be overlooked should be brought to the prospects' attention. But it's better to say too little than too much.

We've talked about the condition of the property. Good condition pays off when you're showing prospective buyers. I don't want to bore you with this, but I must reiterate that few things sell a house better than condition. When you're about to show, make sure that the house is picked up and everything is as much in place as possible. Turn on all the lights that are necessary to make the house as bright as possible. Open up all the window shades during the day, except for windows that have a particularly bad view.

If it is summer, make sure the cooling unit is set low enough to make the home comfortable. If you have fans in any of the rooms, turn them on low speed.

If it is winter, and you have a fireplace, have a nice fire going when you show. Some soft music, played *softly*, will also help. The television *must* be turned off.

THE IMPORTANCE OF SMELL

Try not to show the property when you've just cooked, or are in the process of cooking, something with a very strong aroma, especially fish. If you can, though, try to have some bread or cookies cooking in the oven. That aroma can make a house feel very homey.

If you have pets, make sure they're out of the way. There's nothing worse than a dog bouncing all over your prospective buyers. If you have children, teach them to be calm and quiet when prospects are viewing the home.

I don't believe in taking buyers through a guided tour of a house. Let them browse around at their leisure. One disadvantage you'll have over a real estate salesman is that with you in the house, the buyers can't take psychological possession of the property. So you must make them feel at home as much as possible. The way to do it is to stay out of their way and let them browse.

PUT YOUR VALUABLES AWAY

While you have the house on the market, put all your valuables in hiding. That way you can allow the buyers to look through without having to follow closely behind. That's very uncomfortable for them.

If they have many questions, you might want to stay with them the first time around. If they show a lot of interest, ask them to walk around some more and take their time. Then let them wander around alone while you stay in one end of the house or, preferably, in the back yard.

Once they've looked around, ask them to follow you to the best room of the house. It may be the family room, or a den, or the living room—whichever has the most outstanding features. Ask them to have a seat, and allow them to get comfortable and relaxed. Offer them something to drink, and tell them you'd like to answer any questions about the house, the neighborhood, or the city. Answer all questions as best you can.

Be enthusiastic, act cheery, but don't oversell—that is, don't exaggerate.

Accentuate the positive. Tell the buyers about the most outstanding features of the house, of its location and surroundings. If they seem unusually enthused about certain features, dwell on those a bit longer, and help them build up even more enthusiasm.

DON'T EXPECT EVERYONE TO LIKE YOUR HOUSE

Not everybody will like your house, and some may like it but will dislike some things about it. Accept that fact, and don't worry about the people that don't like it. For those who have objections about some things, do everything you can to counter their objections with good points. For example, someone may say, "Your bedrooms are too small."

You can answer, "Oh, but just think of all the cabinet space you have in the kitchen, where you'll spend so much of your time." Every objection should be countered with a positive statement, preferably reinforcing some of the things the buyers have already indicated they like, or good points they may have overlooked.

Never argue with a buyer. If he says your nice, spacious garage is small, remember that everything is relative; he may have unusually large cars or a lot of things to store in a garage.

Be impartial. Remove yourself from the role of the homeowner while you're talking to the buyers. Never feel offended. Always remember that no matter how many people dislike your house, or certain parts of it, there will always be someone for whom it will be a dream home. I've sold some very distressed property to the best people; one man's garbage is another man's treasure.

BE A GOOD LISTENER

Be attentive and listen to what the buyer tells you. Don't do all the talking; listen more than you talk. Good salespeople realize that we have two ears and one mouth, so we can do twice as much listening as we do talking.

When the buyer hints that he's ready to buy, ask him, "Would you like possession June 15th or July 1st?" If he says that July first would be just fine, *STOP!* Say no more. He has bought. He's taken the bait and all you have to do is reel him in . . . gently. Pull out your earnest-money contract, ask him how he wants his name to read, and start filling in the blanks.

ASK EVERYONE FOR A CONTRACT

You can't sell if you don't ask for the order. Ask everyone who looks at your property if they would like to buy it. If they say "No," ask why not. They may have an objection you can overcome with a few answers. For example, the husband says, "We'll have to think it over." If they have to think it over, that means there are unanswered questions. At that point start asking questions. Here's a typical conversation:

"Are the bedrooms big enough?" you ask.
"Yes, they're just fine," the wife answers.
"Is there enough cabinet space in the kitchen?"
"Yes, I think so."
You continue this line of questioning until you hit the jackpot. "Is the garage large enough?"

The buyer says, "Well, as a matter of fact, we have a large boat and it may not fit along with our station wagon."

You ask, "Can you think of any other reason why you could not buy this home?"

They both shake their heads.

You smile and say, "In that case, why don't we measure the garage and go over to your house and measure your boat and see if it will fit in along with your station wagon. If it will, then you won't have to waste any more time looking at houses. You've found the right one for you."

Always look for the buying objections. Oftentimes they're minor and you can overcome them. If they're major and you can't overcome them, then you won't be hoping this buyer calls you back. He won't. *Rarely* do people call you back when they say they'll think it over.

OPEN HOUSES

Open houses are fine for real estate agents. Rarely does one sell the house being shown—very rarely. But if the house is in a location that has plenty of traffic, and the house has good curb appeal, then there's a multitude of clients to be met at the open house. Those clients can be pursued for a sale on a more suitable house, or one that more closely meets their economic conditions.

For you as a FSBO, I suggest you spend your time more constructively going after the free advertising I've previously suggested, instead of holding open houses. But if you must have an open house, follow these simple rules:

☐ Run your ads for the open house at most a day or two before the open house. Cancel the ads if the weather looks like it will storm on your selected day.

☐ If you're on a busy street, just put out your open house sign on a beautiful Sunday, without any other advertising.

☐ The house must be neat and clean. Observe all the rules I've given in this chapter.

☐ Have lookers sign a guest register, with their name and phone number so you can call them later.

☐ Have plenty of your brochures available to hand out. Have other information handy to answer questions—things such as utility bills, maps showing schools and shopping, etc.

☐ Make sure you don't schedule an open house on a holiday, or on a day of the World Series or the Super Bowl, or when your local college team is playing. You won't have a soul attend your event if you do.

8

Selling Your Co-op or Condo

SELLING A CO-OP OR CONDOMINIUM INVOLVES GOOD KNOWLEDGE OF YOUR PROD-
uct. Let's start this chapter by looking at the different types of condominiums.

Condominium refers to a form of ownership in which there are individually
owned units in a multiple-unit project. Unit ownership is a specific cancelling of
the common-law doctrine that "he who owns the soil owns everything below
to the center of the earth and everything to the heavens." So condominium
ownership is often described as *horizontal* property ownership, or more
accurately, a freehold interest in a horizontal piece of vertical air.

In my selling and building experience, I've encountered three distinct forms
of condominiums, as well as a fourth type of residential dwelling that is not really
a condominium but many buyers look upon as a condominium:

- Single-family attached units
- Duplex townhouses
- Multi-unit townhouses
- Apartment condominiums

SINGLE-FAMILY ATTACHED UNITS

This is a relatively new development that sprouted from the old townhome
design. In the larger, older cities of the U.S., as well as in many other parts

of the world, homes were, and are, built with a front and back yard, but with no side yards. Each owner's home abuts the neighbors' homes on the sides.

Here's a variation of this theme. Normal subdivision lots are developed in narrow pairs. Actually, a normal lot is split in half and called two lots. A duplex is built on the two little lots, and each person owns his half, which is on its own separate lot. There is no homeowners association; there are no maintenance fees. Everyone takes care of his own half of the duplex. These are called *single-family attached units*. It's possible to build this type of home as a duplex, triplex, or fourplex.

While this is not a condominium, you have the disadvantages of selling an attached unit, and also the advantages of small yards and minimum maintenance of true condominiums. This appeals to many people. You also have no homeowners association to deal with, and no dues to pay. That's often a plus.

DUPLEX TOWNHOUSES

Duplex townhouses are much like the single-family attached units I discussed above. The big difference is a homeowners association. If you have a homeowners association, you must sell buyers on the advantages of a homeowners association: no maintenance chores for the homeowners, the entire project looks neat.

The duplex townhouse allows everyone to have not only a front and back yard, but also one side yard. There is almost the privacy of a single-family detached home, but there is economy of construction, and the units can look imposing because there are two homes in what looks like one house on one lot.

MULTI-UNIT TOWNHOUSES

The true townhouse, in my opinion, is a home that is attached to others in a row composed of anywhere from three to ten, twelve, even twenty separate structures, each with a front yard, a back yard, all the ground below it to the center of the earth, and all the air above it.

These *multi-unit townhouses* are almost always a condominium-type dwelling, with a homeowners association, some common areas, and common amenities such as pools and other recreational facilities. They allow more privacy than an apartment condominium, and give the owner a condominium's freedom from exterior maintenance.

APARTMENT CONDOMINIUMS

Apartment condominiums are actually individually-owned apartments. The owner enjoys ownership of only a block of airspace within the building. He also has rights to not only use the amenities that come with the entire condominium complex, but also the areas leading to his own unit.

Many people call this type of unit a condominium, and all other types townhomes or townhouses. It's probably a good way to distinguish the difference between condominiums that have separate use of land below and air above from those that do not.

CO-OPS

Co-ops—short for *cooperatives*—are generally built like the apartment condominiums discussed above. The big difference is that the owner doesn't own a unit individually, but is a shareholder in a nonprofit corporation which owns the building. As a stockholder, the resident is entitled to lease space in the building, and to use the facilities that come with the building.

WHO BUYS CONDOMINIUMS?

You should direct your advertising to the people who buy condominiums. Seek them out, find out where they work and play, and see if you can get your message to them about your home. They include:

- Retirement-age people with moderate to above-average wealth. This group has a much higher preference for condominiums as compared with other consumer groups, primarily because of convenience and amenity characteristics of condominiums.

- New or young households with higher-than-average incomes who either don't expect to have children, or who will wait several years to have them.

- Childless middle-aged households with higher-than-average income and/or wealth who:

  - would like to move out of rental units in order to build up equity and get the tax advantages of home ownership.

  - hope for property appreciation while retaining the conveniences of rental units.

  - would like to move out of single-family housing to enjoy the conveniences of condominiums.

- Young single or divorced people, especially single women, who have reasonably good income and are tired of paying rent in apartments, but like the conveniences of apartment living.

- Small families who want a nice home, but can't afford one because single-family detached units are beyond their means.

DEFINITIVE ADVERTISING

In a buyers' market, where there are more houses than buyers, as a general rule you'll have more trouble selling a condominium than a single-family detached home. The reason is that you'll lose the buyers who are in the last group above. Small families who otherwise couldn't afford a detached home and would buy your condominium will find that, in a buyers' market, some detached homes will be within their grasp. Forget about them in your advertising if you're in this situation.

But in any market, you must concentrate getting your advertising to those folks in the other four groups. Look for newspapers that cater to the young apartment dwellers, to singles, and to older and retired people.

If there are areas near your home with a large concentration of apartments, find the grocery stores near them, and use their bulletin boards.

You may not be able to use a sign in front of your condo. But look for ways you can advertise on-site. How about a club house, meeting, or recreation area? Your neighbors may have friends or acquaintances who would like to buy your condo. Put your information sheet in everyone's mailbox.

How about areas near singles bars and other night-life where singles and childless couples are found? Often you'll be able to leave information in restaurants and stores that are frequented by prospective buyers.

KNOW YOUR PRODUCT

You must know your product to a greater degree when selling a condominium than when selling a single-family dwelling. There simply are more details.

Condo and co-op buyers enter the marketplace with various degrees of knowledge. It's critical that you be prepared to furnish them complete information. You have to know what the legal documents say, and you must be able to explain, in simple terms, the information in FIG. 8-1.

Knowledge Is More Critical with a Co-op

With a co-op, the situation is much more critical. If you didn't read your papers when you originally bought, you should do so at this time. You must be well-informed to deal effectively with the questions your buyers will throw at you.

Fig. 8-1

CONDO/CO-OP INFORMATION CHECKLIST

- ☐ Limited common areas
- ☐ General common areas
- ☐ Airspace
- ☐ Common expenses
- ☐ Homeowners association
- ☐ Assessment fees and what they include
- ☐ Tax assessments on the community
- ☐ Limited liability
- ☐ Functions of the board of directors, president, and manager
- ☐ Unit conveyance (especially with co-ops)
- ☐ Pets
- ☐ Noise
- ☐ Acceptable behavior of children
- ☐ Exterior modifications of a unit
- ☐ Posting of signs
- ☐ Parking for cars, boats, trailers, vans, and trucks

- ☐ Use of patios
- ☐ Use of common amenities and facilities
- ☐ Designated play areas
- ☐ Control of keys
- ☐ Utility costs
- ☐ Window coverings
- ☐ Assessments
- ☐ Reserve account
- ☐ Special assessments
- ☐ Annual budget
- ☐ Insurance
- ☐ Guest parking
- ☐ Mail and parcel delivery
- ☐ Trash and refuse
- ☐ Social benefits (social life)
- ☐ Neighborhood profile
- ☐ Sound control features
- ☐ Your reasons for selling
- ☐ Possession date

Take out your papers, and outline the important points so you can go over them with buyers. If you need special permission from the other owners for the sale, you should know exactly how to go about obtaining it, and how long it may take to get it.

Single-family detached homes are easier to sell because everyone is familiar with that type of ownership. With condominiums you have to explain ownership to many who may be interested but are not at all familiar with them. And even fewer people are familiar with co-ops. The more information you have, and the easier you make it for the prospective purchaser to understand that information, the simpler it will be for you to make a sale.

SELL THE AMENITIES

You need to have handy a list of the amenities to explain to the first-time condo or co-op prospect why he or she would enjoy buying your unit. Here's a partial roll:

- Freedom from upkeep responsibility

- Property management by professionals
- Low cost through group sharing
- Neighborhood consistency
- Security
- Cheaper utilities

OBTAIN A RESIDENT PROFILE FROM THE DIRECTORS

Let the president, board of directors, and manager know that your unit is for sale. They'll know you care, and they'll help answer any questions a prospect may have.

Ask them for a profile of the other owners and/or residents in your development. Find out how many units are owner-occupied and how many are rented. If you have some particularly distinguished owners in the development, that fact can be a real selling feature that you should use to maximum advantage.

EDUCATE THE BUYER

For first-time buyers, you will have to go through an educational process of what condos are. Be prepared to take them step-by-step so they understand the real benefits, especially if they are single.

For repeat buyers, skip the basics and talk about the things that interest them, once you've found out what they need. So it's important to qualify prospects early on, to determine what they're looking for. You must explain in detail those things that interest them which your unit has, and let them savor each bit of information.

THE RIGHT OF FIRST REFUSAL

Some associations have *right-of-first-refusal conditions*. That means when you find a buyer, the association has the right to purchase the property from you for the amount the buyer is offering. You need to be able to explain to the buyer why this right of first refusal is necessary. Your original prospectus will probably give a good explanation that you can use.

Appendix C is a right of first refusal affidavit. You need to use this form with your contract of sale, unless your association has another form they request you to use.

QUALIFY YOUR PROSPECT

As soon as you first talk with your prospect and see that he is interested, qualify him to make sure he will fit with the type of unit you are selling. Ask some of these questions:

- Are you married?
- How many children do you have?
- What are the ages of the adults and children?
- Do you have any pets?
- What kind of pets do you have?
- How many pets do you have?
- What size are the pets?
- What are your social needs?

You should make prospective home buyers aware that a condominium is not just a structure, but a method of owning property. It's actually a way of life.

MORE IDEAS ON CO-OPS

The board of directors usually has the right to approve or reject prospective buyers of shares. They also have the right to approve or reject prospective sublessees.

Most states require a prospectus from the developer of a cooperative. If your complex has a prospectus, get a copy of the original one. Also have handy:

- Names, addresses, and phone numbers of the members of the board of directors

- An engineer's or inspector's report on the general physical condition of the building or buildings (if available)

- A current report on the financial background of the building (the underlying mortgage, reserve funds, recent taxes, and assessments)

- The proprietary lease

- A copy of your subscription agreement

- A breakdown of your monthly maintenance charges

- The board of directors' financial restrictions for buyers
- Information on your personal loan on the co-op, and whether it is assumable or not

CONDO/CO-OP FINANCING

The sale of a condo should be no different than the sale of a home, as a general rule. Because there are exceptions to everything, you should talk with lenders who are familiar with your area and your complex to see if you should look into different avenues for financing your buyer. Most of the ideas in the chapters on financing should work with condos.

Co-ops are a different case. Banks typically loan from 60–85% of the purchase price of new co-op units. The prospective buyer of a co-op cannot obtain new financing for the unit itself, but must adhere to the provisions of the sole mortgage on the building. If the original mortgage is 50% paid off, the buyer has to come up with 50% of the purchase price.

It doesn't mean he has to come up with the down payment in cash, or that he can't make some kind of deal with you for your equity. If the buyer has anything of value that is paid for (or that he has substantial equity in), the value of which you can ascertain with relative ease, then you might suggest a trade.

If you look at some of the concepts in the financing chapters you'll come up with ideas that can work in the sale of your co-op.

Since you might be more inclined to offer owner financing when selling your co-op, make sure you follow all the rules the big boys use when loaning money to a purchaser of real estate. Use a good credit application, make sure the buyer fills in all the blanks, and check all his credit references—in **Appendix K** you'll find a blank credit application to copy and have handy for your buyer. Then have him obtain a copy of his credit report from the local credit bureau. It will take a few days, but the wait will be well worth it to you.

If your buyer has an unstable job, has been on the job a very short time, or has shown an inability to keep up with his economic obligations—unless he can prove to you unusual circumstances that should not reoccur—don't be tempted to risk future headaches with what I might bluntly call a bum.

DUMPING YOUR UNIT

If you have a lot of equity in your unit, unless you do owner financing, you may find it hard to sell in a tough buyers' market if you are wanting cash. As I said above, you don't have to take cash. There are other forms of payment that can be equally if not more rewarding than cash at the time of sale. I say this because, in the long run, these forms of payment may bring you cash quicker, and more of it, than if you simply wait for the cash to come only as a result of the sale of your property.

You might try exchanging. Offer your unit in exchange for *anything*. That means real estate, planes, yachts, another condo or co-op, diamonds, furs, etc.

There are a lot of people in larger cities and smaller towns who may not have a lot of disposable cash, but who have plenty of paid-off assets, or what I call "toys," and who will trade an asset they've tired of for another asset they hunger for.

A relatively wealthy, retired Wyoming rancher may no longer have a need for his $100,000 Beechcraft airplane, but he may yearn for, and indeed need, your $100,000 co-op in New York. You can swap. You might be able to use the plane. Or it might be much quicker to sell than the co-op—say, two months instead of six.

TAXES

What can you consider profit when selling your condo or co-op? Simply, profit is the difference between the original purchase price and the sales price minus: all closing costs from the purchase and sale, the cost of any improvements you have previously made on the property, and finally, improvements and repairs made specifically to strengthen the sale of the property within 90 days after signing the sales contract.

In the sale of a co-op, the seller can also subtract the portion of his monthly maintenance fees that went toward reducing the principal of the cooperative's underlying mortgage.

Condos don't have an underlying mortgage, but you can subtract the cost of any additional assessments that you've paid out for improvements to the common areas, such as fixing up the swimming pool and other recreational amenities.

9

Negotiating with Buyers

THERE IS A CERTAIN AMOUNT OF NEGOTIATING THAT GOES WITH THE PURCHASE of any property. The price you receive for your property, how soon you sell it, and how soon you close the deal all depend on your negotiating ability.

THE IMPORTANCE OF VALUE

Knowing value is the most important way of getting the highest possible price for your property. A professional appraisal is *very* convincing. But even if you don't have one, if you can have a long list of addresses of similar properties with prices being asked, and another list with actual prices received in completed transactions, you'll be a long way towards your goal of receiving top dollar for your property.

Assume you're selling your house for $80,000. How does the buyer know that's a good price? You may be selling it way below value, yet the buyer may not know it. Even if you stress the price is way below market, will he believe you? He may even think you're actually trying to sell it above value. He'll then come to you with a low offer.

Value is of utmost importance. The buyer must feel certain that what he's purchasing is worth at least the asking price. But the prospect often wants to do better than that. After all, everybody loves a bargain; and let's face it, most buyers don't give a hoot about the seller. The buyer is generally only interested in his bargain. So let's give him his bargain.

He tells you, "Mr. Jones, I realize that perhaps your house is worth $80,000. But all I can afford to pay for it is $75,000."

You've got a smart buyer. He's done some quick mental calculations and has deducted a real estate commission from your asking price. After all, if you were selling it through a broker you'd have to pay it, and this is like him giving you full price under those circumstances.

You could be insulted at his low offer, but that never helps. You remain very friendly and very impartial. You smile and show him again your proof that the house is worth every penny of the $80,000 asking price. You say, "Mr. Smith, I can appreciate that. While my price is certainly not engraved in stone, I feel $75,000 is simply too low for me to consider."

At this point you'll know if you have a serious buyer, or simply a bargain hunter who's willing to look at every house in town and wait for the desperate seller who will dump his house. If he says that's his lowest offer and he walks out, then you had a bargain hunter. You might give him a call in a week or so and see if you can prod him up to a reasonable figure. If that doesn't work, drop him and go to greener pastures.

On the other hand, he might get serious and say, "Look, Mr. Jones, let's not fool around and waste time. I'll give you $77,000 and not a dime more."

Now you're dealing with an interested buyer, one who wants a bargain but is realistic enough to realize you want close to the true value for your property. This is the time for careful negotiation. This is actually the start of negotiation.

GET THE OFFER IN WRITING

You're $3,000 apart. At this point you are $1,800 ahead of a full price offer if you had the house listed at 6% with a broker. Your job now is to see how much better you can do without scaring off the buyer. If you really need to make the sale, you might simply take out your earnest-money contract and hand it to him. You'll reply, "I'm not saying I'll take your offer, but I won't consider it unless you show me that it's a serious offer." Here again, you'll find out whether or not you have a serious buyer.

If you have plenty of time to make your sale, and you feel the $3,000 is too great a spread, then try to make his offer better. Tell him that you're $3,000 apart and that you might consider splitting the difference with him if he's willing to put his offer down on paper and put some earnest money down on it.

Or you can say that you can't accept any offer until you have it in writing and your lawyer has looked at it. Say that if he puts it in writing, you'll have your lawyer look at it early the next day and you'll get back with him before noon.

The First Offer Is Often the Best. As a rule of thumb, if the first offer is not too far off from what you expected to net, you should go ahead and accept it. Unless the market is bristling with buyers, often the first offer is the best one you'll get for your property.

Don't Be the First to Drop the Price. Your buyer may ask, "How much less will you take for it?" If he does, don't give him an answer. Rather, answer the question with another question: "How much are you willing to pay for it?" You never know. His top price may be higher than your lowest price. Most people are not very shrewd buyers. So always let the buyer make the first offer below your asking price. Until he does, your price is set in stone.

Know Your Market. If you're *very* familiar with your market, you'll have the upper hand in the negotiating process. You can be very demanding if you're in a hot sellers' market. You'll get top dollar and perhaps more. Don't be afraid to let buyers bid up your asking price if you find that, all of a sudden, you have several who are anxious to buy the home. There are times when people will pay more than the asking price. We'll go into that later in this chapter.

If the market is stable, then you'll want to consider each offer carefully, as the next offer may be a while in coming. And stay in tune with the market. It could change against you in a month or two.

TAKE THE ORDER

The best real estate salespeople are the ones who, in a sense, force the sale. They keep contract forms handy. When they feel someone is showing strong signs of interest in a house, they pull out an appropriate contract form and ask, "Mr. and Mrs. Jones, if you were to make an offer on this home, how would you take title to the property?"

The buyers will have one of two responses to this question:

- They'll give their legal names, in which case the salesperson writes the names on the purchase form. By answering the question, they are consenting to the purchase. They're saying it's okay to fill out the offer, because they will sign it.

- They will back away immediately. When they see the contract form and the salesperson's intention of filling it out, they get scared. When this happens, the good salesperson will say, "I haven't asked you to sign it. I simply want to show you how the offer could be written up. You're welcome to take it with you and take a better look at it later."

In the latter case above, the salesperson is preparing to push for the sale, and if he doesn't get it on that house, then it will be easier on the next one.

You, of course, have no "next one." You have only one. But if you find prospects who show a real interest in the property, that little push can get them to buy. And if they back away you can answer, "I'm sure you want to think about it, and this way you can take the papers with you and study them carefully."

The strong professional salesperson will fill out the offer form even when the prospects forcefully object to his doing so. Then when he has it filled out, he'll put it in front of the prospects and say something like, "Now, Sam, this house has everything you and Mary have requested, from the lovely rock fireplace to the large backyard. It's got your names written all over it." He'll hand him the pen and continue, "If you'll just give us your okay right here, Mary can start deciding exactly where she'll place her furniture."

Does this seem too easy? Sure, but it works at least half the time. Just remember this: many salespeople fail not because they don't know the product, or because they don't do a good selling job, but simply because *they fail to ask for the order.*

"I'LL THINK IT OVER"

You'll get all kinds of objections from prospects for not buying, but this is the classic put-off: "I'll think it over."

There's a good way to pin them down. Your dialogue will go something like this:

> I don't blame you for wanting to think it over. It's an important purchase. It sounds like it's just the right house for you, and I wouldn't want to see you lose it if I sell it tomorrow to someone who's already seen it. So I'll write up the offer just as if you were going to buy it right now. But you won't give me a deposit, and we'll make it subject to your acceptance tomorrow at seven in the evening. Then, if someone else does make me an offer in the meantime, I'll honor yours till seven tomorrow evening. After you've thought about it, when you decide this is the right house, simply bring me your earnest money before seven tomorrow, and we'll have a firm contract.

If they're truly interested, they'll let you write the offer. If they're just tire kickers, or if they just don't like the house, they'll tell you not to bother, but that they'll think it over and call you back.

They won't. Or at least, they rarely do. But now you won't waste time thinking that these buyers will come through with a contract.

The ones who are interested will go back home with "their contract" and begin to think "home ownership." They'll tell their friends and relatives they've found a house, to get their comments. They'll have psychologically bought without going through the normal "buyers' remorse" had they signed, sealed, and delivered the contract to you.

More important than that, it'll force them to make a decision *soon*. They'll either buy, or they won't. And if they don't, at least you won't waste your effort waiting for their call. You'll simply forget them and go on to another prospect.

RECEIVING BIDS

If at all possible, you should wait to sell in a sellers' market. That's when there are more buyers than there are homes to satisfy the need. I don't mean to imply that you sit around for the next three years for the market to change. But you're better off to wait a few months if one of the following is the case:

- It's early December and nobody is looking to purchase a house, but only thinking about the coming Christmas season.

- Portnoy Broom Manufacturing Company has announced they will hire another 2,000 employees four months from now, and you know the currently stable housing market will be a sellers' market when the new employees begin to arrive from out of town.

When you determine there will be more folks wanting your property than you can satisfy, that's when you must prepare yourself for a different type of negotiation. In fact, it can't even be called negotiation; it's really just a bidding process. Again, if you know your market, you won't be tempted to jump at the first offer when it comes in soon after you place the for-sale sign on your lawn. In a sellers' market you *will* receive one, two, even more offers as soon as you start advertising your property. You have to maximize your return at this point.

Keep two thoughts in mind in this situation. The first is to *not* advertise price, at least not a definite price. To do so would be to lock yourself in to the first contract that comes along. Of course, you don't have to accept anyone's offer, even if you've advertised an exact price. But in this country, anyone can sue anyone else. If someone were to fall in love with your property *at your advertised price*, they could cause you legal problems. The second is to advertise that you will *not* work with brokers or agents. You certainly won't need them if the market's that hot for sellers.

Let's say you're selling your house for $140,000. You'll take more, if possible, unless you have an appraisal that won't support more and you have to sell with a new loan. So when your prospects call and ask the selling price, you tell them you'd like them to come see the property and make you an offer. You explain that your home is worth "somewhere in the $140s." You can even say, "It's worth somewhere in the mid $100s."

You're not going to make many friends with this tactic, but business is business. Your business is to get the most money from a situation in which the deck is stacked entirely in your favor.

Prospective buyers won't hesitate to give you written offers in this type of market. Before you take a prospect's offer, explain that you're taking offers, and are looking for the best one. Set a time for the end of the period for taking offers, and tell him you'll get back with him on that date. And do so.

Don't set your time period too far in the future. The market could change. If the market's really that good as a sellers' market, a week will be enough to land you several good offers.

The one disadvantage to keeping offers for any amount of time is that any buyer may withdraw his or her offer at any time before the seller accepts it. You can't hold a buyer to a contract that isn't a contract yet. At any time before you sign it, the buyer may call you and back out without any legal consequences.

GRADING THE OFFERS

In a bidding situation, I suggest you also take a filled-out credit application with each offer if the house will be sold with some form of financing—other than cash. At the end of the time period, look at the credit applications and take the highest bid with a *good* credit application: good income, long and stable employment, some savings, etc. If you get a contract for $10,000 more than the next bidder and that high bidder can't qualify for financing, you'll just have to start all over again.

If you really want to get serious about finding a qualified buyer, you'll ask the top two bidders to get a copy of their credit report at the credit bureau. Accept the offer from the prospect who qualifies from the standpoint of credit as well as income and lack of overwhelming monthly obligations. Avoid working with people who have credit problems, unless they're paying cash.

KEEP A BACKUP CONTRACT

In a sellers' market, keep at least one backup contract. Assuming you've received five offers, accept the No. 1 offer, the one that's in your best interest, and let the others know how their offer came out. Let the prospect who had the No. 2 offer know that you'd like to keep his offer as a backup, in case No. 1 is not able to obtain financing, or in case he backs out and doesn't close for one reason or another.

More than likely, he'll accept and remain as a backup. Make a note on the contract form that his offer is a backup offer and that it will become the No. 1 offer if the existing No. 1 fails to close. Of course, No. 2 has a right to withdraw his offer at any time until you advise him in writing that his offer is No. 1.

You would do well to advise the prospect with the No. 3 offer to remain as a second backup, just in case both of the others fail. In hot markets for sellers, or on unusually desirable properties, it's not uncommon to see three or four backup offers.

THE EARNEST MONEY

In a normal market, the norm in your area might be to take an amount equal to 1% of the purchase price for *earnest money*. So on a $200,000 house you'd accept $2,000. Or it might be that a fixed amount of $500 or $1,000 is standard. Whatever the case, in a sellers' market try to get earnest money equal to twice what is normally acceptable. In a sellers' market you're calling the shots, so the more earnest money you take, the less likely it will be that someone will pull out of a contract because he finds a better deal elsewhere.

10

Qualifying Buyers

RIGHT FROM THE VERY MOMENT YOU START WORKING WITH A PROSPECT, YOU need to *qualify* him. You must make sure he can buy your house. Because if he can't buy for one reason or another, you're wasting your time with him. Too many FSBOs, and entirely too many real estate agents, especially green ones, waste their time trying to sell unqualified buyers.

Qualifying the buyer is a crucial step in the sale of a property. Qualifying means determining whether the buyer can afford the property or not. When selling a co-op, it means not only being able to afford the property, but it also means meeting board standards. So you need to know what the standards for your building are right from the start.

Qualifying is a simple process that can save you a lot of time. If you determine that the buyer can afford to make the down payment and monthly payments it takes to purchase your home, then you won't be wasting your time trying to sell to someone who isn't really a buyer. An unqualified buyer isn't really a buyer, but simply a looker. I might add here also that, under normal circumstances, a person who has not sold his existing home is also not a buyer, but still a seller— merely a looker.

PROFESSIONAL LOOKERS

"Professional lookers" are people who make a hobby of looking at property that's for sale: model homes, used-home open houses, and any property that's available for viewing. You won't see many of these, but you will deal with some folks who can't afford your property and don't know they can't afford it.

The qualifying process is a much simpler task for a broker than it is for you. When you delve into people's finances, it's a personal matter that many won't want to discuss with you. But when someone shows real interest in your property, you'll have to qualify him, or at least explain to him what it will take in income, and to what extent he must be debt-free, in order to be able to purchase your property. If you don't do this, you may attempt to sell the house to someone who can't buy it because he won't qualify with a lender. The big problem for you is that if you put that unqualified buyer on contract, you'll be needlessly taking your property off the market while you try to get him financing.

QUALIFYING PROCEDURES

Let's look at borrower qualifying procedures so you can understand how lenders determine whether a person can afford a particular loan. It'll keep you out of an embarrassing situation when you go to a lender with your buyer.

Most lenders work under the 28/36 rule. That means the buyer is allowed to borrow an amount wherein monthly payments for principal, interest, taxes, and insurance will be no more than 28% of the gross monthly income, and where those payments plus any other fixed monthly obligations—car payments, furniture payments, credit card payments, but not insurance or utility payments—will be no more than 36% of the gross monthly income.

Principal and Interest (PI). We'll use a $54,000 loan as an example. Assume you need to find the payments for a new loan at 13% interest, payable over 30 years. If you look at Appendix D in the back of the book, you'll find the factor for 13% to be 11.062. Multiply 54 by 11.062 to determine the payment, $597.35. At 9% interest you would multiply 54 by 8.0462 and get a payment of $434.49. These are the figures for principal and interest on the loan.

Taxes and Insurance (TI). You must now add taxes and insurance, which are always paid with the monthly payment. Assume the monthly payment for taxes and insurance is $126.60. Now add that to the principal and interest to come up with the total monthly payment for *p*rincipal, *i*nterest, *t*axes, and *i*nsurance—*PITI*. On the 13% loan this totals $723.95.

The 28% Rule. PITI should be no more than 28% of the gross monthly income of the buyer (or the buyer and his or her spouse). To see if the buyer(s) qualify, simply divide the payment by .28 (28%):

Payment ÷ .28 = Minimum Gross Monthly Income
$723.95 ÷ .28 = $2,585.54

Now multiply $2,585.54 times 12. That's approximately $31,000, the minimum yearly income needed to qualify for this loan.

To show you the effects of interest rates on your ability to sell a property, let's figure out what the buyer would need to earn on the 9% loan:

$$\$561.09 \div .28 = \$2,003.89$$

Now multiply the total times 12. That's approximately $24,000 in yearly income needed to qualify. This is a big difference indeed.

The 36% Rule. You probably won't be lucky enough to find someone who has no other payments. Too many people buy cars, boats, and even airplanes before they decide they want to purchase a home. Too much debt can kill your house sale.

These other payments come under the 36% guideline. In the example above, if they had an income of $31,000 per year, then their total monthly payments—for house, cars, boats, credit cards, and other fixed loans—could be no more than $31,000 × .36 ÷ 12, which is $930 per month. Now subtract the house payment from this total:

$$\$930 - \$723.95 = \$206.05.$$

This means that their total fixed monthly obligations, *other than the house payment,* must not be more than $206.05.

If your buyer made the same income, but the loan was at 9% interest, then the calculation would be:

$$\$930 - 561.09 = \$368.91.$$

Now their total fixed monthly payments for everything other than the house payment can be as high as $368.91.

Some lenders will allow a little leeway; they have less strict guidelines. The VA and the FHA have different guidelines, but if you use the above method you should be in the ball park when qualifying your buyer.

Of course, if the buyer doesn't have to qualify for the loan—let's say he assumes your loan and you take a second lien for the entire balance of your equity—then you must use your own good judgment as to whether the buyer can afford the house. You'll understand this better when you read the chapters on financing. I would not deviate too much from the 28/36 rule. It makes good sense.

Some lenders will use a 25/33 ratio. This is especially true with conventional loans where the buyer is only required to have a 5% down payment. The less the down payment, the more stringent are many lenders' qualifying guidelines.

Use the Qualifying Sheet (Appendix E) to do your calculations.

Good Credit Is a Must for a New Loan. Once you've qualified the buyer as to payment ratios, you need to determine if he has a good credit and employment history. A few blemishes on the credit record generally won't disqualify a buyer. But a repossession or recent bankruptcy will usually preclude that buyer from obtaining a normal loan.

Job Stability. The buyer should have been on the job for at least two years, unless he's moved from one company to another with the same type of job. Someone coming out of college with a year or less on the job would probably qualify. Your best bet is to check with several lenders to see what each requires.

GETTING THE INFORMATION FROM THE BUYER

It's not easy to pry into people's private lives. Getting information on their finances is private to most folks. But you *must* know where the buyer stands. Good real estate agents get this information from the prospect within the first five minutes.

You can be blunt: "How much do you and your wife make as a combined gross income per month?" That's simple and straightforward, but it may offend the prospect. Especially if you're 25 years old and he's 60.

One of my salesmen, John Halpine, is extremely articulate with his use of English. He'll say, "What do you and your spouse enjoy as a total yearly income?"

It doesn't matter how you ask it. The fact is that you must have that information. The easiest way to start the qualifying process is to ask the prospect what he considers to be the most he can comfortably handle monthly for a house payment. Let's see how to handle Mr. Jones:

"Mr. Jones, you told me a few minutes ago that you've been renting a three-bedroom home. There is a nice tax advantage when buying as compared to renting. Are you aware of that?" (If he says no, you'd explain that, depending on his income he'll save 15-20% of his entire payment every month because the interest and property taxes he pays on his loan are deductible, whereas renting doesn't give him a tax break.)

He tells you, "Yes, that's one of the reasons we're looking for our own home."

"That's very shrewd of you. How much is rent running on a three-bedroom home like yours?"

"We pay $750, and we're tired of throwing our money away," he replies.

"I know what you mean. Now this home, with the $7,000 that you folks wish to put down, should run about $1,000 a month. Would that be a comfortable figure for you?"

"We'd really like to keep it at $900."

"At $1,000, your true after-tax cost should be no more than $800 to $850."

He insists, "Yes, but we still don't want to pay more than $900 per month." You may hear this often in the sale of a house. He either can't afford more than $900, or he doesn't want to pay more than that.

You can ask, "Do you feel you won't qualify for a $1,000 payment, or have you set a limit on what you want to spend?"

If he says he doesn't think he can qualify, you ask, "How much do you folks enjoy as a gross monthly income at this time?" Then you pull out your qualifying sheet at the end of this chapter, sit down, and fill it out with him. He needs your help.

If he says, "That's the limit on what we want to spend per month," he's probably a shrewd buyer and has a good handle on running his finances.

Then ask him, "Do you understand how a mortgage company qualifies a lender?"

"Yes, we've talked to a mortgage banker and know what kind of loan we'd qualify for." With this information, you don't have to delve into his private finances. They know what they can afford.

Your response would be, "There are a couple of ways you can bring the payment down to $900. You could put down another $10,000, approximately, or we could use a *buydown* to get your payment down to $900." Of course, you need not mention the fact that the third way to bring down his payment is for you to cut the price of your home by $10,000! That's out of the question.

More than likely, he'll say that coming up with another $10,000 is also out of the question. So you'll explain the buydown. As you'll read in the financing chapters, buydowns are a way of bringing down the buyer's payments, either temporarily or permanently, through the use of yours or the buyer's funds.

KNOW YOUR BUYER

In closing this chapter, I want to impress on you that you'll only waste your time if you don't know your buyer. You must know:

- how much he makes,
- how much he pays, and
- how good his credit is.

11

Loans

TO MOST PEOPLE, FINANCING IS THE BIGGEST HURDLE ON THE ROAD TO BECOM-
ing a homeowner. There are so many different types of loans available that it
takes a true "professional" real estate broker to be able to understand and easily
work with all of them. Because you only need to sell one home every now and
then, it would not be worth your while to try to memorize all the types of loans:
VA, FHA, ARM, GPM, PAM, RAM, SAM, VRM, ROM, FLIP, GPAM, and
countless others.

But to sell your home, you must understand financing to a certain extent
and have some handy reference you can turn to when you need information on
what's best and easiest for your buyer. Therefore, I'll give you the information
in the following chapters so you can easily flip to whichever one you need to review.

First I'll explain what I call traditional financing:

- Veterans Administration Loans—Chapter 12

- Federal Housing Administration Loans—Chapter 13

- Conventional Loans—Chapter 14

Then, in Chapters 15 through 17, I'll go over other forms of financing available
for your buyer.

TRADITIONAL FINANCING

In traditional financing, the buyer comes up with little or no down payment, some closing costs, and excellent credit and work history. The house goes through an appraisal, and if both house and buyer qualify, the lending company makes a loan to pay you the balance between the down payment and the selling price of the property.

If you are in a well-balanced market, with comfortable interest rates, you can use traditional financing avenues for helping your purchaser obtain financing.

When you're looking for traditional financing money, you'll need to check with the following sources, more or less in the following order:

- Savings and loans have been the largest providers of mortgage money in America. They account for almost half of all the home loans made.

- Mortgage companies, also called mortgage bankers, are companies that deal only in real estate mortgages.

- Commercial banks were not traditionally providers of funds for long-term mortgages, but recently they have come on strong in this field.

- Mutual savings banks operate like savings and loans, but provide a much smaller percentage of the mortgages.

- Credit unions are becoming more and more active in long-term mortgage money.

- Life insurance companies were strong mortgage lenders in the past, but now provide very little money for home loans.

All of these lenders use their own money to fund the loans they make, but many of them sell their loans on the *secondary market*.

The secondary market works as follows. A lender uses its funds to originate a series of loans, let's say $5 million worth. He then packages them and sells them to secondary investors such as the Federal National Mortgage Association (FNMA, also called Fannie Mae), the Federal Home Loan Mortgage Corporation (FHLMC, also called Freddie Mac), or the Government National Mortgage Association (GNMA, also called Ginnie Mae). There are several others of lesser importance.

If you find that a lender is particularly careful about lending money to your buyer, it is because if the loans are not made correctly he may not be able to sell them on the secondary market. That means the lender would be stuck with a long-term loan using money that he's borrowed on a short-term basis. Too many of these can bankrupt a lender when short-term money rates climb.

ALTERNATIVE FINANCING

If you have a property that's tough to move, then you might wish to use *alternative financing*, covered in Chapter 15. The chapter explains working with traditional financing, but with added twists to allow the qualifying of buyers who would not qualify under the traditional financing methods. It also explains situations where the buyer will purchase entirely with his own funds.

CREATIVE FINANCING

If it's a buyers' market (where there are more homes than there are buyers), or if interest rates are sky-high, then *creative financing* will sell the property under almost any bad situation. Chapter 16 will explain what to do if you find yourself in such a predicament. It will illustrate trades, assumptions, owner financing, wraparounds, second and third mortgages, etc.

THE BLEAK SITUATION

Chapter 17 deals with a favorite subject of mine: helping the seller who's in a pickle. It counsels the homeowner who's desperate for a buyer because he needs to move quickly, or because the market's cards are so stacked against him that it seems like he can't even give his house away.

SELECT YOUR FINANCING BEFORE THE SALE

The type of financing you use will be dictated by the marketplace and prevailing interest rates. At this point you will have determined which situation more or less fits your position in relation to your competition and market demand.

Before you start your advertising, decide which one of the following four situations best describes your market. Then concentrate on your plan of attack:

- **The Sellers' Market**—Houses are moving briskly. You won't have trouble finding several buyers. You don't need to waste your time dealing with marginal buyers. Follow the traditional financing route. Study Chapters 12, 13 and 14 carefully. You don't need to worry about Chapters 15, 16 and 17.

- **The Normal Market**—The market is well-balanced. There are about as many houses as there are buyers. It will take some effort to sell your property. Become familiar with traditional financing, and study alternative financing in Chapter 15.

- **The Buyers' Market**—The market's flooded with houses, and there aren't that many folks looking to buy. You'll spend a good deal of effort trying to move your property. Look at traditional as well as alternative financing routes. But become very familiar with Chapters 16 and 17 as well.

- **The Impossible Situation**—There just aren't any buyers out there. Or perhaps your home is in the worst location in town, or it's the worst property in the county. Concentrate heavily on Chapter 17. It may be the only way you can dispose of your property.

Regulations, customs, and lender requirements change often. You'll want to make a few calls to several lenders concerning the type of loan you feel will be the one you'll more than likely use for your buyer.

DRAWING UP THE PURCHASE AGREEMENT

Once you've decided which type of financing will most help your buyer, you should use the correct contract form for that type of financing. Chapter 18 will talk about drawing up a purchase agreement, and appendices give sample completed and blank forms for various kinds of contract forms designed for different financing situations.

12

VA Loans

UNLESS A BUYER CAN BORROW MONEY FROM A RELATIVE UNDER BETTER TERMS, there is no loan better than a *VA (Veterans Administration) loan*. Keep in mind that the VA does not loan money. They guarantee the lender that the borrower will pay his mortgage.

Only about 12 million VA loans have been made since 1942, so there are well over 20 million veterans who have never used their benefits. The first thing you must ask your buyer, then, is if he is eligible for a VA loan. Not only can a veteran and his or her spouse get a VA loan, but here are other examples of VA benefits:

- Widows of veterans who haven't remarried are eligible for VA mortgage loans.

- A common-law spouse is equal to a spouse, so her income can be used as well as his in qualifying for a VA loan.

- Two veterans can purchase a home together to help qualify for a loan. A veteran can also get a co-signer to help him qualify.

The veteran does not have to contact or deal with the Veterans Administration unless he doesn't have his Certificate of Eligibility. If he doesn't have the Certificate, the VA will help him obtain one.

Once he has his Certificate, he deals directly with the lender. The lender will make sure it gets its loan guarantee from the Veterans Administration.

As a seller, you don't need to worry about working with the VA. You must only determine that the prospective buyer is eligible for a VA loan. If he's not sure, he'll have to contact the Veterans Administration directly. You won't be able to do it for him.

A TRADITIONAL LOAN

A VA loan is one of the three traditional loans I referred to in the preceding chapter. There is no down payment, so it is the easiest to obtain for those who are veterans. As in other forms of traditional financing, the veteran must have the following:

- Excellent credit record
- Enough income to make the monthly payments
- Lack of other, excessive payment obligations
- Stable job

Interest Rate. The VA sets the maximum interest rate that lenders may charge. If the market rate for loans is 10% and the VA has set their rate at 9%, then the lender will charge the seller *points* to make up the loss in income. A point is 1% of the loan amount.

Maximum Amount. A veteran can obtain a loan of $144,000 with no down payment required. Loans are available for more than $144,000 with a down payment. If the veteran has full eligibility, then he needs to have a down payment of 25% of anything over the $144,000, depending on individual lender requirements.

Some Great Advantages. At first it may seem like there's no advantage to using the VA loan when the buyer has to come up with a down payment. But look at these great pluses for the buyer:

- Assumability.
- No cost for mortgage insurance.
- Less strict qualifying guidelines.
- Second mortgages can be used in conjunction with new VA loan.

Assumability. Loans made prior to March 1, 1988 are fully assumable with no qualifying and no change in interest rate. That means that if you have an 8% VA loan, the buyer can pay you your equity and he can assume the loan under the exact same terms as you've had.

Beginning March 1, 1988, the assumability changed. VA loans are now assumable after qualifying ($500.00 assumption fee + ½% funding fee, the latter to be paid by the purchaser). The new buyer has to qualify with the lender, but the terms of the note are the same as for the original owner. It's still almost as good a loan as before.

No Need For Mortgage Insurance. There is no need for mortgage insurance with a VA loan. Let's suppose the veteran is buying a house for $174,000. His total down payment will be 25% of the difference between the purchase price and $144,000. That's $7,500. The loan would be for $166,500. The down payment is just slightly more than 4% of the purchase price. *If* the buyer could obtain a conventional loan for this home with only 4% down, he would need mortgage insurance. That could add $40 to $60 per month to his payment.

Easier Qualifying Guidelines. The VA's guidelines for qualifying the buyer are less strict than those of other programs. The veteran doesn't need to make as much money, because of the way the VA looks at income, size of family, other obligations, and size of house.

Use of Junior Mortgages. The VA loan can also be used to buy more expensive housing if you will carry a second mortgage on the amounts that are not guaranteed by the VA. For example, let's say your home sells for $200,000. The deal can be structured this way:

VA first lien	$144,000
Down payment	40,000
Second lien to you	16,000
Sales price of home	$200,000

Certificate of Eligibility. In order for the veteran to receive the benefits of a VA loan, he must have a Certificate of Eligibility. All veterans are entitled to the full eligibility of $36,000 as of 1988, even though their Certificate states less. The $36,000 entitles them to a full $144,000 loan with no down payment.

Some Disadvantages. There are some disadvantages to VA loans. For example, it sometimes happens that a VA appraisal will come in at a lower value than a conventional appraisal. This used to be the rule, though it is now more an exception to the rule; but it could cause you some problems. Also, loan processing time can be two or three weeks longer than with a conventional loan.

If the interest rates on conventional loans are higher than on VA loans, the points required by the lenders for VA loans could cause you some grief, so you need to do some checking with lenders before you offer a VA loan.

Multi-Family Dwelling Units and Acreages. The VA will allow homes, as well as duplexes, triplexes, and fourplexes to be financed under its program. And any number of acres are allowed, including farms if the veteran will be occupying the house on the farm.

BUYDOWNS ARE GOOD SELLING TOOLS

To help you sell your home, you can offer *buydowns* for the buyer, just like new home builders do. Buydowns are subsidies given to a home buyer by the seller or by anyone else—parents and other relatives. Buydown money goes either to get the payments down for the first few years (temporary buydowns), or to buy the interest rate down for the life of the loan (permanent buydowns).

Temporary Buydowns

These are very good marketing ploys. For example, if the normal rate on a VA loan is 10%, then you can offer the buyer a temporary interest rate buydown up to a maximum of 3% during the first three years. So the buyer would pay 7% the first year, 8% the second year and 9% the third year. On the fourth year, the normal 10% would be set all the way through to the 30th year. This example is called a 3-2-1 buydown: 3% off during the first year, 2% off during the second, and 1% off in the third.

Even though you're sacrificing some of your profit, the buydown is an excellent way to handle getting someone qualified who might be marginal. You can get top dollar for your home by offering more comfortable payments to the buyer during his first few years of ownership. Your cost is a total of the difference in the payments during those first three years. For example, if you offer an $80,000 loan at 10% with a 3-2-1 temporary buydown, the payments would be as follows:

Year	Rate	Normal Payment	Actual Payment
1	7%	$702.01	$532.24
2	8%	702.01	587.01
3	9%	702.01	643.70
4	10%	702.01	702.01

In this example, the buyer saves $169.77 per month the first year, $115.00 per month the second year and $58.31 per month during the last year of the buydown. If you take all these savings and multiply them by 12 and add them all together, the savings to the buyer is $4,116.96. It will cost you almost that much for the buydown (you get a rebate for some interest while the money is not being used). But in a tough market, or with a marginal buyer, you'll make the sale, because the buyer is qualified on the first year's payments.

Permanent Buydowns

As with any new loan, you can also do a permanent buydown of the interest. If the rates are at 9%, the lenders may quote lower rates with some points: 8½% with four points, 8% with six points and so on.

If you play around with the figures on your home, you'll come up with different variables for VA financing. Keep all the figures handy so you can show them to a veteran who might be interested in buying the home. In fact, you should work up figures on not just VA, but other forms of financing so you can come up with them depending on what type of buyer you get. This is a great sales tool and can easily make the difference in whether or not you make a sale.

GRADUATED PAYMENTS

The VA also has *graduated payment mortgages* that can do almost the same thing as the buydown. The payments start out low and increase 7½% per year (remember, it is the *payment* that increases, not the interest rate) for five years, then remain level for the remaining 25 years. The disadvantage of this program is that there is some *negative amortization* (an increase of the principal due on the loan) during the first few years, and there is a down payment of as high as 12% on some properties.

VA CONTRACT FORM

Appendix F at the back of the book has a filled-in example of a contract form useful when selling using a VA-guaranteed loan. There is also a blank contract form for making copies to use when you need to work with a veteran.

13

FHA Loans

THE FEDERAL HOUSING ADMINISTRATION (FHA) WAS ESTABLISHED IN 1934 TO HELP people obtain long-term home financing which was not available at the time. Presently *FHA loans* only account for about 25% of all the home mortgages, but that's still a significant amount. It works the same as the VA; it does not originate loans, but it insures the loans to the lenders making them.

As with the Veterans Administration, the borrower will not be dealing directly with FHA. All dealings are with the lender. The lender complies with all requirements of an FHA loan, then receives the loan insurance from FHA after paying FHA its mortgage insurance premium (explained below).

Unlike the VA loans, you do not have to be anyone special to qualify for an FHA loan. You can be a veteran, a non-veteran, white, black, old, young, male, or female. You don't even have to be a U.S. citizen. As long as you are a legal resident who qualifies economically, you are eligible for an FHA loan.

ANOTHER TRADITIONAL LOAN

This is another one of the three traditional loans I referred to in Chapter 11. There is a small down payment, as I'll explain in more detail later, and an FHA loan is easier to obtain than a conventional loan, which is discussed in the next chapter. As in other forms of traditional financing, borrowers must have the following:

- Excellent credit record

- Enough income to make the monthly payments

- Lack of other, excessive payment obligations

- Stable job, generally with a minimum of two years tenure

Interest rate. The FHA no longer sets interest rates, as it did in the past. Lenders are allowed to charge the going rate on loans. As a general rule, FHA loans are made for lower rates than conventional loans.

Assumability. All FHA loans made prior to December 1986 are fully assumable, just like the old VA loans (no qualifying). For loans made after that date, there will be a period of 12 months after the closing of each loan wherein the purchaser will have to be approved by the lender in order to take over an FHA loan (24 months for FHA loans that were made to investors). I wouldn't worry too much about this provision. Because of its assumability, the FHA loan is still just about as good as a VA loan for the new buyer.

Mortgage Insurance Premium (MIP). One of the disadvantages of FHA loans, and any conventional loans that are made with less than a 20% down payment, is that the buyer has to pay mortgage insurance. But it won't affect your sale. On a 30-year FHA loan, the buyer has to pay—or finance into the loan—a 3.8% MIP. If the loan is for $90,000, then $3,420 is added to it. That money goes to FHA to cover their expenses plus losses when there are foreclosures. Actually, the FHA is one of the few money-making arms of the Federal Government.

FHA 203b PROGRAM

The FHA program with level payments is the 203b. Most of the loans that FHA insures are of this type. The 203c program is the same as the 203b, but is for condominiums. The 203b program can be used not only for single-family homes, but also for properties with up to four living units, that is, duplexes, triplexes, and fourplexes.

FHA loans require a minimum down payment. With the 203b program the buyer pays $750 on the first $25,000 of the loan, then 5% on anything up to the maximum loan amount of $90,000. If the sales price is under $50,000, the down payment is only 3% of the total purchase price. In some high-cost areas the maximum loan amount is higher, so you'll need to check with a lender.

FHA loans are also made to investors. The down payment is now 25%, but it is a good route for you to use if your home would make a good investment and you find an investor willing to buy it who has the 25% for the down payment. Check with a lender to determine the down payment requirement at the time you find an investor who wants to buy your property.

The FHA will also allow an owner-occupant to purchase the home along with an investor, as long as the owner-occupant owns at least a 55% interest in the property. Each party must make a monthly payment equal to his or her ownership share. If an investor owns 45%, then his share of the payment is 45%. This is an excellent way for young people to buy your home with the help of relatives.

FHA 245 GRADUATED PAYMENT PROGRAMS

The FHA 245 graduated payment programs require a down payment of from 3-12% depending on the program and the interest rate. Total amount of the loan is generally the same as with the 203b program.

The FHA comes up with different programs, or variations of existing graduated payment programs, from time to time. It's a good idea to check with lenders at the time you get ready to sell to see what might work for you, and what you need to do to use the programs that fit your needs.

FHA 245a Program

FIGURE 13-1 will give you an idea of the payments required (for each $1,000 financed) with FHA financing on a 10% loan. The left column is for the standard 203b level payment program; the others are the five plans available under the 245a graduated payment programs.

The 245a plans do develop some negative amortization, so the buyer needs to be aware of it. Plan 1 develops .61% of the original balance after two years, Plan 2 is 2.99% after four years, Plan 3 is 5.52% after four years, Plan 4 is 1.90% after five years, and Plan 5 is 4.7% after six years. So if your buyer borrowed $60,000 and went under Plan 2, at the end of four years, he would owe $61,794. At that point the loan would start amortizing and the principal due at the end of each month would be less than it was the previous month.

The 245a program is good for buyers who don't quite qualify to purchase your home. Remember, FIG. 13-1 is only for a 10% loan. Check with a lender to see what rates are available at the time your buyer goes for loan application.

FHA 245b Program

FHA also offers a 245b graduated payment mortgage, designed to supplement the 203b and 245a programs. The down payment is similar to, and in some cases less than, that for the 203b program. To be eligible, the borrower must *not* be

Fig. 13-1

FHA LOAN PAYMENTS
(PER $1,000 FINANCED, 10% INTEREST RATE)

Year	FHA 203b	FHA 245a Plan 1	Plan 2	Plan 3	Plan 4	Plan 5
1	$8.78	$8.0057	$7.3059	$6.6704	$7.8003	$7.3457
2	8.78	8.2058	7.6712	7.1706	7.9564	7.5661
3	8.78	8.4110	8.0547	7.7084	8.1155	7.7931
4	8.78	8.6213	8.4575	8.2866	8.2778	8.0269
5	8.78	8.8368	8.8804	8.9081	8.4433	8.2677
6	8.78	9.0577	9.3244	9.5762	8.6122	8.5157
7	8.78	9.0577	9.3244	9.5762	8.7845	8.7712
8	8.78	9.0577	9.3244	9.5762	8.9601	9.0343
9	8.78	9.0577	9.3244	9.5762	9.1393	9.3053
10	8.78	9.0577	9.3244	9.5762	9.3221	9.5845
11	8.78	9.0577	9.3244	9.5762	9.5086	9.8720
12	8.78	9.0577	9.3244	9.5762	9.5086	9.8720
13	8.78	9.0577	9.3244	9.5762	9.5086	9.8720
14	8.78	9.0577	9.3244	9.5762	9.5086	9.8720
15	8.78	9.0577	9.3244	9.5762	9.5086	9.8720
16	8.78	9.0577	9.3244	9.5762	9.5086	9.8720
17	8.78	9.0577	9.3244	9.5762	9.5086	9.8720
18	8.78	9.0577	9.3244	9.5762	9.5086	9.8720
19	8.78	9.0577	9.3244	9.5762	9.5086	9.8720
20	8.78	9.0577	9.3244	9.5762	9.5086	9.8720
21	8.78	9.0577	9.3244	9.5762	9.5086	9.8720
22	8.78	9.0577	9.3244	9.5762	9.5086	9.8720
23	8.78	9.0577	9.3244	9.5762	9.5086	9.8720
24	8.78	9.0577	9.3244	9.5762	9.5086	9.8720
25	8.78	9.0577	9.3244	9.5762	9.5086	9.8720
26	8.78	9.0577	9.3244	9.5762	9.5086	9.8720
27	8.78	9.0577	9.3244	9.5762	9.5086	9.8720
28	8.78	9.0577	9.3244	9.5762	9.5086	9.8720
29	8.78	9.0577	9.3244	9.5762	9.5086	9.8720
30	8.78	9.0577	9.3244	9.5762	9.5086	9.8720

able to qualify under the 203b program, and must *not* have enough cash assets to use the 245a program. It is limited to a fixed number of mortgages each year, so you will want to check with a lender for details.

BUYDOWNS

I explained buydowns in the previous chapter, but it's worth repeating. Buydowns are subsidies given to a home buyer by the seller or by anyone else— parents and other relatives. Buydown money goes either to get the payments down for the first few years (temporary buydowns), or to buy the interest rate down for the life of the loan (permanent buydowns).

The FHA program, like the VA program, will work with a temporary or permanent buydown. But with FHA the buydown must not exceed 5% of the sale price of the home. If the 5% is exceeded, then the appraiser is instructed to reduce any comparable sales on a dollar for dollar basis over the 5% allowance. That means your home may not appraise high enough, so the buydowns work best if left at or below the 5% maximum.

FHA CONTRACT FORM

Appendix G at the back of the book has a filled-in example of a contract form useful when selling using an FHA-insured loan. There is also a blank contract form for making copies to use when you need to work with a buyer using FHA financing.

14

Conventional Loans

FOR THE BORROWER, A *CONVENTIONAL LOAN* IS HANDLED THE SAME AS A VA or an FHA loan. The borrower—any borrower regardless of race, creed, color or nationality—goes to a lender and takes out a loan to purchase your property. The differences are in the requirements:

- How much the down payment will be

- How much the borrower must earn

- What is the most the borrower can pay in other monthly obligations

Conventional loans are made by the same lending institutions that originate FHA and VA loans. The big difference to the lender is that some conventional loans don't have another institution insuring the loan in case the buyer defaults. On any non-insured loan, if the borrower defaults, the lender takes the entire loss. Whereas on VA loans the Veterans Administration guarantees to the lender that the borrower will make his payments, and on FHA loans the Federal Housing Administration insures to the lender that the borrower will make his payments. Insured conventional loans are insured by a private mortgage insurance (PMI) company, such as Mortgage Guaranty Insurance Corp. (MGIC), the leader in the field.

Conventional mortgages are primarily used on homes over $100,000, since that's close to the limits of both VA and FHA loans. There are many types of conventional mortgages, and the maximum amounts can be up to a million dollars and, at times, more.

ANOTHER TRADITIONAL LOAN

This is the last of the three traditional loans I referred to in Chapter 11. It is usually the hardest of the three to obtain. As in other forms of traditional financing, borrowers must have the following:

- Excellent credit record

- Enough income to make the monthly payments

- Lack of other, excessive payment obligations

- Stable job, with tenure required varying from lender to lender

Maximum Amount. For FNMA and FHLMC mortgages, that is, mortgages which comply with FNMA and FHLMC guidelines, and which will more than likely be eventually sold to one of those secondary mortgage agencies—the large majority of all mortgages—the maximums are $168,700 for single-family homes, $215,800 for duplexes, $260,800 for triplexes, and $324,150 for fourplexes. Of course, some lenders will exceed these maximums, and some even offer "jumbo" loans in the million-dollar range.

Down Payment. The normal down payment is 20% (80% loan). Loans are also available with 5% down (95% loan) and 10% down (90% loan). With the latter two loans the buyer has to pay a mortgage insurance premium (MIP), although the premium is less than with FHA loans. The MIP is 2½% of the loan amount on the 95% loan, and 2% of the loan amount on the 90% loan. The MIP is payable at closing, or it may be financed. If it is financed, 1% is payable at closing on the 95% loan and an additional ¼% per year is payable each month as part of the house payment. On the 90% loan, ½% is payable at closing and an additional ¼% is payable each month with the house payment.

Assumability. Some conventional loans are assumable at the same interest rate as the original note, but most lenders reserve the right to increase the interest rate when the loan is assumed. Some lenders will negotiate an interest rate that's not quite as high as the prevailing loan rate at the time of the assumption, but higher than the original note.

The nice feature of conventional loans is that it generally only takes two or three weeks to process them. That can be a real benefit to you in getting a quick closing on your house sale.

You may want to check with your local lenders. Some have pulled away from the 95% conventional loans because the PMI companies have taken such tremendous losses in recent years. As a matter of fact, many of them have gone broke, leaving lenders holding the bag.

Qualifying Is More Strict. Lenders are typically more strict in granting conventional loans than VA or FHA loans. But there are certain properties that will not be accepted by VA or FHA. If you have problems getting your home qualified under VA or FHA because of its age or condition, you will usually have better luck by going with a conventional loan.

NO FINANCING MEANS NO SALE

It may seem that I'm placing the burden of financing on you, the seller. It isn't your responsibility, of course. If you have a property to sell for which you are asking $125,000, you don't care how the buyer comes up with the money. All you want is $125,000 cash.

As a practical matter though, if the buyer doesn't have cash, he must borrow money. And if he doesn't know how to obtain the loan necessary to come up with the balance of your $125,000, then you must help him. In fact, to most real estate agents, knowing how to come up with these loans is just as important as the advertising of the property and the procuring of a buyer.

You may come up with a good, qualified buyer, but if you don't help him get a loan that will satisfy both his needs and yours, then you have no sale.

A CONVENTIONAL LOAN CONTRACT FORM

Appendix H at the back of the book has a filled-in example of a contract form useful when selling using a conventional loan. There is also a blank contract form for making copies to use when you need to work with a buyer using conventional financing.

15

Alternative Financing

THE LOAN I'VE BEEN DISCUSSING SO FAR ARE STANDARD OR TRADITIONAL LOANS, ones that have been used for decades. In this chapter I'll touch on alternative avenues for you to use in financing the sale of your home. These loans are made through the same lenders as before.

GRADUATED PAYMENT MORTGAGES (GPMs)

The GPM considerably lowers the buyer's payments during the early years of the loan—generally during the first five years. This is accomplished by charging the buyer's loan the full amount of the payment, but having the buyer pay a smaller amount. The amount that the buyer doesn't pay is added to the principal balance of his loan.

Some people shy away from this type of loan, but if you think about it, on a normal loan that amortizes over 30 years, only 1% of the loan amount is reduced during the first five years. On a negative amortization GPM, the loan amount may increase 7-8% during the first five years. So on a $90,000 "standard" loan, the balance at the end of five years may be $89,000. On the GPM, the balance may be $97,000. But if you figure the difference in payments during those years, you'll generally find that the buyer will have saved at least the $8,000 difference. And if the house increased a nominal 5% per year in value, the home will be worth at least $115,000 at the end of those five years.

What does all this mean for your buyer? Simply, more house than he can afford, or smaller payments so he has enough money left over each month to live and enjoy life more during the first few years of his home ownership. Later on, his salary increases should more than take care of the increases in the loan payment, because the highest the payment will reach is normally not more than 110% of what the payment would have been on a level-payment loan.

ADJUSTABLE RATE MORTGAGES (ARMs)

There are many varieties of ARMs. Most ARMs do not have negative amortization; they are level-payment mortgages that amortize over a certain number of years—30 years, 20 years, even 15 years or less. The advantage of the ARM is that the initial rate of the loan is much less than on a "standard" fixed-rate loan. For example, the initial rate of a fixed-rate loan might be 10%. That same loan as an ARM might be 7%. The main difference between the ARM and a fixed-rate loan is that the lender may change the interest rate and payment periodically according to a pre-set schedule and index. The loan carries an interest rate so many percentage points above the index. Usually 2–3% is the norm.

Lenders use an index that is readily available, such as one-year T-bills. The payments and interest rate can be changed as often as monthly, or more commonly every year, every 3 years, or even every 5 years. The mortgage usually has an annual *payment* or *rate cap*, such as an increase of no more than 7½% of the *payment* within a year, or an increase or decrease of 2% of the loan's interest *rate* within a year. There are also total caps on increases and decreases of the interest rate over the life of the loan, usually 3–5%. So, with a total cap of 5%, a 7% loan will never go above 12%.

The beauty of all these loans is that the buyer qualifies on the first year's payments and not on any payments down the line. The buyer can always buy more home than under "standard" loans. It means if you can sell buyers on some kind of alternative financing, you'll have a greater pool of buyers that can afford your property.

BUYDOWNS

In case you skipped the chapters on VA and FHA financing, I'll reiterate that buydowns are subsidies given to a home buyer by the seller or by anyone else—parents and other relatives. Buydown money goes either to get the payments down for the first few years (temporary buydowns) or to buy the interest rate down for the life of the loan (permanent buydowns).

The most common buydown is the 3-2-1 interest rate buydown, similar to what we looked at with VA loans. On an 11% loan, it will reduce the rate to 8% the first year, 9% the second year, and 10% the third year. On the fourth year it goes to the note rate. A temporary buydown like this will do more to sell your home than a permanent buydown. It will cost you about 5% of the sales price of the home. So if you're in a tough market and are thinking of dropping the price 5%, then by all means you should opt to offer the 3-2-1 buydown and allow more people to qualify for your home.

While a permanent buydown may bring down the buyer's payment $50 per month, the temporary buydown can bring the payment down $200 per month the first year. *The buyer qualifies for the loan on the first year's payment.*

CASH

You might find a buyer who has all cash and wants to buy your home, pay all your equity and assume any existing loans on the property. This is a rare occurrence. If you find such a buyer, keep some of these thoughts in mind:

- The buyer, since he's using all his cash, is generally more careful—much more picky—about how the house looks, how the contract is written, and how the deal is closed.

- Once you've written the contract, close as soon as you can. No deal is complete until it closes and *funds*. The cash buyer has all possibilities open to him. Don't give him time to think it over and back out. Close quick, get your money, and run.

- Try to get as much earnest money as possible. On an $80,000 house, $500 earnest money is less than 1% of cash buyer's investment, but it is over 6% of the investment for a buyer putting a 10% down payment and financing the rest.

The cash buyer will typically ask for more of a discount than the buyer who has to finance. In most cases, he is justified in doing so. If you had expected to pay points and additional closing costs for the buyer to obtain a loan, be realistic and give the buyer credit for those costs. You'll make the sale quickly, and your competition will offer the same discounts. But if you're in a sellers' market, you may not need to be quite so generous.

CASH CONTRACT FORM

Appendix I at the back of the book contains a blank cash sale contract form. Make copies of it to use with cash buyers.

16

Creative Financing

CREATIVE FINANCING IMPLIES ANY TYPE OF LOAN WHERE THE SELLER PARTICI-
pates in the lending process. There are assumptions, wraparounds, second
mortgages (second liens), even third and fourth mortgages, contracts for deed
(sale on contract) and many others. Creative financing also includes buydowns
to a certain extent, but we've covered those in previous chapters.

Creative financing is the financing of choice in a poor market. You *do not*
want to use it for the sale of your house if you have plenty of time to sell it and
your housing market is either normal or good from your point of view.

ASSUMPTIONS

Under a straight assumption, the buyer pays the seller the difference between what is owed on the first mortgage, and the sale price. A $70,000 house
with a $50,000 first lien requires a $20,000 down payment. If you have an FHA
or a VA loan, then an assumption will work well for you. If you have $20,000
equity and you find someone who will give you the $20,000, then you just transfer
your loan to him and move on.

Be Creative. You can also get a little more creative with the straight
assumption. Let's suppose the buyer doesn't have $20,000 cash, but he has a
$10,000 car that's paid for, and a lake lot that's worth $10,000 and is also paid

for. Why not take them in on trade if you don't need the money to move on to another house? You could use the car and/or the lot as a down payment to buy your next home from a builder. Builders, especially custom builders, are very much into this type of creativity in the sale of their homes.

You may also find another seller who will go along with a trade if you're moving up. To a lender the car and lot should qualify as a required down payment in the purchase of your next home.

All Assumptions Are a Risk to the Seller. All assumptions carry a certain risk to the seller. If the buyer defaults on the loan, the lender can also look to the seller, whose name is on the original loan instruments (the note and mortgage in some states, or the note and deed of trust in other states).

If the buyer put down a substantial down payment, then the lender probably won't bother with the seller in case of default; there's enough equity in the property for the lender to get his money back when he eventually sells the property.

If you don't have an FHA or VA loan, things get a bit more complicated. Early in the 1970s, lenders started using the *due-on-sale clause* in their conventional mortgages to protect themselves from being locked into 30 years of low interest mortgages when interest rates escalate. Today almost all conventional mortgages have the due-on-sale clause. There are ways to go around the due-on-sale clause. One method is the *contract for deed*. But you must be aware of the pitfalls.

CONTRACTS FOR DEED

Under a *contract for deed*, also known as a *sale on contract* or even a *land contract*, the buyer makes a down payment—oftentimes a very nominal down payment—makes payments to the seller, and purchases the home without receiving title at the time of purchase. The seller receives payments on his buyer's loan and keeps making payments on his own original loan. The lender never finds out you sold the house. This is the easiest form of creative financing, but it is also the one with the greatest number of pitfalls and risks.

Advantages. The major advantages are little or no down payment, no qualifying for the loan (the seller is the lender), perhaps a low interest rate, and immediate possession. For the seller the advantages are that he has no discount points to pay, the sale can be made rather quickly (normally without a broker), without worry that the property won't appraise for the sale price, and with no closing costs. Under certain conditions this is a good way to sell a home.

Disadvantages. The major disadvantage is that the buyer is not the owner of record until all the terms of the contract are fulfilled; in other words, the buyer does not receive a deed to record at the county courthouse to show he is the rightful owner. Problems could arise if the seller cannot deliver a valid title to the buyer after the buyer has met the conditions of the contract.

If the seller has any judgments filed against him, or goes through a bankruptcy or a devastating divorce settlement and does not make payments on his loan, then there could be liens on the property that would have to be paid before the seller can give clear title to the buyer (who may have promptly made all his payments to the seller). If the seller can't clear the liens, the buyer may have paid for a house that he can't get clear title to.

With the serious pitfalls this type of sale can have, there should be an agreed-upon course of action should any of them arise. The safe course for the buyer is that he obtain title to the property as soon as he has enough equity, through appreciation and mortgage principal reduction (usually sometime between the second and fifth years), and that the seller then take back a mortgage or deed of trust to guarantee his remaining loan. But the buyer must understand that if the first lienholder calls the loan due, the buyer must at that point refinance.

In most states, if the contract for deed is recorded, it will protect the buyer sufficiently in case the seller does encounter economic setbacks down the road. If your loan is with an out-of-town lender, then the contract can be safely recorded. The lender would probably never find out that you sold the home. The due-on-sale clause in your mortgage would probably never be triggered.

The buyer can also be protected if you give him a second lien on the property. The second lien would cover the contract for deed. Because the contract for deed would not be recorded in this case, the lender would not be aware of ownership transfer.

SECOND MORTGAGES

A *second mortgage* is used when the buyer does not have enough money to pay the seller his entire equity. If the seller is asking $60,000 for his home, and he has an assumable VA mortgage that carries an interest rate of 8% with a balance of $30,000, then the buyer has to come up with the difference of $30,000 for the equity. Not too many people are able to pay 50% down for a house, and even if they could, the smart buyers won't part with that much money.

So let's say the buyer puts down 10% (most lenders require 10% as a minimum) or $6,000, and gets a second mortgage (second lien) from a commercial lender for $24,000 to pay the seller the balance of his equity. Usually that second mortgage will be at an interest rate two to four percentage points higher than the going rate for new first mortgage loans. The second mortgage will also usually be for a shorter term than the 25 or 30 years available on first mortgages. Twelve or 15 years is the standard length of term.

In the above example, if the interest rate on the second mortgage is 14%, the combined interest rate on the entire amount of the mortgages is still only 10.67%. You find the average by multiplying the first lien amount by its interest rate, multiplying the second lien amount by its interest rate, adding the two totals, and divide that amount by the total of the first and second lien amounts. In this example it is as follows:

$$\$30,000 \times 8\% = \$2,400 \quad \text{First lien}$$
$$\$24,000 \times 14\% = \underline{\$3,360} \quad \text{Second lien}$$
$$\$5,760 \div \$54,000 = 10.67\%$$

If the rate you get by blending the two together is less than the going rate for new loans, considering all costs it would take for a new loan, then this is a good way for you to finance your buyer. One problem: even though this blended interest rate is lower than the prevailing rates for new first liens, the monthly payment may not be any better because the second lien will be payable sooner. But that can be an advantage for the buyer; he'll have the house paid off sooner.

GETTING MORE CREATIVE

Now let's get a little more creative. Assume we have the same circumstances, but the seller decides to take back a second mortgage instead of making the buyer go to a commercial lender to get one. If the seller takes $6,000 as a down payment and carries the $24,000 at 9%, then the combined interest rate on both mortgages is about 8.45%. That's much better. If you don't want to wait 15 years to get all your money, then put a balloon payment at the end of the third, fifth, or seventh year, or whatever feels comfortable to you.

Alternately, the buyer could use a commercial second lien, and you take a third lien; each of which would be for $12,000. You'll end up with more cash than in this example, and the rate will still be lower than if the buyer had gone the straight commercial second lien route.

The big disadvantage of your taking a third lien is that if the buyer defaults on the first or second mortgages, *you* must foreclose on the buyer or else the other lienholders will wipe you out when they foreclose.

WRAPAROUNDS

A *wraparound mortgage* is an excellent way to sell your house for top dollar. Let's say you have a first lien with a balance of $52,000 at 13% interest, and it's an FHA assumable loan. Your payments for principal and interest are $575 and the taxes and insurance are $100, for a total payment of $675. The market is slow. The house is worth $80,000, but in this slow market you'll probably have to discount it by 10% to find a buyer.

Now let's also assume you don't need all your cash right away and are willing to do owner financing with a wraparound. Here's how you could sell quickly.

Run an ad in the classifieds that says something like this:

> **$1,900 DOWN,** owner financing, 9.5%
> loan. Only $765/month. Pretty 3-2-2
> with large corner lot. 555-5555

Normally, this type of situation will get you a buyer within a week or two. What you're doing is selling the house for $79,900, taking $1,900 down, and financing $78,000. You act as the lender. Your loan to the new buyer is at 9.5% interest—the higher the sales price, the lower the interest rate if you don't change the payment—with principal and interest payments of $655 plus taxes and insurance of $110, for a total payment of $765. This is $90 per month more than what you pay on your FHA loan. And the $90 is all profit.

This is a marvelous seller's gimmick. This type of advertising will get you a multitude of calls, and in the end you may be able to talk one of these prospects into going for an alternative form of financing instead of owner financing.

You can sell the house with the above financing and put a balloon payment on the loan in three to six years. The beauty of this is that you avoid closing costs, points, and fees when the buyer refinances.

ASSUMPTION AND OWNER-FINANCED CONTRACT FORMS

Appendix J at the back of the book has a filled-in example of a contract form useful when selling using assumptions. The contract form in Appendix I is filled-in for an owner-financed sale, but could have been used for a cash sale as well. Blank contract forms are also included in these appendices.

17

Financing for the Desperate Seller

I'D LIKE TO GIVE YOU OPTIONS THAT SELLERS HAVE USED WHEN THEY'RE UP against a wall in trying to get a sale. I don't endorse all or any of these methods. But I've been in the business long enough to have seen every trick in the book used by sellers who needed to make a sale.

Financing can affect a sale in an absolutely astounding manner. In 1986 U.S. car manufacturers couldn't sell their remaining 1986 cars before the 1987 model year came out. So they dropped their financing rates under 3% and had buyers swarming into their showrooms. Did they discount the price? No, they raised their prices and discounted the financing rate. It was just another smart gimmick. First a word of caution, then I'll show you some gimmicks.

Scrutinize Your Buyer. Before we go deeper into this chapter, I'd like you to remember to scrutinize your buyer. I've mentioned this before in the chapter on condos and co-ops, but it's worth repeating here in case you're dealing with a single-family home and skipped over that chapter. When you will do owner financing, emulate the professionals. Use a good credit application, make sure the buyer fills out all the blanks, and check all his credit references—Appendix K is a blank credit application you can make a copy of to have handy for your buyer. Have him obtain a copy of his credit report from the local credit bureau. It will take a few days, but the wait will be well worth it to you. If your buyer has an unstable job, has been on the job a very short time, or has shown an inability to keep up with his economic obligations don't be tempted to risk future headaches with him—unless he can prove to you unusual circumstances that should not reoccur.

NO MONEY DOWN

Let's say you have a house that will appraise for $60,000. You need to sell it soon. Assume it cost you $42,000. If you pay $3,000 in points and closing costs for the buyer's loan, your cost will be up to $45,000. If you really need to sell it soon and get your cash, you might discount the house 10%, and *give* the buyer the down payment. He gets a loan for $54,000 and gets the house. You still make a $9,000 profit. He gets a good deal and you make a profit and get rid of your house in a hurry. Even with only a 5% discount, the buyer would still be able to show a 5% down payment, which is enough to buy the house under most loan plans.

The mechanics of the above plan are easy. You write a contract for $60,000 with a $6,000 down payment. The lender will want to verify that the buyer has the money to pay the down payment. The buyer can do one of two things: he can borrow the money from a relative and put it in his savings account until closing, or he can get a *gift letter* from a relative, preferably one with good assets. The latter is the best way to do it.

The Gift Letter. In the gift letter the relative will say that he'll give the buyer the money for the down payment and does not expect the buyer to repay him. At closing you give the buyer back his down payment, and he repays the relative.

Even if you don't want to give the buyer such a discount, you can still work out a plan where you loan him the money after closing and he gives you a second lien on the property and makes payments to you on that loan for the down payment.

Have the Buyer Borrow the Down Payment. Let's look at another variation. Suppose your buyer has some credit and is able to borrow $3,000 on his signature, or perhaps on a car or boat to which he has a clear title. The money from that loan can be used to purchase the $60,000 house with a 5% down payment, as long as you will pay *all* of the closing costs as well as the *prepays* (that is, any closing costs he would have been responsible for and any amounts to be escrowed by the lender for hazard insurance, taxes, mortgage insurance, and the first year's hazard insurance premium—as much as the lender will allow).

The mortgage company will want to know if the debt is a furniture loan or a car loan, etc. There's nothing wrong with the buyer having a number of debts, as long as he qualifies for the house loan. But the buyer shouldn't come out and say that he's borrowed the down payment.

Using a Third Lien. Most sellers are familiar with selling a house where they allow the buyer to assume their mortgage company's first lien, and they take a second lien for a part or all of their equity. Or the second lien comes from a commercial lender who loans the buyer money to purchase the property. The buyer pays the mortgage company on the first lien, and also pays the seller, or the second lienholder as the case may be, on the second lien every month.

If you are willing to take back a third lien, then you should have no trouble selling your house to a buyer with no money down. You can write an offer showing that he pays a 10% down payment. He borrows the down payment, then goes to a second lien lender and borrows enough to cover the equity. When you close on the deal, you give him back his down payment and file your third lien. He pays off his down payment loan. He now makes payments to you for the down payment; he makes a total of three payments each month. If you have a house with high equity, this works well. You get most of your money at closing—generally at full price because of the excellent terms—and you receive payments on the balance of your equity.

Before you do this, please read again the chapter on qualifying buyers. You must make sure you're not placing your buyer in a financially hazardous position.

You're in a third lien position, so if you have an unqualified buyer—one whose income won't be enough to meet all of his obligations *comfortably*—you jeopardize not only your loan, but the buyer's credit. These plans are *only* for buyers who are short of down payment funds, not for those who are short of necessary income to qualify for the entire amount of the house payment.

In situations where you have a double contract—in other words, you are telling the lender that you're doing one thing on the contract, and going behind his back and doing another—you must be careful that you don't do anything that could be construed as fraud. In other words, double contracts are illegal. The best way to go around this is to be creative in the way the buyer gets his money—or discount from you—for the down payment.

For example, you can buy an asset from the buyer (even though it has a lien), such as a car, motorcycle, or boat. He gets money for the down payment. After closing, you sell it back to him and he gives you an IOU for it. Or he can do some service for you for which you will generously compensate him so that he has funds for his down payment.

How about this: his brother "gives" him the down payment, and you buy something from his brother, then sell it to the buyer on terms after he closes on the house. If you find a buyer who *really* wants to purchase your property—how many won't with no money down?—then you and he can sit down and brainstorm for a way to go around the double contract problem.

Everybody will buy a house with no money down and comfortable payments. In a tough market that's what will sell your house. If you'll use these ideas you will come up with something that works and is legal. In other words, it doesn't matter where the buyer gets his cash for the down payment, as long as the agreement between you and the buyer, which you give to the lender, is the same as the *true* agreement between you and that buyer.

But if you have an agreement to purchase something from his brother, and his brother will in turn *give* that money to the buyer, it doesn't matter to you or to the lender if that buyer will at some point give his brother some money and that the brother will give you some money, etc., etc.

ADDITIONAL CREATIVE FINANCING IDEAS

There are countless ways to make a house more saleable due to the terms. I'll briefly describe some ideas you may want to try.

Adjustable Owner Financing. The seller's financing might start at 5%, go to 6% the second year, and increase each year until it reaches a specified limit, so the buyer's payments can be easier at first.

Negative Amortization Owner Financing. How about selling your house with the same terms as lenders do? It's better than renting it. You'll have a very interested party living in the house who won't hound you for repairs.

No Interest Owner Financing. You might want to carry a second lien loan for the buyer at no interest. You will get a higher price for the house than what the market warrants, so in effect you would be getting interest. It's a good selling gimmick.

Several years ago, when new loan rates were at their highest, I worked with a seller of a townhouse who hadn't had any luck with another real estate broker. He wanted $58,900 for the property. I listed it, raised the price to $63,900 and advertised that the buyer could assume the seller's 8% FHA loan. The seller would carry a 0% interest second lien payable over 10 years with $10,000 down. The property sold in a couple of weeks.

Most real estate agents do not really understand real estate financing. With the right type of financing, I was able to personally sell over 40 homes in three months in a depressed Texas market in 1986.

With some thought and ingenuity, you can sell your home quickly, perhaps better and quicker than if you had it listed with an agent. But you cannot hope for the impossible. You won't get $100,000 cash for your $95,000 home in a tough market. But you will get $105,900 for it if you offer great terms through owner financing. For example, assume you owe $60,000 on a 9% FHA loan, and your monthly payments are $600 per month PITI. You need to sell, but you don't need much cash. You feel a buyer will pay just under $1,000 per month PITI. So you offer the home for $105,900 with $2,500 down and payments of $995 PITI. If you work it out, you'll find that you'll be selling it at under 8% fixed interest. The buyer won't care that the house is at the top of the retail value range. The fact is that you'll have a product others don't have: owner financed; low interest; low down payment; comfortable monthly payments.

18

Drawing Up a
Purchase Agreement

A *PURCHASE AGREEMENT* IS ANOTHER NAME FOR A *CONTRACT*, AND A CON-tract is simply a written record of your oral agreement with the purchaser. A legal written agreement can be very simple and not much different from the way you would make an oral agreement. For example you could state it this way:

> We, John and Mary Smith, agree to sell our house at 245 N. Main St., Anywhere, USA, to Ted and Julie Jones for $150,000. They've given us $1,000 earnest money. They will apply for a loan from XYZ Mortgage Company within 10 days after the date of this agreement, and if they qualify for a 90% loan, they will close at ABC Title Company within 60 days from the date they apply for the loan. If the loan is not approved they will receive the earnest money back and this contract is terminated.

That's a good purchase agreement as long as everyone signs it. It would stand up in most courts if you, the seller, wanted to back out of the deal, or if the buyer backed out and you wanted to keep his earnest money.

But selling a house is a bit more complicated than selling a bicycle. So you want to spell out things in more detail, such as the legal description, what personal property goes with the real estate, what happens if there are problems with the title, what happens if there are problems with the property, and what happens if it were to partially burn before closing.

Any contract simply spells out as clearly as possible the what, where, when, and how of the deal you and the buyer are proposing. Any good form contract will have the basics. The contract forms I've included in this book are standard forms originally used in Texas and promulgated by the Texas Real Estate Commission. They are simpler to use, and shorter than, the current Texas forms. I think they're good forms, and they give you the basics without flooding you with details. They should work in your state, though real estate people in your area will undoubtedly use different forms. Forms more appropriate to your state, and probably simpler forms, should be available at your local office supply store.

THE BASICS OF A GOOD CONTRACT

I'm not an attorney, but I've been around many of them and have seen a great number of their contract forms. I've noticed that the more an attorney charges, the more complicated are his contract forms. The more complicated forms usually are a bit more specific; often they're merely more verbose. Here are the specifics of a good contract form for selling your home:

- ☐ Full legal names of all parties
- ☐ Complete description of the property
- ☐ Purchase price and how it's to be paid
- ☐ Type of financing and its conditions
- ☐ Details of the earnest money
- ☐ Details on clear title
- ☐ Details on property condition
- ☐ Fees to brokers or agents
- ☐ Details on closing date
- ☐ When buyer will have possession
- ☐ Who will pay what expenses
- ☐ Casualty loss before closing
- ☐ What happens if one party defaults
- ☐ Who pays attorneys fees in litigation
- ☐ Additional details to be inserted by parties

Appendices at the back of the book contain forms and instructions for writing the following types of purchase contracts:

- Purchase with a VA-guaranteed loan
- Purchase with an FHA-insured loan
- Purchase with a conventional loan
- Purchase for cash or with owner financing
- Purchase with an assumption of your existing loan
- Property condition addendum for use with the above forms

You'll learn exactly how to fill out each one of the contract forms (also called purchase agreements or residential earnest money contracts) and be able to explain each form to a prospective purchaser. While you don't need a separate form for each type of financing, it's easier to have all the details of the financing spelled out on the form. Using these forms will simplify your selling process.

While much of the information I've given is the same for one form as for the other—and it may all seem somewhat redundant—I think that by setting each one off in a section all its own, you'll be able to turn to that section and proceed step-by-step with your contract without having to guess at anything.

The appendices contain sample completed forms, along with blank forms you can make photocopies of to use on your sale. I suggest you make a couple of copies of each blank. When a buyer is ready to give you earnest money and sign on the line, you *must* have a line he can sign on.

WHEN TO USE A LAWYER

These forms are fine if you have a "standard" sale. On the other hand, if you have a complicated transaction—one with many contingencies, complicated financing, complicated terms—and you'll have to delete and add much to the form, then it's *well worth the money* to have a lawyer draw up the contract. A few hundred dollars in legal fees could save you thousands in later headaches.

The problem with using a lawyer is that you lose momentum. When someone is really interested in writing up a contract, you will want to fill in the blanks, sign it, have the buyers sign it, and take the earnest money. You'll want to have it over and done with quickly.

If you agree to have a lawyer write up the contract, he could take several days to do so. Meanwhile, your buyers could get cold feet and back out. Or they may find another house they like better. Most people, once they've found a house and signed a contract, drop any efforts to find a better deal or a more suitable house.

I've seen lawyers kill deals. They try to make a contract so iron-clad that they scare the buyer. So if you see the need to use a complicated form, have your lawyer prepare it in advance. That way you'll have it available for immediate use.

If preparing one beforehand is impractical, then write a short memorandum of agreement in your own handwriting that simply states that you and the buyer will have an attorney draw up a contract for the sale of the property. Take the earnest money from the buyer, and state in the memorandum that the house will remain off the market and that if either of you fail to agree on the terms of the formal contract by a certain date, the earnest money will be refunded and neither will have any obligation towards the other.

This will accomplish two things. First, it'll get you earnest money, showing that the buyer is serious. Second, the buyer will have psychologically bought the house. That will discourage him from looking at any more houses till you get the final contract signed.

THE SELLER MUST SELL

In most parts of the country, the seller *must* sell once he's signed a purchase offer and the buyer has signed and accepted it and has given earnest money. So, if you make a mistake on the terms or the price in the contract, you could be forced to sell under those terms and at that price. Be very careful, and make sure all important items are covered and are correct on your purchase offer.

The flip side of the coin in this situation is that in most parts of the country, buyers *don't* have to buy if they have a change of heart about the purchase. Most of the time you get to keep their earnest money, and they walk away.

You might wonder why there is this inequity. Well, it's because the buyer can file the signed contract at the county courthouse and legally tie up the title to your property if you decide to back out. But if the buyer backs out, what can you tie up? Only his earnest money. If you want more, you have to go to court and sue for specific performance. And if you win, what happens if the buyer has nothing you can attach? You have nothing but a large lawyer's bill for the lawsuit.

19

What Happens at the Closing

THE *CLOSING* IS WHERE AND WHEN THE SALE IS CONSUMMATED. KEEP IN MIND throughout your sales endeavor that you *do not* have a sale until the deal is closed *and funded.* Closing is when you sign all the papers; funding is when the money is disbursed by the *escrow agent,* a disinterested third party who handles the closing for the buyer, seller, and lender. Only when you have your money in hand do you have a sale.

While most deals close, enough do not close to make it prudent for you not to make any commitments predicated on a successful closing. In other words, don't go out and buy another house without making the closing *and funding* of the sale of your present house, within a specified time, a condition to your purchase of the other home.

More than once I've been at the closing table and witnessed one or both of the buyers get up and leave without closing. And, to my and the sellers' great chagrin, I've seen too many people back out of a deal, either the day after the contract is signed (commonly known as *buyers' remorse*) or just before closing because a marriage breaks up, the buyers found a better deal, the buyers were transferred by an employer, etc.

I sold one young couple a house they fell completely in love with. They were truly qualified, and the house was perfect for them and their young son. I knew I had a strong deal and gave it a 95% chance of closing and funding. Lo and behold, my perfect deal fell flat on its face the day the young couple went for their loan application. The innocent young wife explained to the loan officer, to her husband's disbelief, that she had failed to get a divorce from her first husband before marrying the present one. Was it true, or was it their ploy to back out of the deal? I'll never know, but the perfect deal fell apart.

So I repeat again, make all home purchasing deals contingent on the sale, closing, and funding of your present home. Even if you think you can keep the present home and the new home for a few months until the present home sells, be careful. Often the market will change, and the present home won't sell. Are you prepared to keep it as a rental, or keep making payments for a long time while it remains vacant? Think it through carefully.

PREPARING FOR THE CLOSING

If you're selling the first home you ever purchased, you may not remember what went on at the closing when you bought it. You might want to pull out your copies of the closing papers and review them. But that should not take the place of preparing for the closing.

Preparing for the closing means making sure all final papers reflect the seller's and the buyer's full agreement as specified in the contract. You won't know that everything is as you understood the contract to say unless you read and *understand* the closing documents.

At least a day before the closing, go to the escrow agent's office and review the documents. In this chapter are filled-out examples of the documents in a typical closing:

- HUD Settlement Statement (FIG. 19-1). Look at the back page first. The far right column shows your expenses. Those expenses are transferred to the front page to deduct, along with other charges, from the sales price to give you the "Cash to Seller," which is your net.

- Note (FIG. 19-2). This instrument is of prime importance to the lender, which is usually a mortgage company. But you may be the lender if you are carrying a second or third lien, or carrying a lien through "wraparound" financing. In that case you'll want to review the note to make sure it coincides with your agreement with the purchaser.

- Deed of Trust (FIG. 19-3). This is called a mortgage by some people, but there's a difference. In your state you may see an instrument something similar to this one. If your state doesn't use a deed of trust, then you'll have a true mortgage. Just as with the note above, this document won't be of concern to you unless you're carrying the paper on some or all of the financing.

Fig. 19-1

HUD-1 Rev. 5/76

Form Approved
OMB NO. 63-R-1501

A.	U.S. DEPARTMENT OF HOUSING AND URBAN DEVELOPMENT	B. TYPE OF LOAN

B. TYPE OF LOAN

1. ☒ FHA 2. ☐ FmHA 3. ☐ CONV. UNINS.
4. ☐ VA 5. ☐ CONV. INS.

6. File Number

7. Loan Number

SETTLEMENT STATEMENT

8. Mortgage Insurance Case Number:

C. NOTE: This form is furnished to give you a statement of actual settlement costs. Amounts paid to and by the settlement agent are shown. Items marked "(p.o.c.)" were paid outside the closing; they are shown here for informational purposes and are not included in the totals.

D. NAME OF BORROWER:	E. NAME OF SELLER:
John and Jane Dough	Richard and Ruth Rowe

F. NAME OF LENDER:	G. PROPERTY LOCATION:
Points Galore Mortgage Co.	39 Wistful Vista, Anytown, TX

H. SETTLEMENT AGENT: Cloud 9 Title Co.	PLACE OF SETTLEMENT: 345 Mechanic's Lane, Anytown, TX	I. SETTLEMENT DATE: 2-4-85

J. SUMMARY OF BORROWER'S TRANSACTION		K. SUMMARY OF SELLER'S TRANSACTION	
100. GROSS AMOUNT DUE FROM BORROWER:		**400. GROSS AMOUNT DUE TO SELLER:**	
101. Contract sales price	87,000.00	401. Contract sales price	87,000.00
102. Personal property		402. Personal property	
103. Settlement charges to borrower (line 1400)	4207.89	403.	
104.		404.	
105.		405.	
Adjustments for items paid by seller in advance		*Adjustments for items paid by seller in advance*	
106. City/town taxes to		406. City/town taxes to	
107. County taxes to		407. County taxes to	
108. Assessments to		408. Assessments to	
109.		409.	
110.		410.	
111.		411.	
112.		412.	
120. GROSS AMOUNT DUE FROM BORROWER	91,207.89	420. GROSS AMOUNT DUE TO SELLER	87,000.00
200. AMOUNTS PAID BY OR IN BEHALF OF BORROWER:		**500. REDUCTIONS IN AMOUNT DUE TO SELLER:**	
201. Deposit or earnest money	500.00	501. Excess deposit (see instructions)	
202. Principal amount of new loan(s)	72,200.00	502. Settlement charges to seller (line 1400)	2954.00
203. Existing loan(s) taken subject to		503. Existing loan(s) taken subject to	
204. Refund due on Credit Report ✓ Appraisal ✓ ✓ ✓	7.00 25.00	504. Payoff of first mortgage loan thru 2/4 Heritage Bank Savings	62,882.08
Rent Deposit Credit	900.00	Earnest Money from Buyers Rent deposits to Buyers	500.00 900.00
205.		505. Payoff of second mortgage loan	
206.		506.	
207.		507.	
208.		508.	
209.		509.	
Adjustments for items unpaid by seller		*Adjustments for items unpaid by seller*	
210. City/town taxes 1985 to TAXES		510. City/town taxes 1985 to TAXES	
211. County taxes 1-1-85 to 2-4-85	115.15	511. County taxes 1-1-85 to 2-4-85	115.15
212. Assessments to		512. Assessments to	
213.		513.	
214.		514.	
215.		515.	
216.		516.	
217.		517.	
218.		518.	
219.		519.	
220. TOTAL PAID BY/FOR BORROWER	73,747.15	520. TOTAL REDUCTION AMOUNT DUE SELLER	67,351.23
300. CASH AT SETTLEMENT FROM/TO BORROWER		**600. CASH AT SETTLEMENT TO/FROM SELLER**	
301. Gross amount due from borrower (line 120)	41,207.89	601. Gross amount due to seller (line 420)	87,000.00
302. Less amounts paid by/for borrower (line 220)	(73,747.15)	602. Less reductions in amount due seller (line 520)	(67,351.23)
303. CASH (☐ FROM)(☐ TO) BORROWER	17,460.74	603. CASH (☐ TO)(☐ FROM) SELLER	19,648.77

L. SETTLEMENT CHARGES

700. TOTAL SALES/BROKER'S COMMISSION based on price $ @ % =	PAID FROM BORROWER'S FUNDS AT SETTLEMENT	PAID FROM SELLER'S FUNDS AT SETTLEMENT
Division of Commission (line 700) as follows:		
701. $ *N/A* to		
702. $ to		
703. Commission paid at Settlement		
704.		
800. ITEMS PAYABLE IN CONNECTION WITH LOAN		
801. Loan Origination Fee 1 %		696.00
802. Loan Discount 1.50 % POINTS GALORE MORTGAGE CO.		1,083.00
803. Appraisal Fee P.D.C. $300.00		
804. Credit Report P.D.C. $50.00 to		
805. Lender's Inspection Fee		
806. Mortgage Insurance Application Fee to		
807. Assumption Fee		
808. Messenger Fees		25.00
809. Tax Service Fee		42.00
810. Processing Fee		100.00
811. Recording Fee		5.00
900. ITEMS REQUIRED BY LENDER TO BE PAID IN ADVANCE		
901. Interest from 2-4 to 3-1-85 @ $ 25.07 /day	626.75	
902. Mortgage Insurance Premium for FHA MIP months to	2,644.80	
903. Hazard Insurance Premium for 1 years to Tom Jones Ins.	374.00	
904. years to		
905.		
1000. RESERVES DEPOSITED WITH LENDER		
1001. Hazard Insurance 2 months @ $ 31.17 per month	62.34	
1002. Mortgage Insurance months @ $ per month		
1003. City property taxes months @ $ per month		
1004. County property taxes months @ $ per month		
1005. Annual assessments months @ $ per month		
1006. 1985 TAXES 5 months @ $ 100.00 per month	500.00	
1007. months @ $ per month		
1008. months @ $ per month		
1100. TITLE CHARGES		
1101. Settlement or closing fee to		
1102. Abstract or title search to		
1103. Title examination to		
1104. Title insurance binder to		
1105. Document preparation to POINTS GALORE MORTGAGE CO./CLOUD 9		60.00
1106. Notary fees to		
1107. Attorney's fees to CLOUD 9 TITLE		
(includes above items numbers:		
1108. Title insurance to CLOUD 9 TITLE		697.00
(includes above items numbers:		
1109. Lender's coverage $ 64,600.00		
1110. Owner's coverage $ 87,000.00		
1111. Escrow Fees		50.00
1112. Restrictions		5.00
1113. Tax Certificates		15.00
1200. GOVERNMENT RECORDING AND TRANSFER CHARGES		
1201. Recording fees. Deed $ 5.00 : Mortgage $ 11.00 : Release $ 5.00		21.00
1202. City/county tax/stamps: Deed $: Mortgage $		
1203. State tax/stamps: Deed $: Mortgage $		
1204.		
1205.		
1300. ADDITIONAL SETTLEMENT CHARGES		
1301. Survey to BIG STATE Land Surveyors		155.00
1302. Pest inspection to		
1303.		
1304.		
1305.		
1400. TOTAL SETTLEMENT CHARGES (enter on lines 103. Section J and 502, Section K)	4,207.89	2,954.00

HUD-1 Rev. 5/76

Attached to and made part of Disclosure/Statement File # _____

I (we) acknowledge receipt of a copy of the Disclosure/Settlement Statememt and confirm same as correct. Buyer's/Seller's signature hereunder acknowledges his approval of tax prorations, and signifies his understanding that prorations were based on figures for preceding year, or estimates for current year, and in the event of any change for current year, all necessary adjustments must be made between Buyer and Seller direct.

Seller _____ Buyer _____

Seller _____ Buyer _____

By: _____
                    closer

- Warranty Deed (Appendix M). This transfers title from you to the buyer. You don't need to concern yourself too much with this document. But take a look to make sure your names are spelled correctly. If they're not, you might have to make a trip back to the escrow agent's office to sign a corrected one.
- Deed of Trust to Secure Assumption (FIG. 19-4). If you're in a deed-of-trust state, you'll see one of these if you're allowing someone to assume your loan. If the buyers fail to pay the lender, this instrument gives you the right to step in and foreclose on the buyers and take over the property. Of course, *you'd* have to make up any back payments and charges on the original loan.

YOUR ATTORNEY

In some states, it is common practice for the buyer and seller to have their respective attorneys present at the closing. In other areas, the attorneys simply review the documents before the closing, but don't actually attend the closing. Check with a title or escrow company to see what the norm is in your state.

In your area, attorneys may rarely be involved. If you read the documents carefully and understand them, then you won't need to spend money for an attorney, but if you're doing some of the financing by carrying a lien, the cost of an attorney is cheap insurance. Have him review the documents.

BUYER'S REVIEW OF THE DOCUMENTS

You'll avoid any problems at the closing if the buyer reviews the documents and/or has his lawyer look at them also. In fact, if both you and the buyer can look at the documents several days before the closing, you'll have a smooth closing. That way anything that would have been a surprise or a problem on the day of closing can be worked out without pressure on either party.

You certainly don't want to have all your furniture in a moving van on the day of closing only to find out that the buyer won't sign the closing papers because of additional settlement charges he doesn't agree with, or because of wording in the loan papers he won't go along with. Be safe, look ahead.

THE CLOSING

On closing date, if everyone has looked over the papers, you should expect no problems. Both parties to the contract sign, and the deal is consummated.

If the buyer has not looked over the papers, you should be prepared to be flexible. Many wrenches can be thrown into the works to foul things up. For

Fig. 19-2

NOTE

LOAN # __1234567__

US $ __90,000.00__   City __Dallas__, State __Texas__

Nov. 12 _____, 19 __87__

FOR VALUE RECEIVED, the undersigned ("Borrower") promise(s) to pay __Olive Oil's__ __Investment Corporation__ _____ on order, the principal sum of __Ninety thousand and 00/100 ($90,000.00)------------------__ Dollars, with interest on the unpaid principal balance from the date of this Note, until paid, at the rate of __12__ percent per annum. Principal and interest shall be payable at __323 Brick Rd., Dallas__ __Texas__ _____, or such other place as the Note holder may designate, in consecutive monthly installments of __one thousand twenty eight and__ __62/100-----------------------------__ Dollars (US$ __1028.62__), on the __1st__ day of each month beginning __January 1__ _____, 19 __88__. Such monthly installments shall continue until entire indebtedness evidenced by this Note is fully paid, except that any remaining indebtedness, if not sooner paid, shall be due and payable on __Dec. 1, 2017__.

If any monthly installment under this Note is not paid when due and remains unpaid after a date specified by a notice to Borrower, the entire principal amount outstanding and accrued interest thereon shall at once become due and payable at the option of the Note holder. The date specified shall not be less than thirty days from the date such notice is mailed. The Note holder may exercise this option to accelerate during any default by Borrower regardless of any prior forebearance. If suit is brought to collect this Note, the Note holder shall be entitled to collect all reasonable costs and expenses of suit, including, but not limited to, reasonable attorney's fees.

Borrower shall pay to the Note holder a late charge of __four (4)__ percent of any monthly installment not received by the Note holder within __fifteen (15)__ days after the installment is due.

Borrower may prepay the principal amount outstanding in whole or in part. The Note holder may require that any partial payments (i) be made on the date monthly installments are due and (ii) be in the amount of that part of one or more monthly installments which would be applicable to principal. Any partial prepayment shall be applied against the principal amount outstanding and shall not postpone the due date of any subsequent monthly installments or change the amount of such installments, unless the Note holder shall otherwise agree in writing. If, within five years from the date of this Note, Borrower make(s) any prepayments in any twelve month period beginning with the date of this Note or anniversary dates thereof ("loan year") with money lent to Borrower by a lender other than the Note holder, Borrower shall pay the Note holder (a) during each of the first three loan years __-0-__ percent of the amount by which the sum of prepayments made in any such loan year exceeds twenty percent of the original principal amount of this Note and (b) during the fourth and fifth loan years __-0-__ percent of the amount by which the sum of prepayments made in any such loan year exceeds twenty percent of the original principal amount of this Note.

Presentment, notice of dishonor, and protest are hereby waived by all makers, sureties, guarantors and endorsers hereof. This Note shall be the joint and several obligation of all makers, sureties, guarantors and endorsers, and shall be binding upon them and their successors and assigns.

Any notice to Borrower provided for in this Note shall be given by mailing such notice by certified mail addressed to Borrower at the Property Address stated below, or to such other address as Borrower may designate by notice to the Note holder. Any notice to the Note holder shall be given by mailing such notice by certified mail, return receipt requested, to the Note holder at the address stated in the first paragraph of this Note, or at such other address as may have been designated by notice to Borrower.

This indebtedness evidenced by this Note is secured by a Deed of Trust dated __Nov.__ __12, 1987__, and reference is made to the Deed of Trust for rights as to acceleration of the indebtedness evidenced by this Note.

Lady N. Shoe

123 Candlestick Lane
Dallas, Texas 77777

Property Address   *(Execute Original Only)*

Fig. 19-3

DEED OF TRUST

THIS DEED OF TRUST is made this _12th_ day of _November_
19 _87_, among the Grantor, _Lady N. Shoe, a single woman_
_____ (herein "Borrower"), _John Smith_
_____ (herein "Trustee"), and the Beneficiary,
Olive Oil's Investment Corporation _____, whose address is_____
323 Brick Road, Dallas, Texas _____(herein "Lender").

BORROWER, in consideration of the indebtedness herein recited and the trust herein created, irrevocably grant and conveys to Trustee, in trust, with power of sale, the following described property located in the County of _Dallas_, State of _Texas_:

Being Lot 5, in Block 9 of Forest Park, an Addition to the City of Dallas, Texas, according to the Map thereof recorded in Volume 188, Page 2179, Map Records of Dallas County, Texas

which has the address of _123 Candlestick Lane, Dallas, Texas 77777_

_____(herein "Property Address");

TOGETHER with all the improvements now or hereafter erected on the property, and all easements, rights, appurtenances, rents (subject however to the rights and authorities given herein to Lender to collect and apply such rents), royalties, mineral, oil and gas rights and profits, water, water rights, and water stock, and all fixtures now or hereafter attached to the property, all of which, including replacements and additions thereto, shall be deemed to be and remain a part of the property covered by this Deed of Trust; and all of the foregoing, together with said property (or the leasehold estate if this Deed of Trust is on a leasehold) are herein referred to as the "Property";

TO SECURE to Lender (a) the repayment of the indebtedness evidenced by Borrower's note dated _November 12, 1987_ (herein "Note"), in the principal sum of _ninety thousand and 00/100 ($90,000.00)_ Dollars, with interest thereon, providing for monthly installments of principal and interest, with the balance of the indebtedness, if not sooner paid, due and payable on _December 1, 2017_; the payment of all other sums, with interest thereon, advanced in accordance herewith to protect the security of this Deed of Trust; and the performance of the covenants and agreements of Borrower herein contained; and (b) the repayment of any future advances, with interest thereon, made to Borrower by Lender pursuant to paragraph 21 hereof (herein "Future Advances").

Borrower covenants that Borrower is lawfully seized of the estate hereby conveyed and has the right to grant and convey the Property, that the Property is unencumbered, and that Borrower will warrant and defend generally the title to the Property against all claims and demands, subject to any declarations, easements or restrictions listed in a schedule of exceptions to coverage in any title insurance policy insuring Lender's interest in the Property.

UNIFORM COVENANTS. Borrower and Lender covenant and agree as follows:

1. **Payment of Principal and Interest.** Borrower shall promptly pay when due the principal of and interest on the indebtedness evidenced by the Note, prepayment and late charges as provided in the Note, and the principal of and interest on any Future Advances secured by this Deed of Trust.

2. **Funds for Taxes and Insurance.** Subject to applicable law or to a written waiver by Lender, Borrower shall pay to Lender on the day monthly installments of principal and interest are payable under the Note, until the Note is paid in full, a sum (herein "Funds") equal to one-twelfth of the yearly taxes and assessments which may attain priority over this Deed of Trust, and ground rents on the Property, if any, plus one-twelfth of yearly premium installments for hazard insurance, plus one-twelfth of yearly premium installments for mortgage insurance, if any, all as reasonably estimated initially and from time to time by Lender on the basis of assessments and bills and reasonable estimates thereof.

The Funds shall be held in an institution the deposits or accounts of which are insured or guaranteed by a Federal or state agency (including Lender if Lender is such an institution). Lender shall apply the Funds to pay said taxes, assessments, insurance premiums and ground rents. Lender may not charge for so holding and applying the Funds, analyzing said account or verifying and compiling said assessments and bills, unless Lender pays Borrower interest on the Funds and applicable law permits Lender to make such a charge. Borrower and Lender may agree in writing at the time of execution of this Deed of Trust that interest on the Funds shall be paid to Borrower, and unless such agreement is made or applicable law requires such interest to be paid, Lender shall not be required to pay Borrower any interest or earnings on the Funds. Lender shall give to Borrower, without charge, an annual accounting of the Funds showing credits and debits to the Funds and the purpose for which each debit to the Funds was made. The Funds are pledged as additional security for the sums secured by this Deed of Trust.

If the amount of the Funds held by Lender, together with the future monthly installments of Funds payable prior to the due dates of taxes, assessments, insurance premiums and ground rents, shall exceed the amount required to pay said taxes, assessments, insurance premiums and ground rents as they fall due, such excess shall be, at Borrower's option,

1 to 4 Family—6/75—FNMA/FHLMC UNIFORM INSTRUMENT

either promptly repaid to Borrower or credited to Borrower on monthly installments of Funds. If the amount of the Funds held by Lender shall not be sufficient to pay taxes, assessments, insurance premiums and ground rents as they fall due, Borrower shall pay to Lender any amount necessary to make up the deficiency within 30 days from the date notice is mailed by Lender to Borrower requesting payment thereof.

Upon payment in full of all sums secured by this Deed of Trust, Lender shall promptly refund to Borrower any Funds held by Lender. If under paragraph 18 hereof the Property is sold or the Property is otherwise acquired by Lender, Lender shall apply, no later than immediately prior to the sale of the Property or its acquisition by Lender, any Funds held by Lender at the time of application as a credit against the sums secured by this Deed of Trust.

3. Application of Payments. Unless applicable law provides otherwise, all payments received by Lender under the Note and paragraphs 1 and 2 hereof shall be applied by Lender first in payment of amounts payable to Lender by Borrower under paragraph 2 hereof, then to interest payable on the Note, then to the principal of the Note, and then to interest and principal on any Future Advances.

4. Charges; Liens. Borrower shall pay all taxes, assessments and other charges, fines and impositions attributable to the Property which may attain a priority over this Deed of Trust, and leasehold payments or ground rents, if any, in the manner provided under paragraph 2 hereof or, if not paid in such manner, by Borrower making payment, when due, directly to the payee thereof. Borrower shall promptly furnish to Lender all notices of amounts due under this paragraph, and in the event Borrower shall make payment directly, Borrower shall promptly furnish to Lender receipts evidencing such payments. Borrower shall promptly discharge any lien which has priority over this Deed of Trust; provided, that Borrower shall not be required to discharge any such lien so long as Borrower shall agree in writing to the payment of the obligation secured by such lien in a manner acceptable to Lender, or shall in good faith contest such lien by, or defend enforcement of such lien in, legal proceedings which operate to prevent the enforcement of the lien or forfeiture of the Property or any part thereof.

5. Hazard Insurance. Borrower shall keep the improvements now existing or hereafter erected on the Property insured against loss by fire, hazards included within the term "extended coverage", and such other hazards as Lender may require and in such amounts and for such periods as Lender may require; provided, that Lender shall not require that the amount of such coverage exceed that amount of coverage required to pay the sums secured by this Deed of Trust.

The insurance carrier providing the insurance shall be chosen by Borrower subject to approval by Lender; provided, that such approval shall not be unreasonably withheld. All premiums on insurance policies shall be paid in the manner provided under paragraph 2 hereof or, if not paid in such manner, by Borrower making payment, when due, directly to the insurance carrier.

All insurance policies and renewals thereof shall be in form acceptable to Lender and shall include a standard mortgage clause in favor of and in form acceptable to Lender. Lender shall have the right to hold the policies and renewals thereof, and Borrower shall promptly furnish to Lender all renewal notices and all receipts of paid premiums. In the event of loss, Borrower shall give prompt notice to the insurance carrier and Lender. Lender may make proof of loss if not made promptly by Borrower.

Unless Lender and Borrower otherwise agree in writing, insurance proceeds shall be applied to restoration or repair of the Property damaged, provided such restoration or repair is economically feasible and the security of this Deed of Trust is not thereby impaired. If such restoration or repair is not economically feasible or if the security of this Deed of Trust would be impaired, the insurance proceeds shall be applied to the sums secured by this Deed of Trust, with the excess, if any, paid to Borrower. If the Property is abandoned by Borrower, or if Borrower fails to respond to Lender within 30 days from the date notice is mailed by Lender to Borrower that the insurance carrier offers to settle a claim for insurance benefits, Lender is authorized to collect and apply the insurance proceeds at Lender's option either to restoration or repair of the Property or to the sums secured by this Deed of Trust.

Unless Lender and Borrower otherwise agree in writing, any such application of proceeds to principal shall not extend or postpone the due date of the monthly installments referred to in paragraphs 1 and 2 hereof or change the amount of such installments. If under paragraph 18 hereof the Property is acquired by Lender, all right, title and interest of Borrower in and to any insurance policies and in and to the proceeds thereof resulting from damage to the Property prior to the sale or acquisition shall pass to Lender to the extent of the sums secured by this Deed of Trust immediately prior to such sale or acquisition.

6. Preservation and Maintenance of Property; Leaseholds; Condominiums; Planned Unit Developments. Borrower shall keep the Property in good repair and shall not commit waste or permit impairment or deterioration of the Property and shall comply with the provisions of any lease if this Deed of Trust is on a leasehold. If this Deed of Trust is on a unit in a condominium or a planned unit development, Borrower shall perform all of Borrower's obligations under the declaration or covenants creating or governing the condominium or planned unit development, the by-laws and regulations of the condominium or planned unit development, and constituent documents. If a condominium or planned unit development rider is executed by Borrower and recorded together with this Deed of Trust, the covenants and agreements of such rider shall be incorporated into and shall amend and supplement the covenants and agreements of this Deed of Trust as if the rider were a part hereof.

7. Protection of Lender's Security. If Borrower fails to perform the covenants and agreements contained in this Deed of Trust, or if any action or proceeding is commenced which materially affects Lender's interest in the Property, including, but not limited to, eminent domain, insolvency, code enforcement, or arrangements or proceedings involving a bankrupt or decedent, then Lender at Lender's option, upon notice to Borrower, may make such appearances, disburse such sums and take such action as is necessary to protect Lender's interest, including, but not limited to, disbursement of reasonable attorney's fees and entry upon the Property to make repairs. If Lender required mortgage insurance as a condition of making the loan secured by this Deed of Trust, Borrower shall pay the premiums required to maintain such insurance in effect until such time as the requirement for such insurance terminates in accordance with Borrower's and Lender's written agreement or applicable law. Borrower shall pay the amount of all mortgage insurance premiums in the manner provided under paragraph 2 hereof.

Any amounts disbursed by Lender pursuant to this paragraph 7, with interest thereon, shall become additional indebtedness of Borrower secured by this Deed of Trust. Unless Borrower and Lender agree to other terms of payment, such amounts shall be payable upon notice from Lender to Borrower requesting payment thereof, and shall bear interest from the date of disbursement at the rate payable from time to time on outstanding principal under the Note unless payment of interest at such rate would be contrary to applicable law, in which event such amounts shall bear interest at the highest rate permissible under applicable law. Nothing contained in this paragraph 7 shall require Lender to incur any expense or take any action hereunder.

8. Inspection. Lender may make or cause to be made reasonable entries upon and inspections of the Property, provided that Lender shall give Borrower notice prior to any such inspection specifying reasonable cause therefor related to Lender's interest in the Property.

9. Condemnation. The proceeds of any award or claim for damages, direct or consequential, in connection with any condemnation or other taking of the Property, or part therof, or for conveyance in lieu of condemnation, are hereby assigned and shall be paid to Lender.

Fig. 19-2. Continued.

In the event of a total taking of the Property, the proceeds shall be applied to the sums secured by this Deed of Trust, with the excess, if any, paid to Borrower. In the event of a partial taking of the Property, unless Borrower and Lender otherwise agree in writing, there shall be applied to the sums secured by this Deed of Trust such proportion of the proceeds as is equal to that proportion which the amount of the sums secured by this Deed of Trust immediately prior to the date of taking bears to the fair market value of the Property immediately prior to the date of taking, with the balance of the proceeds paid to Borrower.

If the Property is abandoned by Borrower, or if, after notice by Lender to Borrower that the condemnor offers to make an award or settle a claim for damages, Borrower fails to respond to Lender within 30 days after the date such notice is mailed, Lender is authorized to collect and apply the proceeds, at Lender's option, either to restoration or repair of the Property or to the sums secured by this Deed of Trust.

Unless Lender and Borrower otherwise agree in writing, any such application of proceeds to principal shall not extend or postpone the due date of the monthly installments referred to in paragraphs 1 and 2 hereof or change the amount of such installments.

10. Borrower Not Released. Extension of the time for payment or modification of amortization of the sums secured by this Deed of Trust granted by Lender to any successor in interest of Borrower shall not operate to release, in any manner, the liability of the original Borrower and Borrower's successors in interest. Lender shall not be required to commence proceedings against such successor or refuse to extend time for payment or otherwise modify amortization of the sums secured by this Deed of Trust by reason of any demand made by the original Borrower and Borrower's successors in interest.

11. Forbearance by Lender Not a Waiver. Any forbearance by Lender in exercising any right or remedy hereunder, or otherwise afforded by applicable law, shall not be a waiver of or preclude the exercise of any such right or remedy. The procurement of insurance or the payment of taxes or other liens or charges by Lender shall not be a waiver of Lender's right to accelerate the maturity of the indebtedness secured by this Deed of Trust.

12. Remedies Cumulative. All remedies provided in this Deed of Trust are distinct and cumulative to any other right or remedy under this Deed of Trust or afforded by law or equity, and may be exercised concurrently, independently or successively.

13. Successors and Assigns Bound; Joint and Several Liability; Captions. The covenants and agreements herein contained shall bind, and the rights hereunder shall inure to, the respective successors and assigns of Lender and Borrower, subject to the provisions of paragraph 17 hereof. All covenants and agreements of Borrower shall be joint and several. The captions and headings of the paragraphs of this Deed of Trust are for convenience only and are not to be used to interpret or define the provisions hereof.

14. Notice. Except for any notice required under applicable law to be given in another manner, (a) any notice to Borrower provided for in this Deed of Trust shall be given by mailing such notice by certified mail addressed to Borrower at the Property Address or at such other address as Borrower may designate by notice to Lender as provided herein, and (b) any notice to Lender shall be given by certified mail, return receipt requested, to Lender's address stated herein or to such other address as Lender may designate by notice to Borrower as provided herein. Any notice provided for in this Deed of Trust shall be deemed to have been given to Borrower or Lender when given in the manner designated herein.

15. Uniform Deed of Trust; Governing Law; Severability. This form of deed of trust combines uniform covenants for national use and non-uniform covenants with limited variations by jurisdiction to constitute a uniform security instrument covering real property. This Deed of Trust shall be governed by the law of the jurisdiction in which the Property is located. In the event that any provision or clause of this Deed of Trust or the Note conflicts with applicable law, such conflict shall not affect other provisions of this Deed of Trust or the Note which can be given effect without the conflicting provision, and to this end the provisions of the Deed of Trust and the Note are declared to be severable.

16. Borrower's Copy. Borrower shall be furnished a conformed copy of the Note and of this Deed of Trust at the time of execution or after recordation hereof.

17. Transfer of the Property; Assumption. If all or any part of the Property or an interest therein is sold or transferred by Borrower without Lender's prior written consent, excluding (a) the creation of a lien or encumbrance subordinate to this Deed of Trust, (b) the creation of a purchase money security interest for household appliances, (c) a transfer by devise, descent or by operation of law upon the death of a joint tenant or (d) the grant of any leasehold interest of three years or less not containing an option to purchase, Lender may, at Lender's option, declare all the sums secured by this Deed of Trust to be immediately due and payable. Lender shall have waived such option to accelerate if, prior to the sale or transfer, Lender and the person to whom the Property is to be sold or transferred reach agreement in writing that the credit of such person is satisfactory to Lender and that the interest payable on the sums secured by this Deed of Trust shall be at such rate as Lender shall request. If Lender has waived the option to accelerate provided in this paragraph 17, and if Borrower's successor in interest has executed a written assumption agreement accepted in writing by Lender, Lender shall release Borrower from all obligations under this Deed of Trust and the Note.

If Lender exercises such option to accelerate, Lender shall mail Borrower notice of acceleration in accordance with paragraph 14 hereof. Such notice shall provide a period of not less than 30 days from the date the notice is mailed within which Borrower may pay the sums declared due. If Borrower fails to pay such sums prior to the expiration of such period, Lender may, without further notice or demand on Borrower, invoke any remedies permitted by paragraph 18 hereof.

NON—UNIFORM COVENANTS. Borrower and Lender further covenant and agree as follows:

18. Acceleration; Remedies. Except as provided in paragraph 17 hereof, upon Borrower's breach of any covenant or agreement of Borrower in this Deed of Trust, including the covenants to pay when due any sums secured by this Deed of Trust, Lender prior to acceleration shall give notice in the manner prescribed by applicable law to Borrower and to the other persons prescribed by applicable law specifying: (1) the breach; (2) the action required to cure such breach; (3) a date, not less than 30 days from the date the notice is mailed to Borrower, by which such breach must be cured; and (4) that failure to cure such breach on or before the date specified in the notice may result in acceleration of the sums secured by this Deed of Trust and sale of the property at public auction at a date not less than 120 days in the future. The notice shall further inform Borrower of (i) the right to reinstate after acceleration, (ii) the right to bring a court action to assert the non-existence of a default or any other defense of Borrower to acceleration and foreclosure and (iii) any other matter required to be included in such notice by applicable law. If the breach is not cured on or before the date specified in the notice, Lender at Lender's option may declare all of the sums secured by this Deed of Trust to be immediately due and payable without further demand and may invoke the power of sale and any other remedies permitted by applicable law. Lender shall be entitled to collect all reasonable costs and expenses incurred in pursuing the remedies provided in this paragraph 18, including, but not limited to, reasonable attorney's fees.

If Lender invokes the power of sale, Lender shall give written notice to Trustee of the occurrence of an event of default and of Lender's election to cause the Property to be sold. Trustee and Lender shall take such action regarding notice of sale and shall give such notices to Borrower and to other persons as applicable law may require. After the lapse of such time as may be required by applicable law and after publication of the notice of sale, Trustee, without demand on Borrower, shall sell the Property at public auction to the highest bidder at the time and place and under the terms designated in the notice of sale in one or more parcels and in such order as Trustee may determine. Trustee may postpone sale of the Property for a period or periods not exceeding a total of 30 days by public announcement at the time and place fixed in the notice of sale. Lender or Lender's designee may purchase the Property at any sale.

Trustee shall deliver to the purchaser Trustee's deed conveying the Proprety so sold without any covenant or warranty, expressed or implied. The recitals in the Trustee's deed shall be prima facie evidence of the truth of the statements made therein. Trustee shall apply the proceeds of the sale in the following order: (a) to all reasonable costs and expenses of the sale, including, but not limited to, reasonable Trustee's and attorney's fees and costs of title evidence; (b) to all sums secured by this Deed of Trust; and (c) the excess, if any, to the person or persons legally entitled thereto, or the clerk of the superior court of the county in which the sale took place.

19. Borrower's Right to Reinstate. Notwithstanding Lender's acceleration of the sums secured by this Deed of Trust, Borrower shall have the right to have any proceedings begun by Lender to enforce this Deed of Trust discontinued at any time prior to the earlier to occur of (i) the tenth day before sale of the Property pursuant to the power of sale contained in this Deed of Trust or (ii) entry of a judgment enforcing this Deed of Trust if: (a) Borrower pays Lender all sums which would be then due under this Deed of Trust, the Note and notes securing Future Advances, if any, had no acceleration occurred; (b) Borrower cures all breaches of any other covenants or agreements of Borrower contained in this Deed of Trust; (c) Borrower pays all reasonable expenses incurred by Lender and Trustee in enforcing the covenants and agreements of Borrower contained in this Deed of Trust and in enforcing Lender's and Trustee's remedies as provided in paragraph 18 hereof, including, but not limited to, reasonable attorney's fees; and (d) Borrower takes such action as Lender may reasonably require to assure that the lien of this Deed of Trust, Lender's interest in the Property and Borrower's obligation to pay the sums secured by this Deed of Trust shall continue unimpaired. Upon such payment and cure by Borrower, this Deed of Trust and the obligations secured hereby shall remain in full force and effect as if no acceleration had occurred.

20. Assignment of Rents; Appointment of Receiver; Lender in Possession. As additional security hereunder, Borrower hereby assigns to Lender the rents of the Property, provided that Borrower shall, prior to acceleration under paragraph 18 hereof or abandonment of the Property, have the right to collect and retain such rents as they become due and payable.

Upon acceleration under paragraph 18 hereof or abandonment of the Property, Lender, in person, by agent or by judicially appointed receiver, shall be entitled to enter upon, take possession of and manage the Property and to collect the rents of the Property, including those past due. All rents collected by Lender or the receiver shall be applied first to payment of the costs of management of the Property and collection of rents, including, but not limited to, receiver's fees, premiums on receiver's bonds and reasonable attorney's fees, and then to the sums secured by this Deed of Trust. Lender and the receiver shall be liable to account only for those rents actually received.

21. Future Advances. Upon request of Borrower, Lender, at Lender's option prior to full reconveyance of the Property by Trustee to Borrower, may make Future Advances to Borrower, Such Future Advances, with interest thereon shall be secured by this Deed of Trust when evidenced by promissory notes stating that said notes are secured hereby.

22. Reconveyance. Upon payment of all sums secured by this Deed of Trust, Lender shall request Trustee to reconvey the Property and shall surrender this Deed of Trust and all notes evidencing indebtedness secured by this Deed of Trust to Trustee. Trustee shall reconvey the Property without warranty and without charge to the person or persons legally entitled thereto. Such person or persons shall pay all costs of recordation, if any.

23. Substitute Trustee. In accordance with applciable law, Lender may from time to time appoint a successor trustee to any Trustee appointed hereunder who has ceased to act. Without conveyance of the Property, the successor trustee shall succeed to all the title, power and duties conferred upon the Trustee herein and by applicable law.

24. Use of Property. The Property is not used principally for agricultural or farming purposes.

IN WITNESS WHEREOF, BORROWER has executed this Deed of Trust.

_____

_____ Lady N. Shoe _____ Borrower

_____

_____ Borrower

STATE OF ___Texas___, ___Dallas_____County ss:

On this __12th__ day of __Nov.___, 19_87_, before me the undersigned, a Notary Public in and for the State of ___Texas_____, duly commissioned and sworn, personally appeared ___Lady N. Shoe_____
_____ to me known to be the individual(s) described in and who executed the foregoing instrument, and acknowledged to me that _____she_____ signed and sealed the said instrument as ___her___ free and voluntary act and deed, for the uses and purposes therein mentioned.
WITNESS my hand and official seal affixed the day and year in this certificate above written.

My Commission expires:
_____
_____
Notary Public in and for the State of _____ residing at:

REQUEST FOR RECONVEYANCE

To TRUSTEE:
The undersigned is the holder of the note or notes secured by this Deed of Trust. Said note or notes, together with all other indebtedness secured by this Deed of Trust, have been paid in full. You are hereby directed to cancel said note or notes and this Deed of Trust, which are delivered hereby, and to reconvey, without warranty, all the estate now held by you under this Deed of Trust to the person or persons legally entitled thereto.

Date: _____

_____

(Space Below This Line Reserved For Lender and Recorder)

Fig. 19-4

Prepared by the State Bar of Texas for use by lawyers only. Revised 1-1-76. Revised to include grantee's address (art 6626, RCS) 1-1-82.

DEED OF TRUST TO SECURE ASSUMPTION

(WHERE BENEFICIARY IS LIABLE ON NOTE ASSUMED)

THE STATE OF TEXAS

COUNTY OF Tarrant

} KNOW ALL MEN BY THESE PRESENTS:

That   Edward J. Barnett and wife Sally S. Barnett

of Tarrant County, Texas, hereinafter called Grantors (whether one or more) for the purpose of securing the indebtedness hereinafter described, and in consideration of the sum of TEN DOLLARS ($10.00) to us in hand paid by the Trustee hereinafter named, the receipt of which is hereby acknowledged, and for the further consideration of the uses, purposes and trusts hereinafter set forth, have granted, sold and conveyed, and by these presents do grant, sell and convey unto Sam Kerrs , Trustee, of Tarrant County, Texas, and his substitutes or successors, all of the following described property situated in Tarrant County, Texas, to-wit:

Lot 37, Block 6/7789 Cozy Acres Addition to the City of Fort Worth, Texas according to the Map thereof recorded in Volume 893, Page 467 Map Records of Tarrant County, Texas.

TO HAVE AND TO HOLD the above described property, together with the rights, privileges and appurtenances thereto belonging, unto the said Trustee and to his substitutes or successors forever. And Grantors named herein do hereby bind themselves, their heirs, executors, administrators and assigns to warrant and forever defend the said premises unto the said Trustee, his substitutes or successors and assigns forever, against the claim, or claims, of all persons claiming or to claim the same or any part thereof.

This conveyance, however, is made in TRUST for the following purposes:
WHEREAS, Burt W. Higgs and wife Ernestine D. Higgs

hereinafter called Beneficiary, by deed of even date herewith conveyed the herein described property to Grantors named herein, who, as part of the consideration therefor assumed and promised to pay, according to the terms thereof, all principal and interest remaining unpaid upon that one certain promissory note in the original principal sum of $ 100,000.00 , dated 9/23/79 , executed by Burt W. Higgs and wife Ernestine D. Higgs

and payable to order of Big City Mortgage Company

which said note is secured by a Deed of Trust recorded in Volume 645 , Page 743 , Records of Tarrant County, Texas, the obligations and covenants of the grantors named in said Deed of Trust were also assumed by Grantors named herein, and in said Deed the superior title and a vendor's lien were expressly reserved and retained by Beneficiary until said indebtedness and obligations so assumed are fully paid and satisfied, and should Grantors do and perform all of the obligations and covenants so assumed and make prompt payment of the indebtedness evidenced by said note so assumed as the same shall become due and payable, then this conveyance shall become null and void and of no further force and effect, it being agreed that a release of such indebtedness so assumed and of the liens securing the same by the legal owner and holder thereof prior to the advancement and payment thereon by Beneficiary of any sum or sums required to cure any default, shall be sufficient to release the lien created by this instrument as well as said vendor's lien so retained, without the joinder of Beneficiary. Unless, prior to the filing of a release of the indebtedness so assumed and of the liens securing the same in the office of the County Clerk of the County where said real property is situated, Beneficiary shall have filed in the office of the County Clerk of said County a sworn statement duly acknowledged and containing a legal description of the real property hereinbefore described and setting forth any and all sums that Beneficiary may have so advanced and paid, it shall be conclusively presumed that no sum or sums have been advanced and paid thereon by Beneficiary.

Grantors agree that in the event of default in the payment of any installment, principal or interest, of the note so assumed by Grantors, or in the event of default in the payment of said note when due or declared due, or of a breach of any of the obligations or covenants contained in the Deed of Trust securing said note so assumed, Beneficiary may, at his option, advance and pay such sum or sums as may be required to cure any such default, and that any and all such sums so advanced and paid by Beneficiary to cure such default shall be paid by Grantors to Beneficiary at 12345 Main Street

, in the City of Grand Prairie, Texas 66666

County, Texas, within five (5) days after the date of such payment, without notice or demand, which are expressly waived.

Grantors covenant to pay promptly to Beneficiary, without notice or demand, within the time and as provided in the foregoing paragraph, any and all sums that may, under the provisions of the foregoing paragraph, be due Beneficiary.

In the event of a breach of the foregoing covenant, it shall thereupon, or at any time thereafter, be the duty of the Trustee, or his successor or substitute as hereinafter provided, at the request of Beneficiary (which request is hereby conclusively presumed), to enforce this Trust, and after advertising the time, place and terms of the sale of the above described and conveyed property, then subject to the lien hereof, for at least twenty-one (21) days preceding the date of sale by posting written or printed notice thereof at the Courthouse door of the county where said real property is situated, which notice may be posted by the Trustee acting, or by any person acting for him, and the Beneficiary (the holder of the indebtedness secured hereby) has, at least twenty-one (21) days preceding the date of sale, served written or printed notice of the proposed sale by certified mail on each debtor obligated to pay the indebtedness secured by this Deed of Trust according to the records of Beneficiary, by the deposit of such notice, enclosed in a postpaid wrapper, properly addressed to such debtor at debtor's most recent address as shown by the records of Beneficiary, in a post office or official depository under the care and custody of the United States Postal Service, the Trustee shall sell the above described property, then subject to the lien hereof, at public auction in accordance with such notice at the Courthouse door of the county where such real property is situated (provided where said real property is situated in more than one county, the notice to be posted as herein provided shall be posted at the Courthouse door of each of such counties where said real property is situated, and said above described and conveyed property may be sold at the Courthouse door of any one of such counties, and the notices so posted shall designate the county where the property will be sold), on the first Tuesday in any month between the hours of ten o'clock A.M. and four o'clock P.M., to the highest bidder for cash, and make due conveyance to the Purchaser or Purchasers, with general warranty binding Grantors, their heirs and assigns; and out of the money arising from such sale the Trustee shall pay, first, all expenses of advertising the sale and making the conveyance, including a commission of 10% to himself and, second, to Beneficiary the full amount of all sums so advanced and paid and that are then owing to Beneficiary under the provisions hereof, rendering the balance of the sales price, if any, to the person or persons legally entitled thereto; and the recitals in the conveyance to the Purchaser or Purchasers shall be full and conclusive evidence of the truth of the matters therein stated, and all prerequisites to said sale shall be presumed to have been performed, and such sale and conveyance shall be conclusive against Grantors, their heirs and assigns; said sale and deed to be made subject to the then unpaid part of the indebtedness so assumed by Grantors and the lien or liens securing the same, and it is agreed that such sale shall not in any manner affect any indebtedness which may thereafter become due and owing to Beneficiary under the covenants and provisions of this Deed of Trust, it being agreed that this Deed of Trust and all rights of Beneficiary shall be and remain in full force and effect so long as the obligations and indebtedness so assumed by Grantors or any part thereof remains unsatisfied or unpaid; that a sale by the Trustee or Substitute Trustee hereunder shall not exhaust the right of the Trustee or Substitute Trustee in event of any subsequent default hereunder, and at the request of Beneficiary, to thereafter enforce this trust and make sale of said property as herein provided.

Beneficiary shall have the right to purchase at any sale of the property, being the highest bidder and to have the amount for which such property is sold credited on the total sums owed Beneficiary.

Beneficiary in any event is hereby authorized to appoint a substitute trustee, or a successor trustee, to act instead of the Trustee named herein without other formality than the designation in writing of a substitute or successor trustee; and the authority hereby conferred shall extend to the appointment of other successor and substitute trustees successively until the full and final payment and satisfaction of the indebtedness and obligations so assumed by Grantors, and each substitute and successor trustee shall succeed to all of the rights and powers of the original Trustee named herein.

The term "Grantors" used in this instrument shall also include any and all successors in interest of Grantors to all or any part of the herein described and conveyed property as well as any and all purchasers thereof at any sale made hereunder by the Trustee or Substitute Trustee, and the provisions of this Deed of Trust shall be covenants running with the land.

If this Deed of Trust is or becomes binding upon one person or upon a corporation, the plural reference to Grantors shall be held to include the singular and all of the agreements and covenants herein undertaken to be performed by and the rights conferred upon Grantors, shall be binding upon and inure to the benefit of not only Grantors respectively but also their respective heirs, executors, administrators, grantees, successors and assigns.

It is expressly stipulated that the liability of Grantors to Beneficiary, arising by virtue of the assumption by Grantors of the payment of the note herein described and of the obligations of the Deed of Trust securing said note, as well as the liability to Beneficiary of any and all persons hereafter assuming payment of said note and performance of the obligations of said Deed of Trust, shall in no wise be discharged or released by this instrument or by the exercise by Beneficiary of the rights and remedies herein provided for, it being agreed that this instrument and all rights and remedies herein accorded Beneficiary are cumulative of any and all other rights and remedies existing at law.

Grantors expressly represent that any indebtedness becoming due and payable under and by virtue of the terms and provisions of this Deed of Trust is in part payment of the purchase price of the herein described and conveyed property and that this Deed of Trust is cumulative and in addition to the Vendor's Lien expressly retained in deed of even date herewith executed by Beneficiary to Grantors, and it is expressly agreed that Beneficiary may foreclose under either or both of said liens as Beneficiary may elect, without waiving the other, said deed hereinbefore mentioned, together with its record, being here referred to and made a part of this instrument.

In the event any sale is made of the above described property, or any portion thereof, under the terms of this Deed of Trust, Grantors, their heirs and assigns, shall forthwith upon the making of such sale surrender and deliver possession of the property so sold to the Purchaser at such sale, and in the event of their failure to do so they shall thereupon from and after the making of such sale be and continue as tenants at will of such Purchaser, and in the event of their failure to surrender possession of said property upon demand, the Purchaser, his heirs or assigns, shall be entitled to institute and maintain an action for forcible detainer of said property in the Justice of the Peace Court in the Justice Precinct in which such property, or any part thereof, is situated.

EXECUTED this 12th day of November , A.D. 1987

Mailing address of trustee:

Name: Sam Kerrs
Address: 7878 Division Street
          Arlington, TX 75555

Mailing address of each beneficiary:

Name: Burt and Ernestine Higgs
Address: 12345 Main Street
          Grand Prairie, TX 66666

Name:
Address:

(Acknowledgment)

STATE OF TEXAS
COUNTY OF

This instrument was acknowledged before me on the   day of   , 19   ,
by

My commission expires:

....
Notary Public, State of Texas
Notary's printed name:

....

example, on a new loan the *lock-in period,* or guarantee period, on the points may have expired. If rates have nudged up, the points will have gone up on the buyer's loan if he is to get the rate he expected. So if he expected to get 10% fixed at 3 points, and the rates go to 10¼% at 3 points, then for him to get 10% fixed, the points may now be at 5. Who pays the other two points, the buyer or the seller? You'll have to work that out with him then and there.

A good closer can make things run smoothly in a tough situation. I've seen good closers do a marvelous sales job on a balking buyer—talked them into going through with the closing when they wanted to back out. Unfortunately, you can't judge a good closer from a mediocre one unless you're in the business. But a middle-age person with years of experience is often better than a young person just starting out.

FUNDING

If the buyer is purchasing by obtaining a new loan, you'll have your money as soon as the closing is finished if the mortgage company *table funds.* That means they fund at the closing table. After all papers are signed, the closer will call the lender and get a funding number. That means he's allowed to disburse the lender's funds from a check that will have come with the closing papers.

If the lender does not table fund, then you may have to wait a day or two, or even longer, for your money. The escrow agent will have to send the closing packet to the lender for his approval. Once the lender approves the paperwork, he funds the loan, and the escrow agent disburses the money.

The simplest closings are where they take place at the lender's office, such as a savings and loan or a bank. One of the lender's employees will handle the closing, and as soon as everyone has signed, your funds are released. There are few places where buyers and sellers close in this manner. Usually it's at an escrow company, title company, or attorney's office.

KEEP THE DEAL TOGETHER

After struggling through the advertising, showing, and negotiating to sell your property, don't let a minor glitch spoil your deal. If you stand to receive a $30,000 equity, but the buyer refuses to pay a required $700 in additional points or closing fees, are you going to let the deal sour over that amount? Some people do. But look at it this way. If you were a gambler, would you gamble $30,000 to gain $700? Not likely.

So my point is that, depending on how much you stand to gain, if things go wrong at the closing, don't let principles stand in your way of making money. If you need to put a bit more into the pot to get the sale through, do it. Once you have a bird in hand, don't let him go.

IF YOU'RE DUMPING PROPERTY

If you're merely selling your home in an effort to save your credit, (in other words, you can't make your payments anymore, and you allow someone to assume your loan without giving you any equity), then you don't need the expense of a title company, title insurance, or even a lawyer.

The buyer can have an abstractor search the deed records at the courthouse and, for less than $100, get a title search that will show all liens on the property. If there are none other than the ones you've indicated you have, the buyer can proceed with taking over the property. In that case, make a copy of the blank warranty deed in Appendix M and fill it out like the filled-out example I've included immediately before it.

Sign it and have your signature notarized. The buyer then takes it to the county courthouse and files it at the County Clerk or County Recorder's office. He'll have to pay a small fee for recording, plus any state recording stamps or taxes. He then continues making your payments.

The only drawback here is that if he defaults, your credit will still be affected. Even though he assumed your loan, it still doesn't relieve you of any responsibility. Your name is still on the note and deed of trust, or mortgage. But if you were about to lose the house anyway, there's more to gain in letting someone else try to keep up the loan.

20

How Taxes
Affect Your Sale

UNLESS YOU SELL YOUR HOME AND HAVE NO GAIN OR LOSS, YOU'LL HAVE TO DEAL with the tax implications of a profit or loss on your income tax return. This chapter will answer many of the most common questions.

Tax laws change yearly, so you will need to consult IRS publications if you have a complicated tax situation. Among the more useful publications you can obtain from the IRS are:

- Moving Expenses (#521)

- Basis of Assets (#551)

- Installment Sales (#537)

- Tax Information for Owners of Homes, Condominiums, and Cooperative Apartments (#530)

- Tax Information on Selling Your Home (#523)

- Tax Information for Homeowners Associations (#588)

There are two tax items most people are concerned with, so I'll briefly explain these first. Then we'll go into details on the many ramifications of selling a home and how to handle various tax situations.

- Gain or Loss on the Sale of a Home—If you sell or exchange your personal home at a profit, you are allowed to postpone the tax on all of the gain if, within 2 years before or 2 years after the sale, you buy and live in another home that costs *at least* as much as the adjusted sales price of the old home. On the other hand, if you sell or exchange your personal home at a loss, you cannot deduct the loss on your federal tax return.

- Exclusion of Gain at Age 55 or Older—You may exclude from your gross income up to $125,000 of gain on the sale or exchange of your principal home if you were 55 or older on the date of the sale, if you owned and lived in your principal home for at least 3 years out of the 5-year period ending on the date of the sale, and you or your spouse have never excluded gain on the sale or exchange of a home after July 26, 1978. This election may be made only once in a lifetime.

Now let's look at the tax laws in more detail.

TREATMENT OF GAIN

Tax on part or all of the gain from the sale of your principal residence may be postponed. If you buy a new (meaning ''newly purchased'') home, and its purchase price is at least as much as the adjusted sales price of your old home, you may be able to postpone the tax on all the gain from the sale. If you do not buy another home, or if the purchase price of the new home is less than the adjusted sales price of the old home, you will be subject to tax on some or all of the gain, unless you qualify to exclude the gain (as explained later).

If you are on active duty in the armed forces, or if your tax home is outside the United States, the two-year period may be suspended.

Purchase Price Less Than Sales Price

If the purchase price of your newly purchased home is less than the adjusted sales price of your old home, and you buy and live in the new home within the time period given above, the gain taxed in the year of the sale is the lesser of:

- The gain on the sale of the old home, or

- The amount by which the adjusted sales price of the old home is more than the purchase price of the new home.

Postponing the Gain

You *must* postpone the gain if you replace your old home within the required period. If you have more than one home, you postpone the gain only on the sale of your *principal* home.

The tax on the gain is *postponed*, not forgiven. You subtract any gain that is not taxed in the year you sell your old home from the cost of your new home. This gives you a lower basis in the new home. If you sell the new home in a later year and again replace it, you may continue to postpone any tax on your gain.

For example, let's assume you sold your home in 1986 and had a $5,000 gain. Within two years you bought another home for $60,000, which is more than you received for the old one. The $5,000 gain will not be taxed in 1986 (the year of sale), but you must subtract it from the $60,000. This makes the basis of your new home $55,000. If you later sell the new home for $66,000, and do not buy and live in a replacement home within the required time, you will be subject to tax on the $11,000 gain ($66,000 minus $55,000) in the sale year.

Separate Funds

You need not use the same funds received from the sale of your old home to buy or build the new home. For example, you may use less cash and increase the amount of your mortgage loan.

Loss on Sale

You may not deduct a loss on the sale or exchange of your home. The loss has no effect on the basis of your new home.

Employer Reimbursements

If your employer transfers you to a new location, any reimbursements from your employer covering the loss on the sale or exchange of your home or for the expenses of the sale or exchange must be included in your *income*. Do not include the payment as part of the selling price. Include it in your gross income as compensation for services.

Estimated Tax Payments

If you have a gain from the sale of your home and you do not plan to replace it, or you do not meet the requirements for postponing the gain, then you may have to make estimated tax payments.

Basis

Basis is a way of measuring your investment in property for tax purposes. Whether you bought your home, hired a contractor to build it for you, built it yourself, or received it in another way, it is important that you know its basis. The basis of property you buy is usually the cost or purchase price. But you must know your home's *adjusted basis* to figure gain or loss when you sell or otherwise dispose of it. You also must know the adjusted basis at the time of a casualty to determine your deductible loss from the casualty.

If you change your home to rental or business use, your depreciation is based on the fair market value of the home or its adjusted basis at the time of the change, whichever is less.

Purchase. The original basis of a home you bought is the purchase price or cost of the property to you. This includes your down payment and any debt, such as a first or second lien, or notes you gave to the seller. Certain settlement or closing costs are added to or deducted from your basis, as you'll see later.

New Construction. If you contracted to have your house built on land that you own, your original basis is your basis of the land plus the amount it cost you to complete the house. This includes the cost of labor and materials, or the amounts paid the contractor, and any architect's fees, building permit charges, utility meter and connection charges, and legal fees that are directly connected with building your home. If you built all or part of your house yourself, its original basis is the total amount it cost you to complete it. You cannot include in the cost of the house the value of your own labor or any other labor you did not pay for.

Gift. If someone gave you your home, its original basis to you is whatever the donor's adjusted basis was when the gift was made. However, if the donor's adjusted basis was more than the fair market value of the home when it was given to you, you must use that fair market value as your basis for measuring any possible loss if you later sell or exchange the home. You still use the donor's adjusted basis to measure any gain.

If the fair market value was more than the donor's basis at the time of gift, your basis is the donor's adjusted basis at the time you received the gift. For gifts made before 1977, increase your basis by any federal gift tax paid on the gift. However, this increase can never raise the basis to more than the fair market value of the home when it was given to you.

If you received a gift after 1976, your basis is the donor's adjusted basis increased by the part of the gift tax paid that is due to the net increase in value of the gift. This part is figured by multiplying the gift tax paid on the gift by a fraction. The numerator (top part) of the fraction is the net increase in value of the gift and the denominator is the amount of the gift. The net increase in value of the gift is the fair market value of the gift less the donor's adjusted basis.

Inheritance. If you inherited your home, the original basis of the home is its fair market value at the date of the decedent's death or the later alternate valuation date if that date was used for federal estate tax purposes. If an estate tax return was filed, the property value listed there is generally your basis. If no return was filed, you should use the best available objective evidence of fair market value, such as a competent appraisal.

Trade. If you acquired your home in a trade for other property, the original basis of your home is the adjusted basis of the property you gave up, plus any recognized gain or cash difference you paid, and minus any recognized loss or cash difference you received.

Adjusted Basis

This is your original basis increased or reduced by certain amounts. Certain expenditures allow you to increase your basis, thereby decreasing your tax liability, and some forms of income will decrease your basis, thereby increasing your tax liability. For example, you must increase your basis by the cost of improvements, additions, and other capital items. You may also add to your basis any assessments for local benefits, such as streets and sidewalks. You must reduce the basis by any depreciation you have claimed, any deductible fire or other casualty payments you receive, and the value of any easements or rights-of-way you give up.

If you claimed any residential energy credit before 1986 and the items for which you took the credit increased the basis of your home, you must reduce the amount of that increase by the credit you took on those items.

Points and Closing Costs. You may not add to your basis certain settlement fees or closing costs such as points, fire insurance premiums, mortgage insurance premiums, or charges for services concerning occupancy of the house.

Improvements. Improvements add to the value of your home, prolong its useful life, or even adapt it to new uses. Do not confuse *improvements*, which you add to the basis of your property, with *repairs*, which you do not add to the basis. Repairs simply maintain your home in good condition. They do not add to its value or prolong its life.

Improvements would include putting a recreation room in your unfinished basement, adding another bathroom or bedroom, putting up a fence, putting in new plumbing or wiring, putting on a new roof, or paving your driveway. On the other hand, repainting your house inside or outside, fixing your gutters or floors, mending leaks or plastering, and replacing broken window panes are examples of repairs. However, if items that would otherwise be considered repairs are done as part of an extensive remodeling or restoration of your home, the entire job is considered an improvement.

Purchase Credit. The tax credit on the purchase of a new home acquired and occupied after March 12, 1975, and before January 1, 1977, has no effect on its basis.

Energy Credit. You must reduce the basis of your home by the amount of the residential energy credit allowed for energy saving and renewable energy source items you installed before 1986. You should add the cost of the items to the basis of your home.

Recordkeeping. You should save receipts and other records for all improvements, additions, and other items that affect the basis of your home. Keep them for at least three years after the year you sell or otherwise dispose of your home.

Principal Home

Usually, the home in which you live is your principal home (residence). The home that you sell and the one you buy to replace it must both qualify as your principal home.

Houseboats, Mobile Homes, and Co-ops. A houseboat or mobile home may be your principal home. Likewise, if you own a co-op, that apartment may be your principal home. Your basis in the apartment is usually the cost of your stock in the co-op housing corporation, which may include your share of a mortgage on the apartment building.

Condominiums. A condominium home or apartment may be your principal home. Your basis is your cost, which also may include your share of the mortgage on the common parts of the development or structure.

Furniture. Furniture, appliances, and similar items that are not *fixtures* (permanent parts of the property) generally are not part of your principal home. But appliances that are attached are part of the home, such as dishwashers, central vacuum systems, etc.

Land. If you sell the land on which your principal home is located, but not the house itself, you may not postpone any gain you have from the sale of the land. For example, you sell the land on which your principal home is located. Within the replacement period, you buy another piece of land and move your house to it. This sale is not considered to be a sale of your principal home and you may not postpone any gain on the sale. This rule applies to sales after March 27, 1983.

More Than One Home. If you have more than one home, only the sale of your principal home qualifies for postponing the tax. For example, if you own and live in a house in town and also own beach property which you use in the summer months, the town property is your principal home; the beach property is not.

If you have two homes and live in both of them, your principal home is the one you live in most of the time.

If you own a house, but live in another house for which you pay rent, the rented home is your principal home. But if a house you own is your principal home, you may temporarily rent it out before its sale without changing its character as your principal home.

Amount Realized and Selling Expenses

Your gain is the amount realized minus the adjusted basis of the home. The amount realized is the selling price minus selling expenses. The selling price is the total amount you receive for the property, including money, all notes, mortgages, or other debts that are part of the sale, and the fair market value of other property you receive. If, on the sale of your old home, you receive a note or mortgage with no stated interest or a low rate of interest, see the discussion of unstated interest in IRS Publication #537.

If you have to sell your home because of a job transfer, and your employer pays you for a loss in value of your home, do not include the payment as part of the selling price. Include it in your gross income as compensation for services.

The selling expenses include commissions, advertising, and legal fees. Loan charges paid by the seller, such as loan placement fees or points, are usually a selling expense.

If your move is job related, some expenses of selling a home may be deducted as moving expenses. For more information see IRS Publication #521.

Adjusted Sales Price

The adjusted sales price of the old home is used to figure the part of the gain on which tax is postponed. The adjusted sales price is the amount realized minus any fixing-up expenses you might have. Compare the adjusted sales price with the cost of the new home to find the gain on which tax is postponed. Fixing-up expenses must:

- be for work done during the 90 days before you sign the contract to sell, and

- be paid within 30 days after the sale, and

- not be deductible in arriving at your taxable income, and

- not be used in figuring the amount realized, and

- not be capital expenditures or improvements.

Be careful though, because you consider fixing-up expenses only in finding the gain on which tax is postponed. You may not deduct them in figuring the actual profit on the sale of the old home.

Special Situations

Trading Homes. If you trade your old home for another home, the trade is treated as a sale and a purchase.

Property Partly Used As Your Home. You may use your property partly as your home and partly for business or to produce income. Examples are a working farm on which your house is located, an apartment building in which you live in one unit and rent out the others, or a store building with an upstairs apartment in which you live. If you sell the whole property, you postpone only the tax on the part used as your home. This includes the land and outbuildings, such as a garage for the home, but not those for the business or the production of income.

When you buy a new home you must reinvest in the new home only the part of the selling price for the part of the old home used as your home, in order to have the tax on that part of the gain postponed. If you use only part of the new property as your home, only the cost for that part counts as reinvestment. You should look at the whole transaction as the sale of two properties.

Business Use of Your Home. If, in the year of sale, you deduct expenses for the business use of your home, you cannot postpone the tax on the gain on the part of the home used for business. In figuring the amount of gain you may postpone, you must make an allocation for the business-use portion of the home.

Home Changed to Rental Property. You may not postpone tax on the gain on rental property, even though it was once used as your home. Once you change its use, you have investment property. For more information, see IRS Publication #527.

Temporary Rental of Principal Home. If you temporarily rent out your old principal home before selling it, or your new principal home before living in it, as a matter of convenience, or for some other nonbusiness purpose, any gain on the sale of the property will qualify for treatment as the sale of a principal residence.

If you place your home with a real estate agent for rent or sale and it is not rented, it will not be considered business property or property held for the production of income.

Condemnation. If your home is condemned for public use and you have a gain, you may either postpone the tax on the gain, or you may choose to treat the transaction as an involuntary conversion. The replacement periods allowed under the two treatments may be different and you should compare the replacement periods under both.

If you treat the transaction as an involuntary conversion, to postpone tax on the gain, you must buy, within a specified period, replacement property that costs at least as much as the net proceeds received from the involuntary conversion.

In a condemnation, or the threat or imminence of one, the replacement period begins on the date you disposed of the property, or the date condemnation was threatened or was imminent, whichever was earlier. Generally, the replacement period ends two years after the close of the first tax year in which you realize any part of the gain on the conversion.

Gain on Casualty. The tax on a gain from fire, storm, or other casualty cannot be postponed. But you might want to look at IRS Publication #547, *Nonbusiness Disasters, Casualties, and Thefts.*

Options. If you grant an option to buy your home, add the amount you receive for the option to the sale price of your home if the option is exercised. If the option is not exercised, you must report the amount you receive as ordinary income for the year the option expires.

Property Taxes. You may deduct property taxes in the year of sale based on the number of days in the year that you owned the property. It does not matter what part of those taxes you actually paid. If, as part of the contract price of your home, the buyer paid delinquent taxes that you owed, the payment increases the amount you realized on the sale.

Transfer Taxes. You may not deduct as itemized deductions any transfer taxes, stamp taxes, and other incidental taxes and charges on the sale of a home. However, if you pay these amounts as the seller of the property, they are expenses of the sale and reduce the amount you realize on the sale. If you pay these amounts as the buyer, they are included in your cost basis of the property. If you deduct them as moving expenses, you may not use the amount deducted either to reduce the amount realized on the sale of the home or to increase the cost basis of the new home.

Members of the Armed Forces. The replacement period following the sale of your old home is suspended while you serve on extended active duty in the armed forces. You are on extended active duty if you are serving under a call or order for an indefinite period or for more than 90 days. The suspension applies only if your service begins before the end of the two-year period. This time plus any period of suspension is limited to four years from sale of your old home.

If you sell your house after July 18, 1984, the replacement period is suspended while you are stationed outside the United States. The replacement period may also be suspended while you are required to live in on-base quarters following your return from tour of duty outside the United States. In this case, it will be suspended if you are required to live on base because you are stationed at a remote site where the Secretary of Defense has determined adequate off-base housing is not available. The replacement period will not expire until one year after the last day of either of these two periods. The replacement period, plus any period of suspension, is limited to eight years from sale of your old home.

Spouse in Armed Forces. If your spouse is in the armed forces and you are not, the suspension applies to you if you own the old home. Both of you must have used the old home and the new home as your principal home. However, if you are divorced or separated while the replacement period is suspended, the suspension ends for you on the day after the date of the divorce or separation.

Living Abroad. The replacement period after the sale of your old home is suspended while you have your tax home (the place where you live and work) outside the United States. This suspension applies only if your stay abroad begins before the end of the two-year replacement period. The replacement period, plus the period of suspension, is limited to four years from sale of your old home.

If you are married, this suspension of the replacement period lasts while either you or your spouse has a tax home outside the United States, provided that both of you used the old and the new home as your principal home.

Your tax home is considered to be the city or general area of your main place of business, employment, station, or post of duty. It does not matter where your family lives.

New Home

You use the purchase price of your replacement home to find the gain taxed and the gain postponed on the sale of your old home. Purchase price includes costs incurred within the 48-month replacement period for the following items:

- Buying or building the home

- Rebuilding

- Capital improvements or additions

You may not consider any costs incurred before or after the 48-month period. However, if you are a member of the armed forces you may include in the purchase price any costs incurred during the suspension period.

Debts on the New Property. The price of a new home includes debts it is subject to when you buy it and the face amount of your notes or other liabilities (purchase-money mortgage or deed of trust) that you give for it.

Zero Interest Mortgage. If when you bought your home you gave the seller a noninterest-bearing mortgage with payments due over a number of years, the payments due more than six months after the date of purchase must be allocated between principal and interest. This interest is deductible as an interest expense if you itemize deductions. It is not part of the purchase price of the home. You must subtract the interest from the total purchase price in arriving at the cost of the home. For more information, see IRS Publication #537.

Temporary Housing. If a builder gives you temporary housing while your new home is being finished, you must subtract the value of the temporary housing from the total contract price in arriving at the cost of the new home.

Settlement Fees or Closing Costs. You probably paid an amount in addition to the contract price of the property for settlement fees or closing costs. Several expenses connected with the purchase are not included in the purchase price of the home, but are divided between the buyer and seller, according to the sales contract, local custom, or understanding of the parties. You may deduct some of these costs, such as real estate taxes, mortgage interest, and points that are deductible if you itemize your deductions. You can get more information in IRS Publications #530 and #545.

You may also add other costs to the basis of your home, such as attorney fees and transfer taxes, if they are applicable in your area. For more information see IRS Publication #551.

You may not deduct, or add to your basis, certain settlement fees or closing costs. These include points or loan origination fees that are not deductible as interest, fire insurance premiums, FHA mortgage insurance premiums (PMI), charges for the use of utilities, rent for occupancy before closing, and other fees or charges for services concerning occupancy of the house.

Investment in Retirement Home. You have not bought a replacement home if you sell your home and invest the amount you receive for it in a retirement home project that will give you living quarters and personal care but which does not give you any legal interest in the property. Therefore, you must include in income any gain on the sale of your home. However, if you are 55 or older, refer to the "Exclusion of Gain" section later in this chapter.

Allocation Between You and Your Spouse. Sometimes either you or your spouse may own the old home separately, but title to the new one is in both your names as joint tenants. Or, you may own the old home as joint tenants and either you or your spouse may own the new home separately. In such cases, the gain from the sale of the old home on which tax is postponed and the resulting adjustment to the basis of the new home may be allocated between you and your spouse. You may make the allocation only if:

- both of you use the old and new homes as your principal home, and

- both of you file a consent with the IRS. It may be filed in the bottom margin of Form #2119, "Sale or Exchange of Principal Residence," or on an attached statement by writing: "We consent to reduce the basis of the new residence by the gain from selling the old residence." Both of you must sign the consent.

If both of you do not consent, you must figure gain on the sale of the old home in the regular way without allocation.

Separate Homes Replaced by Single Home. The tax on your and your spouse's gains from the sales of homes that had been your separate principal homes before your marriage will be postponed if:

- you buy a new principal home for more than the combined adjusted sales prices of the old homes, and

- you and your spouse each contribute one-half of the purchase price and take joint title to the new home.

Report the sales of the old homes on separate Forms #2119. Divide the purchase price of the new home between you and your spouse.

Title Not Held in Your Name. If you invest the amount you receive from the sale of the old home in a new home in which neither you nor your spouse hold any legal interest, title being held by someone else, such as your child, you may not postpone the tax on the gain on the sale of the old home.

Home Replaced by Two Homes. The postponement provisions apply separately to the gains realized by you and your spouse from the sale of your principal home if you have agreed to live apart and you each bought and lived in a separate replacement home. If your gain is $20,000 on the sale of the old home, and if each of you will keep one-half of that amount, then you report half of the sales price, and your spouse reports half of the sales price. Basically, you consider the sale as if you had each sold a home separately.

Home Combined with Business or Rental Property. If you replace your old home with property used partly as your home and partly for business, you must make allocation between the gain on which tax is postponed and that on which tax is not postponed.

Inheritance. If you inherit or receive any part of your new home as a gift, you cannot use the value of that part in figuring the gain on the sale of your old home on which tax is postponed. You include the basis of that part, however, in the adjusted basis used in figuring the gain when you sell the new home.

No Double Deduction. You may not decrease the amount realized on the sale of your home by the real estate commission or similar expenses you deduct as a moving expense. You may not increase the basis of a new home by the attorneys' fees or similar expenses you deduct as moving expenses. For more information, see IRS Publication #521.

Holding Period. If you postpone tax on any part of the gain on the sale of your old home, you will be considered to have owned your new home for the combined period you owned both the old and the new homes.

If you sell your new principal home within two years after the sale of your old home and any part of the gain was not recognized, you generally may not postpone tax on the gain on the sale of the new home.

The exception to this rule is if you sell or exchange your principal home because of a work-related move for which you can deduct moving expenses. Thus, if certain requirements are met, you may postpone the gain from the sale of more than one principal home during the replacement period. These requirements relate to the distance between your new workplace and your old home, and to the length of time you must work after the move. Your new principal place of work must be at least 35 miles farther from your former home than was your former place of work, or if you had no former place of work, your new place of work must be at least 35 miles from your former home.

If you are an employee, you must work full-time for at least 39 weeks during the first 12 months after you arrive in the general area of your new job location. If you are self-employed, you must work full time for at least 78 weeks during the 24 months after you arrive in the area of your new job location. For more details on the distance and time requirements, see IRS Publication #521.

More Than One New Home. If during the replacement period you buy or build more than one principal home, only the last one bought or built in the period may be treated as the new home in figuring whether you may postpone the tax on the gain from the sale of the old home.

In this case there is also an exception. If you sell your home because of a work-related move to which the exception discussed above applies, you should treat this home as the new home in deciding whether you can postpone tax on the gain from the sale of your old home.

EXCLUSION OF GAIN

You may exclude from your gross income some or all of your gain from the sale of your principal home, if you meet certain age, ownership, and use tests at the time of the sale. You may choose to exclude a gain only once for sales or exchanges after July 26, 1978.

Age, Ownership, and Use

You may choose to exclude from your gross income $125,000 of gain ($62,500 if you are married filing separately) on the sale or exchange of your principal home if:

- you were 55 or older on the date of the sale or exchange, and

- you owned and lived in your principal home for at least three years out of the five-year period ending on the date of the sale or exchange, and

- you or your spouse have never excluded a gain on the sale or exchange of a home after July 26, 1978.

Age 55 at Time of Sale. You must be 55 by the date you sell the home to qualify for the $125,000 exclusion. You do not meet the age 55 test if you sell the property during the year in which you will be 55 but before you actually become 55. The earliest date on which you may sell your home and still qualify for the exclusion is your 55th birthday.

Ownership and Use Test. The required three years of ownership and use during the five-year period ending on the date of the sale or exchange do not have to be continuous. You meet the test if you can show that you owned and lived in the property as your principal home for either 36 full months or 1,095 days (365 × 3) during the five-year period. Short temporary absences for vacations, or other seasonal absences, even if you rent out the property during the absences, are counted as periods of use.

More Than One Owner. If a husband and wife sell their jointly owned home and either one meets the age, ownership, and use tests, they are considered one owner for figuring the gain to be excluded from income. But if the joint owners of a home are other than husband and wife, each individual owner who meets the age, ownership, and use tests may exclude his or her gain on an individual basis.

Each such owner who chooses to exclude gain from gross income must meet the age, ownership, and use tests. If one owner meets the tests, that does not automatically qualify the other owners to exclude their gain from gross income. A choice by one owner does not keep the other owners from making a similar choice in the future.

Previous Home Destroyed or Condemned. For purposes of the ownership and use tests, you may add the time you owned and lived in a previous home that was destroyed or condemned to the time you owned and lived in the home on which you wish to exclude gain. This applies if any part of the basis of the home you sold or exchanged depended on the basis of the destroyed or condemned home. Otherwise, to qualify for the exclusion, you must have owned and lived in the same home that was sold or exchanged for three out of the five years before the sale or exchange.

The ownership and use tests may be met during different three-year periods as long as both tests are met during the five-year period ending on the date of the sale or exchange.

If you meet the age, ownership, and use tests, you may choose to exclude $125,000 of your gain on the sale or exchange of your home. If you are married filing separately, you may choose to exclude only $62,500 of gain on the sale or exchange. Your gain is the amount realized minus the adjusted basis of the home. If there is gain remaining after the exclusion, you may be able to postpone the rest of the gain if, as explained earlier, you buy and live in another home.

Principal Home

Principal home has the same meaning for the exclusion of gain as it has for postponing tax on gain. Also, when you use only part of the property as your principal home, the rules discussed earlier apply only to the gain on the sale or exchange on the part of the property used as your principal home.

Trade Old Home. If you trade your old home for a different home, the trade is treated as a sale and a purchase. Gain on the old home may qualify for exclusion from gross income.

Land. If you sell the land on which your principal home is located, but not the house itself, you may not exclude from income any gain you have from the sale of the land. This rule applies to sales after March 27, 1983.

If Your Home Is Condemned. If your home is condemned for public use, you may treat the transaction as a sale of the home. If you choose to exclude the gain on it from gross income, you must first exclude it, as explained previously. Also, you may postpone the tax on the rest of the gain, or you may postpone it under the rules for an involuntary conversion. This is discussed in IRS Publication #549, *Condemnations and Business Casualties and Thefts.*

Damaged Home. If your home is damaged by fire, storm, or other casualty, you may choose to exclude the gain from insurance proceeds or other compensation. However, unlike a condemnation gain, you may not postpone the tax on the rest of the gain. The rest may qualify, however, for the tax treatment that applies to involuntary exchanges. See IRS Publication #547, *Nonbusiness Disasters, Casualties, and Thefts.*

Jointly Owned Home. Both you and your spouse will meet the age, ownership, and use tests if:

- you hold the home either as joint tenants, tenants by the entirety, or as community property on the date of the sale or exchange, and

- you file a joint return for the tax year in which you sell the home, and

- either you or your spouse is 55 or older on the date of sale and has owned and lived in the property as a principal home for the required time before the sale or exchange.

Home of Spouse Who Died. You will meet the ownership and use tests if on the date you sell your principal home:

- your spouse is deceased, and

- you have not remarried, and

- your deceased spouse had met the ownership and use tests for that principal home, and

- your deceased spouse had not previously chosen or joined in choosing to exclude gain on the sale or exchange of another principal home after July 26, 1978.

Sale by Executor. Gain from the sale of a home by the executor of an estate qualifies for this exclusion, if the sale is made under a contract entered into before death by a taxpayer who met the age, ownership, and use tests.

Effect of Marital Status

You determine your marital status as of the date of sale or exchange of the home. If you are divorced by the date of the sale or exchange, you are not considered married. If you are married at the time you sell or exchange your principal home, you may not choose to exclude the gain unless your spouse joins you in making the choice. Your spouse must join you in the choice even if:

- you or your spouse owned the home separately,

- you and your spouse filed separate returns, or

- the spouse not owning an interest in the home had not lived in it for the required period before the sale or exchange.

If your spouse died after the sale or exchange, but before making the choice to exclude the gain, his or her personal representative (for example, administrator or executor) must join with you in making the choice. You, as the surviving spouse, are considered the personal representative of your deceased spouse if no one else has been appointed.

If the home is not jointly owned, the spouse who owns the property must meet the age, ownership, and use tests discussed earlier. The other spouse must join in making the choice.

If you are married and file a separate return and you meet the tests discussed earlier, you may choose to exclude no more than $62,500 of gain on the sale or exchange of your principal home. Your spouse must show agreement to your choice by writing in the bottom margin of Form 2119 or on an attached statement, "I consent to Part II election" and signing his or her name.

Only One Exclusion

You or your spouse may exclude gain only once. If you or your spouse chooses to exclude gain from a sale or exchange after July 26, 1978, neither of you may choose to exclude gain again for a sale or exchange after that date. If you and your spouse each owned separate homes before your marriage and sold both homes after your marriage, you may exclude the gain on one of them, but not on both.

If, after choosing to exclude gain, you and your spouse divorce, neither of you may exclude gain again. If you remarry, you and your new spouse may not exclude gain on sales or exchanges after your marriage. However, a previous choice may be revoked as you'll see below.

Making and Revoking a Choice to Exclude Gain

You may exclude gain on the sale or exchange of your principal home only once for sales or exchanges after July 26, 1978. You may make or revoke a choice to exclude gain from a particular sale or exchange at any time before the latest of the following dates:

- Three years from the due date of the return for the year of the sale

- Three years from the date the return was filed

- Two years from the date the tax was paid

Making the Choice. You make the choice by attaching a filled-in Form 2119, "Sale or Exchange of Principal Residence," to your income tax return for the year in which you sell or exchange your home. However, if you do not have Form 2119, you can make the choice by attaching a signed statement to your return. The statement must say that you choose to exclude from income the gain from the sale or exchange, and must also include:

- Your name, age, social security number, and marital status on the date of the sale or exchange. If jointly owned, give this information for each owner.

- The dates you bought and sold the home.

- The adjusted sales price and the adjusted basis of the property on the date of sale.

- How long you were away from the home during the five years before the sale, except for vacation and other seasonal absences, even if you rented out the home during these absences.

- Whether you or a joint owner ever chose to exclude gain on the sale of a home, and if you did, when and where you did so. If you revoked the choice, give the date it was revoked.

You may, after originally reporting the gain on the sale of your home, choose to exclude the gain from taxable income. You do so by filing an amended return on Form 1040X. You must send a filled-in Form 2119 or a statement with your amended return.

Revoking the Choice. The spouse who joined you in making the choice must join you in revoking it. If your spouse is deceased, his or her personal representative must join in revoking any choice previously made by you and your deceased spouse, or by you and his or her personal representative. You revoke your choice in a signed statement showing your name and social security number. Include in the statement the year in which you made the choice. Send it to the IRS Service Center where you filed the choice, the Service Center now nearest you, or your local IRS Service office.

If, at the time you revoke your choice, less than a year is left in the assessment period (the time for determining your correct tax) for the tax year for which the choice was made, you must agree, in writing, that the assessment period will not run out before the end of one year after the filing of the statement. You must file this agreement before the end of the assessment period for the tax year in which you made the original choice to exclude gain. The assessment period normally ends on the latest of the dates under the time-to-exclude-gain dates shown earlier.

Filing Your Return

Even if you exclude the gain on the sale of your home from gross income, you must consider that gain in determining whether you had enough income to require you to file a return.

In conclusion, if you have a complicated tax situation, it's always a good idea to get professional help from an accountant or tax attorney.

21

Working with Brokers —If You Must

EVEN AFTER READING AND USING THIS COMPREHENSIVE BOOK, YOU MIGHT FIND that you *must* use a real estate broker. Generally, the *only* reason you'd absolutely need a broker's services is when you're short of time. A broker may be able to procure a buyer sooner than you can. In fact, a good broker *should* be able to get you a buyer much sooner than you can. The reasons for this are readily apparent:

- Real estate is the broker's business; he has a lot of contacts.
- He does a lot of advertising and receives many phone calls.
- He may be tied-in with an excellent relocation system.
- He has many agents working to sell your house.
- He and his agents will use strong closing techniques that can sell the property to a hesitant prospect.

Along with the advantages, you'll find disadvantages that may keep you from using his services on an exclusive right-to-sell contract (explained below). Those disadvantages are:

- The commission: 5–7% of the total sales price

- Showings to unqualified buyers by novice agents

- The hassle of dealing with unqualified agents

I talk with many FSBOs during the course of a week. Many of them shun me like the great plague. As a rule, I think that's a mistake. Real estate brokers and salespeople can help you. If you make them your friend, they may sell your house, and in that case, you gain and they gain.

You might be thinking right now, "But that's totally against the grain of this book."

My answer is, "Not exactly." Let's look at the real estate brokerage business so you can see what I mean.

THE NEGOTIABLE COMMISSION

As you know, everyone has to make a living. Some make a better living than others. Each area of the country seems to have what I call, and what the general public often takes for granted as, a "standard" commission charged a seller for the merchandising of his property by a real estate brokerage firm. It's generally between 5% and 7%.

You should know that, legally, there is no "standard" commission. The commission is *always* a negotiable item. Some brokers will act as if it's not, and stick to their own minimum commission. Of course, everyone has a right to run his business as he sees fit. And not everyone has the same overhead. For example, a firm that's a member of a national franchise system will pay 4–10% of what it earns to the franchise company. So they have to charge a higher fee.

As it goes in most real estate brokerage firms, the commissions are split thus: if the listing contract states 6%, generally half of the commission, or 3%, goes to the listing broker, and the other half goes to the selling broker. If the selling agent and listing agent are from the same brokerage firm, or it's the same individual, so much the better for the company.

Now if a selling broker is happy enough to settle for half of the commission when he sells a house listed by another broker, then he may be happy enough to settle for half of the commission when you, the seller, are your own listing agent and he is the selling agent. Many *are* happy enough to settle for half of the commission, or they *would* be happy enough to settle for half if you would explain to them that there's no difference between selling your house and selling a house listed with another broker.

The Small Broker Is the Most Accommodating

The smaller, independent, non-franchise firms are more likely to work with you this way than the larger and/or franchise-affiliated ones. It makes sense for the smaller firms to work with you—and I know for a fact that many will—because they won't have to spend advertising dollars on your property. They may have a client for whom your home is an exact fit, and they certainly won't want to lose their client. Or their client may be very loyal to them, and the only way that buyer will see your property is through their agent.

Whatever the situation, it can be an ideal thing for you and for the agent, and for the agent's buyer as well. You have to look at your position carefully. If you'll be pressed for time, you might need all the help you can get—and at the least cost possible.

You'll get plenty of calls from agents trying to get your listing. You want to make friends with all of them. Not all will work with you on a reduced commission, but usually enough of them will to serve your purpose.

When they give you their reasons why you should list with them, be very nice and very polite. Tell them you've done your homework, that you've already had the house appraised by a professional appraiser, or you've done a thorough market analysis, and that you would be happy to pay them half of whatever is normal in your community.

You may hear them moan, complain, perhaps even gnash their teeth when you mention such a low commission, but persist with your polite reasoning. Tell them that you know everyone must make a living, and they're entitled to their commission. But under your present circumstances, you feel the normal commission is more than you can afford to pay someone for selling your house.

Let them know you understand how the real estate brokerage business works, and that if they're willing to sell another broker's listing and settle for half of the "standard" commission, then you can't see how they'd not be happy to earn half of the commission on the sale of your house.

You'll hear many objections, and a lot of good excuses why they just can't work that way. A favorite one is, "My broker doesn't allow me to work for anything less than such and such commission because of our extensive and expensive advertising."

You have to determine what is a just commission for someone to bring you a buyer, depending on your particular circumstances. If you have plenty of time to find a buyer, you can go for the lower commission. If you don't have much time, then you can entice them with a little higher rate.

GIVE YOURSELF PLENTY OF TIME TO FIND A BUYER

If you know you must sell your home—and get all your cash— by a certain date, then give yourself plenty of time to find a buyer, *plus* enough time for a real estate agency to find one for you under a regular listing, if all your efforts are fruitless. This is why you must be aware of the market conditions in your area. If things are normal or better, there is absolutely no reason why you can't sell your home yourself or, at worst, pay only half of a normal commission to a real estate agency.

Many folks fail in selling their own homes by not knowing the market. If you *must* make a move in 6 months, then give yourself 2½ or 3 months to find a buyer. After that, let the agent who has impressed you the most—in terms of knowledge and your own feeling about the agent as well as the agency—have the listing and go to work on it full-time. If you wait till the last minute, you could have two problems:

- You'll leave a vacant house. Vacant houses never sell as well as furnished ones, unless a seller has extremely distressed furniture and is a terrible housekeeper.

- If you need to buy where you're relocating, you won't have your equity for the purchase of another property. That'll mean renting and another move sometime soon.

Plan Well in Advance

Once you feel comfortable with an agent, sit down with him or her well in advance, and discuss market time in your area and possible favorable terms that will get you a sale in case your own efforts fail. The "professional" agent—we'll discuss professionals in a moment—will be honest with you and not try to push for a quick listing. He or she will know that if they treat people right, in the end they'll have more than enough business.

LISTING AGREEMENTS

Now then, back to your own efforts. When you've determined what you think is a just commission, tell the agents who call you that you'll be happy to pay them that commission, and to prove it, you'll mail them an information sheet and a signed *open listing agreement*. Get the agent's name, and the name and address of his agency, then excuse yourself politely from the phone conversation, and mail the agent the information sheet and the listing agreement such as the one included in Appendix N.

When you mail it, you'll accomplish two things. First, you'll get your information to the agent, who may find the features of your home interesting enough for a future customer. Second, you'll have given him an open listing which he more than likely would not have taken any other way. After all, if he had come to you and accepted the listing at only 3% (or whatever you've offered), he would have backed down from his otherwise hard-and-set commission rules. But the agent now will have the signed listing and won't be afraid to bring you a buyer, because he knows he'll get his commission if he sells it.

In some states, oral listings are enforceable in court. In that case, your word over the phone is good enough for him to claim his commission if he brings you a buyer. But in other states, only a *written* listing contract is enforceable to collect a commission. A good agent wouldn't try to sell your home without a written listing anyway.

So now the agent has your written listing. But you have not given him an "exclusive right to sell." Let me explain the three types of listings common in residential transactions:

- The *exclusive right to sell* gives the broker an exclusive right to market your property for a certain length of time. The time is negotiable, but it can be anywhere from one day to one year; more commonly, it is three to four months. If at any time during this period a buyer is found—by the broker, by *you*, or by anyone else—then the broker has earned his commission. This is the most common listing agreement used by brokers in residential sales.

- The *exclusive agency* gives the broker the exclusive right to act as the owner's agent. But if the owner finds a buyer himself, then the broker is not entitled to a commission. Brokers don't like this agreement; they feel they're wasting advertising dollars on a home they may not collect a commission on.

- The *open listing* is what you're offering the agents that call you. This form of listing states that if the agent finds the buyer, then the owner will pay a commission as stated in the listing agreement. But if another broker finds a buyer, or if the owner sells the house himself, then the agent receives no commission.

The Open Listing Is Best for You

While the open listing is not popular with real estate agents, it can work out well for *you*, and it also protects the agent and it can work out well for him also. It is commonly used in commercial transactions, so there's no reason why it shouldn't work in residential sales. If the agent brings you a buyer, and you work directly with the buyer, then the agent is still entitled to his commission. But if you find a buyer through your own efforts, the agent is not entitled to a commission just because he has a listing on the property. It's really a fair arrangement. I've used it often and have never had a problem with it.

DEALING WITH AGGRESSIVE AGENTS

Real estate brokers and agents are very aggressive individuals. At least, the good ones are. In fact, the good ones will be at your house asking for the listing before you know it, even if you've made it clear you're not interested in their services.

Here's one technique I employed successfully to get my foot in the door after a seller had emphatically stated that he didn't need my services. I would show up at the seller's door and hand him a very neat packet of information that could help him do a better job of selling his property. I called it my FSBO packet.

My dialogue went something like this: "Good evening Mr. Jones, I'm Maurice Dubois with Dubois Real Estate. I have a complimentary packet of information here that may help you do a better job of selling your own property."

He would take the packet and thank me for it. Then I'd start some small talk about how nice the front of his house looked, what a great neighborhood he lived in, etc. After a minute or two, he'd feel rather comfortable with me. Then I'd ask, "Would you mind if I took a look at the inside of your home."

That usually got me in. Once inside, I could give him or he and his wife a sales pitch about myself and my company while I toured and admired his home.

Once a good, strong salesman is inside a seller's house, he'll often come out with a listing. And if he doesn't, he'll keep calling and chatting with the seller on a weekly basis until the seller relents and gives him the listing.

You should be aware of this strategy. Stick to *your* strategy. When a salesman shows up to preview your property, show him around and give him your open listing. When he calls you on a weekly basis, you know he's serious about selling your house. Insist on his use of your open listing. In fact, you might *call him* every week to see how he's doing in selling your house with your open listing. Do this with enough agents and they'll remember your house when they find a buyer whose needs will be met by your property.

No matter what the salesman's strict instructions from his broker are, no matter how set his principles are against working for lower commissions, the fact is that *all* salesmen work first to make a living, and secondly to help the client. If he finds a buyer for whom your house fits like a glove, he'll bring him out and do the best he can to make the sale. He knows that if he only gets half of a commission, that's all he'd get if he sold someone else's listing anyway.

MAKE THE AGENTS YOUR FRIENDS

So instead of offending the real estate agent, make him your friend. Allow him to help you sell your house. And if he does, he'll earn his commission, and you'll save half of what you'd normally pay if you handed him the normal listing.

As a practical matter, I must state that some brokers would not be able to run their business entirely on half commissions, especially the large ones with proportionately large overheads. But as an active broker, I've always believed in the law of averages. For example, there are many people who have a large equity in their home, and whose time is too valuable to spend selling their own home. These homeowners will list at a regular commission, it won't hurt them to pay the broker's full fee, and the broker will deserve his commission. There are also times when a buyer needs to sell soon, or the property is extremely difficult to sell or finance and it will take a large amount of work and advertising to market it. So there will always be a need for, and the availability of, many full-commission listings.

But if you're willing to put forth the effort, you stand a good chance of selling the home yourself. And if you don't accomplish your task, perhaps you can have an agent sell it for you and save some money. In either case, your efforts will have paid off.

RAISING THE PRICE WHEN SELLING THROUGH BROKERS

Many home sellers, when listing their house with an agency, insist that the price be raised enough to cover the commission. This only works in favor of the agent. The reason is simple. Assume you have a house that's worth $100,000, and you have it priced exactly at value: $100,000. Then let's say Wonderful Willie the agent will list the house for $107,000 to get enough money to cover his commission and your full value. Will the market pay more than your house is worth just because Wonderful Willie is selling it? Not likely. What's more than likely is that you'll still only get $100,000, *minus* Wonderful Willie's commission.

Why do I say that raising the price works only in favor of the agent? By raising the price you are trying to justify listing the property and paying a commission. So you go ahead and list. Wonderful Willie knows that he has time in his favor. He'll do everything he can to bring you back down to reality on your price.

And if reality doesn't work, the offers that come in will. The first offer may be for $98,000 and you'll scream. The second one might come in at $97,000 and you'll scream even louder. But when the third one comes in right at $100,000, he'll take the time to sit down with you and tell you the facts. Those facts are that the house is only worth $100,000, that you've been kidding yourself, and that this is a great offer you should take. And guess what? You will.

Rarely does listing with a real estate agency get you more for the house than what it is worth. And if you receive an offer for $107,000 and the house only appraises for $100,000, what do you do then? That's simple. You let the deal die, or you lower your price.

22

Selecting a Broker

I WOULD BE LESS THAN FAIR IF I DIDN'T TALK ABOUT THE UNHEARD OF: LISTING your property under a standard listing agreement—an exclusive right to sell. In other words, if all your efforts fail, and you *must* sell, then you list with a real estate agent. So let's talk about real estate agents a bit.

Just as there are mediocre doctors, lawyers, and accountants, there are also mediocre real estate agents. I classify real estate agents in the following three categories:

1. **"AMATEURS"**: These are the 50% who lack experience and knowledge. A great many of these are part-timers.

2. **"TAXI DRIVERS"**: These are the 25% who are reasonably competent, though still quite green.

3. **"PROFESSIONALS"**: These are the 25% who are totally competent, and full-time.

The above figures are not, of course, scientific and infallible. But my experience in dealing with other agents and brokers is that half of the ones I meet I would not hire to work for me under any circumstances. Of the remaining half, those in Group #3 I'd hire in a minute and be proud to have them working with me. Those in Group #2 I'd have to think long and hard about hiring. Typically, new agents have only six months of education. They have so much to learn.

Would a law firm hire junior associates with only six months of law school? They'd have to finish educating them. That's a formidable task.

Let's dissect the three groups so you can tell each one from the others.

AMATEURS

Those in this group either just got their license, or have had it a while but work real estate part-time. Some have been in it a while and are full-timers, but their main reason for being in the real estate business is to socialize at the office because they have nothing better to do (while that's often true, I'm being somewhat facetious). They *never* go to a seminar, read a real estate book, or take a salesmanship course. They are totally stagnant.

They generally don't like to work with sellers. Their passion is only to take ad calls over the phone, grab a buyer, and try to sell him a house.

New or inexperienced agents will not know how to do a good job of helping you set the right financing for a speedy sale, negotiate with buyers, and convey to the Multiple Listing Service and other agents the features and benefits of your property.

New agents come on the scene with very little training, and on a part-time basis, they'll be almost as ignorant after a couple of years. By the way, this group has a business mortality rate of a year or two at the most. You're dealing with what is probably your largest investment. Don't leave it in the hands of amateurs.

TAXI DRIVERS

I call those in this group "Taxi Drivers" because their main trick is to take a buyer and drive him and his family in a nice car and show them 35 houses one right after the other. After six hours of this torture the buyers are exhausted. They don't even remotely remember the first 30 houses.

When a Taxi Driver finally wears his buyers down, they'll sign any contract on any house. But when the buyers go for a loan application, the loan officer discovers the husband is looking for a job, the wife doesn't work either, and they filed for bankruptcy two months ago. The Taxi Driver never qualified them. (You laugh; I've seen this happen much too often.)

Taxi Drivers are people who have been around long enough to get some real estate experience, but like the newcomers, also lack education. Some will graduate to Professionals, others will flounder in the Sea of Mediocrity for years.

A lot of these people have been in the business long enough to get by comfortably with innocent buyers. You don't need this type of agent. You need. . .

TRUE PROFESSIONALS

The True Professionals have three outstanding qualities:

1. They are full-time professionals.
2. They have been in the business full-time for several years and started out with a good education in their profession.
3. They keep abreast of their business by going to seminars at least six times a year and reading books on real estate law, finance, and merchandising.

FIND OUT WHOM YOU'RE DEALING WITH

How do you know with whom you're dealing? Ask some questions such as these:

- How long have you been in the business?
- Are you full-time?
- When is the last time you went to a seminar?
- How many educational meetings do you attend per year?
- Can you show me that you *fully* understand residential real estate financing?
- How much experience and education do you have in your profession?
- What will you specifically do to market my property?

You have 25% of all real estate agents to choose from. Ask enough questions and you'll find the right one.

23

Final Hints

I'D LIKE TO GO OVER SOME ADDITIONAL ELEMENTS THAT CAN MAKE YOUR SEL-ling effort easier, more successful, and with less risk of future legal problems.

KNOWN PROPERTY DEFECTS

There's not one house on our entire globe which is free from defects. That's as sure as death and taxes. Yours will have its share. Modern laws and court decisions require that you inform a buyer of latent defects in the structure or equipment.

The more informed the buyer is of the actual, total condition of your proper-ty, the less chance there will be that he'll come at you later with accusations of fraud and misrepresentation because you failed to disclose hidden defects.

That doesn't mean you need to make a 20-page list of every scratch, dent, flaw, blemish, drip, and loose board that's not apparent from a hurried inspection of the house.

It does mean you must let the buyer know about problems with the structure that might substantially reduce the value because of required repairs at time of sale, or within the immediate future.

For example, if there are problems with the roof, you might be able to fool the buyer at the time of sale by not mentioning the defects and hiding any leaks on the inside with paint and spackle. But he could come after you later with a lawsuit that could cost you much more than the cost of fixing the roof in the first place.

In some parts of the country, foundations can shift and cause structural difficulties throughout the entire house. In other parts, basements may leak during very wet times. Don't hide such defects. Either fix them, or tell the buyer you've compensated for the defects in the price you're asking.

OTHER DISCLOSURES

Structural defects are not the only disclosures you must make to your buyer with respect to his new home. What is your duty under many states' laws to disclose information to potential purchasers regarding your knowledge of prior residents or owners? Some examples will help.

In *Reed v. King*, 145 Cal. App. 3d 261, 193 Cal. Rptr. 130 (1983), King sold Reed a home for $76,000. Neither King nor the real estate agent informed Reed that a woman and her four children had been murdered in the subject house 10 years earlier. Both the seller and his agent represented that the house was in good condition and fit for an elderly lady living alone. After Reed moved in, she was informed by neighbors that no one had been interested in purchasing the property because of the stigma following the murders.

The trial court held for the seller and agent, and Reed appealed. The Court of Appeals reversed and held that a vendor of real property has a duty to disclose to the purchaser facts materially affecting the value of said property when those facts are known only to the vendor and are not readily detectable by the purchaser.

That brings up the subject of disclosure of previous residents' or owners' potentially transmittable diseases, specifically AIDS (even though medical authorities are adamant that AIDS can be transmitted only through intimate contact or exchange of blood products). It's almost certain the above case will be cited often as precedent for future cases associated with non-disclosure of the presence of an infection in a vendor. As a matter of fact, it has been referred to in a civil action involving the sale of a California home, *Roberts v. Heramb*, slip op. no. 5943942.

In *Roberts*, the purchaser sought to rescind a purchase agreement and recover a $10,000 escrow deposit when she learned of the death of one of the sellers of hepatitis and of the illness of the other seller with pneumonia. She suspected that at least one of the sellers had AIDS. The case was settled out of court.

A commentator has suggested that in the above type of case, the court must balance the seller's right to privacy with the buyer's right to full disclosure of material facts. Where do you stand as a seller? It's not certain yet. And only time will tell if there will ever be a definite answer. Just be aware of the fact that failure to disclose *any* type of potential problem could cause you big headaches months or years later.

PAYING BIRD-DOG FEES TO NON-AGENTS

All states have real estate commissions that regulate the listing and selling of real property by licensed brokers and agents. Generally, owners and direct employees of owners of real estate (such as builders' salesmen) are not required to possess a real estate license to sell their own or their employers' products.

Bird-dog fees are compensation to a non-licensed individual who doesn't actually make a sale, but simply locates the buyer and directs him to the seller. I doubt that the real estate commission in your state has the manpower, or even the desire, to fine or prosecute you for paying a friend or acquaintance a bird-dog fee for the acquisition of a buyer for your property.

As a matter of fact, it would probably be to your advantage if you let people you are familiar with, *and trust*, know that you'll reward them with a gift, perhaps a substantial gift, if they send someone to you to whom you eventually sell your home. Just make sure you don't give someone who is not licensed what would amount to a listing, whether oral or written.

BUYERS' BROKERS

In the chapters on working with brokers, I discussed *sellers'* brokers, but I didn't mention *buyers'* brokers. That's because sellers' brokers are paid by the seller—that's you. And buyers' brokers receive compensation from the buyer; therefore, you must *always* be accommodating and attentive with buyers' brokers. You won't have to pay them a commission, but they might bring you a buyer.

Actually, when one calls you, he may already have a buyer for your property. Answer all his questions, ask him to preview your home, and encourage him to show it to his clients.

Just be cognizant of the buyers' broker's job: to secure the best house for the best price for his clients. A sellers' broker's client is the seller. He tries to get the highest price for the seller. Now the situation is reversed. The buyer—and his broker—are looking for the *lowest* price. That means there's a good chance you'll be dealing with someone extremely able at negotiating for price concessions. Be firm, keep your temper in solid control, and play his game till you get as close to your price as meets your objectives.

Appendices

Appendix A

HOME IMPROVEMENT CHECKLIST

EXTERIOR

Driveway: OK ☐   Fix _____ Cost _____

Sidewalk: OK ☐   Fix _____ Cost _____

Lawn: OK ☐   Fix _____ Cost _____

Shrubs: OK ☐   Fix _____ Cost _____

Trees: OK ☐   Fix _____ Cost _____

Sprinkler
   system: OK ☐   Fix _____ Cost _____

Brick: OK ☐   Fix _____ Cost _____

Siding: OK ☐   Fix _____ Cost _____

Eaves: OK ☐   Fix _____ Cost _____

Windows: OK ☐   Fix _____ Cost _____

Doors: OK ☐   Fix _____ Cost _____

Roof: OK ☐   Fix _____ Cost _____

Fence: OK ☐   Fix _____ Cost _____

Exterior
   buildings: OK ☐   Fix _____ Cost _____

Other: _____
     OK ☐   Fix _____ Cost _____

Appendix A (cont'd)

INTERIOR

☐ Entry   ☐ Master Bedroom
☐ Living Room   ☐ Bedroom #2
☐ Dining Room   ☐ Bedroom #3
☐ Den   ☐ Bedroom #4
☐ Game/Exercise Room   ☐ Other _____

Floors: OK ☐   Fix _____ Cost _____

Walls: OK ☐   Fix _____ Cost _____

Ceilings: OK ☐   Fix _____ Cost _____

Trim boards: OK ☐   Fix _____ Cost _____

Doors: OK ☐   Fix _____ Cost _____

Windows: OK ☐   Fix _____ Cost _____

Door knobs
  and hardware: OK ☐   Fix _____ Cost _____

Light fixtures: OK ☐   Fix _____ Cost _____

Closets: OK ☐   Fix _____ Cost _____

Cabinets: OK ☐   Fix _____ Cost _____

Other: _____
                   OK ☐   Fix _____ Cost _____

Appendix A (cont'd)

Kitchen

Floors: OK ☐   Fix _____ Cost _____

Walls: OK ☐   Fix _____ Cost _____

Ceilings: OK ☐   Fix _____ Cost _____

Trim boards: OK ☐   Fix _____ Cost _____

Doors: OK ☐   Fix _____ Cost _____

WIndows: OK ☐   Fix _____ Cost _____

Door knobs
   and hardware: OK ☐   Fix _____ Cost _____

Light fixtures: OK ☐   Fix _____ Cost _____

Closets: OK ☐   Fix _____ Cost _____

Cabinets: OK ☐   Fix _____ Cost _____

Countertops: OK ☐   Fix _____ Cost _____

Sinks: OK ☐   Fix _____ Cost _____

Range: OK ☐   Fix _____ Cost _____

Ovens: OK ☐   Fix _____ Cost _____

Refrigerator: OK ☐   Fix _____ Cost _____

Dishwasher: OK ☐   Fix _____ Cost _____

Other: _____

                   OK ☐   Fix _____ Cost _____

Appendix A (cont'd)

Bathroom: ☐ **Master**   ☐ **#2**   ☐ **#3**

Floors: OK ☐ Fix _____ Cost _____

Walls: OK ☐ Fix _____ Cost _____

Ceilings: OK ☐ Fix _____ Cost _____

Trim boards: OK ☐ Fix _____ Cost _____

Doors: OK ☐ Fix _____ Cost _____

Windows: OK ☐ Fix _____ Cost _____

Door knobs
   and hardware: OK ☐ Fix _____ Cost _____

Light fixtures: OK ☐ Fix _____ Cost _____

Closets: OK ☐ Fix _____ Cost _____

Cabinets: OK ☐ Fix _____ Cost _____

Countertops: OK ☐ Fix _____ Cost _____

Mirrors: OK ☐ Fix _____ Cost _____

Faucets: OK ☐ Fix _____ Cost _____

Water closets
   and seats: OK ☐ Fix _____ Cost _____

Shower and
   enclosure: OK ☐ Fix _____ Cost _____

Tub and
   enclosure: OK ☐ Fix _____ Cost _____

Other: _____
          OK ☐ Fix _____ Cost _____

Appendix A (cont'd)

Mechanical

Fireplace: OK ☐   Fix _____ Cost _____

Heating system: OK ☐   Fix _____ Cost _____

Cooling system: OK ☐   Fix _____ Cost _____

Central vacuum
   system: OK ☐   Fix _____ Cost _____

Other: _____

                      OK ☐   Fix _____ Cost _____

Appendix B

PROPERTY INFORMATION SHEET

Attach Picture Here

Owner _____

Address _____

Price _____ **Phone (w)** _____ **Phone (h)** _____

Schools _____

Shops _____

Heating _____ **Air** _____ **Lot size** _____

Garage _____ **Storage** _____ **Roof** _____

Foundation _____ **Fence** _____ **Exterior** _____

L.R. _____ **D.R.** _____ **Kit.** _____

Brkfst. _____ **Den** _____ **Util.** _____

BR 1 _____ **BR 2** _____ **BR 3** _____

BR 4 _____ **BR 5** _____ **Baths** _____

Other rooms _____ **Age** _____

1st Mortgage _____ **Bal.** _____

% Int. _____ **Years** _____ **Date** _____ **Payment** _____

2nd Mortgage _____ **Bal.** _____

% Int. _____ **Years** _____ **Date** _____ **Payment** _____

Lot _____ **Block** _____ **Addition** _____

Taxes _____ **Remarks** _____

Appendix C

RIGHT OF FIRST REFUSAL AFFIDAVIT

State of _____

_____, or County of _____

The undersigned states upon oath as follows:

1. He/she is the duly qualified and elected (title)

_____

of (legal name of association) _____
(hereinafter, the "Association"), a duly qualified non-profit (corporation or partnership) _____ in good standing formed to administer and maintain the condominium complex known as _____ according to the recorded Condominium Map and Declaration thereof (hereinafter, the "Complex").

2. This Affidavit is made and executed pursuant to the provisions of (article or paragraph) _____ of the Condominium Declaration for the Complex, which Declaration was duly recorded in Book _____ at Page _____ in the office of the County Clerk or County Recorder of _____ County of _____ (hereinafter the "Declaration").

3. Timely, written notice giving the terms of the offer of (proposed purchaser) _____ to purchase Unit _____ in Building _____ according to the recorded Condominium Map for the Complex, was duly served upon the Association in accordance with the provision of the Declaration and notice was, in turn, duly given to the other unit owners, members of the Association. The requisite (number of days) _____ day period has expired and neither the Association nor any member nor any group of members submitted an offer to purchase the unit in accordance with the provisions of the Declaration.

Appendix C (cont'd)

4. This Affidavit is made for the purpose of complying with the terms of the Declaration and assuring the purchaser and all others that the Association, as of this date, is satisfied that the Right-of-first-refusal requirements of the Declaration have been met.

Attest: *(Corporate seal if used)*

President _____

Secretary _____

The foregoing instrument was subscribed and sworn to before me this _____ day of _____, 19____ by (president) _____ and (secretary) _____ on behalf of said corporation.

Witness my hand and official seal.

(Notary) _____

(Notary's printed or typed name) _____

(Notary's commission expires) _____

Appendix D

MORTGAGE PAYMENT TABLE
(Payment factors for each $1,000 of a loan)

TERM OF LOAN (IN YEARS)

Rate	5	10	15	20	25	30
5.0%	18.8712	10.6066	7.9079	6.5996	5.8459	5.3682
5.5%	19.1012	10.8526	8.1708	6.8789	6.1409	5.6779
6.0%	19.3328	11.1021	8.4386	7.1643	6.4430	5.9955
6.5%	19.5661	11.3548	8.7111	7.4557	6.7521	6.3207
7.0%	19.8012	11.6108	8.9883	7.7530	7.0678	6.6530
7.5%	20.0378	11.8702	9.2701	8.0559	7.3899	6.9921
8.0%	20.2764	12.1328	9.5565	8.3640	7.7182	7.3376
8.5%	20.5165	12.9386	9.8474	8.6782	8.0523	7.6891
9.0%	20.7584	12.6676	10.1427	8.9973	8.3920	8.0462
9.5%	21.0019	12.9398	10.4422	9.3213	8.7370	8.4085
10.0%	21.2470	13.2151	10.7461	9.6502	9.0870	8.7751
10.5%	21.4939	13.4935	11.0540	9.9838	9.4418	9.1474
11.0%	21.7424	13.7750	11.3660	10.3219	9.8011	9.5232
11.5%	21.9926	14.0595	11.6819	10.6643	10.1647	9.9029
12.0%	22.2444	14.3471	12.0017	11.0109	10.5322	10.2861
12.5%	22.4979	14.6378	12.3252	11.3614	10.9035	10.6726
13.0%	22.7531	14.9311	12.6524	11.7158	11.2784	11.0620
13.5%	23.0098	15.2274	12.9832	12.0737	11.6564	11.4541
14.0%	23.2683	15.5266	13.3174	12.4352	12.0376	11.8487
14.5%	23.5283	15.8287	13.6550	12.8000	12.4216	12.2456

Appendix D (cont'd)

TERM OF LOAN (IN YEARS)

Rate	5	10	15	20	25	30
15.0%	23.7899	16.1335	13.9959	13.1679	12.8083	12.6444
15.5%	24.0532	16.4411	14.3399	13.5388	13.1975	13.0452
16.0%	24.3181	16.7513	14.6870	13.9126	13.5889	13.4476
16.5%	24.5845	17.0642	15.0371	14.2890	13.9824	13.8515
17.0%	24.8526	17.3798	15.3900	14.6680	14.3780	14.2568
17.5%	25.1222	17.6979	15.7458	15.0494	14.7753	14.6633
18.0%	25.3934	18.0185	16.1042	15.4331	15.1743	15.0709
18.5%	25.6662	18.3417	16.4652	15.8190	15.5748	15.4794
19.0%	25.9406	18.6672	16.8288	16.2068	15.9768	15.8889
19.5%	26.2164	18.9952	17.1947	16.5966	16.3801	16.2992
20.0%	26.4939	19.3256	17.5632	16.9882	16.7845	16.7102
20.5%	26.7729	19.6582	17.9335	17.3815	17.1901	17.1218
21.0%	27.0534	19.9932	18.3061	17.7764	17.5966	17.5340
21.5%	27.3354	20.3303	18.6808	18.1728	18.0041	17.9467
22.0%	27.6189	20.6697	19.0576	18.5706	18.4124	18.3598
22.5%	27.9039	21.0112	19.4362	18.9697	18.8215	18.7734
23.0%	28.1905	21.3548	19.8166	19.3700	19.2313	19.1873
23.5%	28.4785	21.7004	20.1988	19.7715	19.6417	19.6015
24.0%	28.7680	22.0481	20.5827	20.1741	20.0526	20.0160
24.5%	29.0589	22.3977	20.9682	20.5777	20.4643	20.4308
25.0%	29.3513	22.7493	21.3553	20.9822	20.8763	20.8458

Appendix E

QUALIFYING SHEET

BORROWER _____ SALES PRICE _____ LOAN AMOUNT _____ LTV _____

CLOSING COSTS

	Conventional		FHA		VA	
	Buyer	Seller	Buyer	Seller	Buyer	Seller
Origination Fee						
Discount Points			•••			
Appraisal						
Credit Report						
Title Policy			•••			
Survey						
Attorney Fees					••	
Restrictions					••	
Underwriting Fee			-0-		-0-	
Tax Service			-0-		-0-	
Escrow Fee					••	
Recording Fee						
Mortgagee Title Policy						
VA Funding Fee/PMI/FHA MIP			•••			
Subsidy Fee						
Processing Fee						
Other						
Total Estimated Closing Costs			•			

ESTIMATED TOTAL MONTHLY PAYMENT

P&I _____

Hazard Insurance _____

Taxes _____

PMI _____

Other _____

TOTAL _____

ESTIMATED PREPAIDS

15 Days prepaid interest_____

14 mo. hazard insurance_____

2 mo. taxes _____

2 mo. PMI _____

TOTAL PREPAIDS _____

LIABILITIES _____

INCOME _____

QUALIFYING

CONVENTIONAL

Payment/Income Ratio _____
Obligations/Income Ratio _____

ESTIMATED CASH FOR CLOSING

Downpayment _____

Closing Costs _____

Prepaids _____

Total _____

Earnest Money_____

Cash For Closing_____

FHA/VA

Total monthly payment_____	
Maintenance _____	+
Utilities _____	+
Total housing payment_____	=
Social Security*_____	+
Liabilities _____	+
Total fixed payment _____	=
Income _____	
Income taxes_____	−
Net effective income _____	=

Expendable income _____
(Net Effective Income less Total Fixed Payment)
*Max. SS $250.25/person (430.50—self-employed)

EXPENDABLE INCOME (FHA/VA)
FHA/VA

1 person	$400	3 people	$670	5 people	$850	7 people	$1030	9 people	$1210
2 people	$570	4 people	$760	6 people	$940	8 people	$1120	10 people	$1300

*Use for FHA submission application for estimated closing costs.
**Veteran may not pay if he pays the loan origination fee.
***Do not include in acquisition costs.

Appendix F
VA Contract Form

USE THIS CONTRACT FOR A SALE TO A VETERAN WHO USES A VA-GUARANTEED LOAN.

Paragraph #1: Write your legal name(s) on the first line, as sellers, and the legal names of the buyers on the next line. Remember to note the marital status of all parties. For example:

- If one of the parties is a married couple, you would write "John M. Doe and wife Mary M. Doe."

- For a single person, you can simply write "John M. Doe," or you can write "John M. Doe, a single person."

- For a divorced person, write "John M. Doe, a divorced person since May 23, 1985."

- For a widower, write "John M. Doe, a widower since May 23, 1985."

- For a corporation, you would write "JMD Industries, Inc., a Texas corporation."

- For a Partnership, you would write "Doe Properties, a Texas General Partnership," or "Doe Properties, a Texas Limited Partnership."

- For a pension and profit-sharing plan, you would write "JMD Industries, Inc., Pension & Profit-Sharing Trust."

- For two individuals not related or married, you would write "John M. Doe and John R. Smith, in indiscriminate interest."

The next blank asks for the name of the county in which the real estate is located, then place the two letter code for the state after the word "County."

The last blank requests the address of the property.

Paragraph #2: This paragraph asks for the legal description of the property. You'll find this information in your copies of your original closing papers. Make *certain* you have the correct description. Write the lot number, the block number, then the name of the addition in the first three blanks. On the fourth blank insert the city in which the property is located.

Paragraph #3:

A. In this space, most of the time you'll want to put "0" since most VA loans are processed with no money down. In some cases, there will be a down payment (if the loan is to be for more than $144,000).

B. Here insert the amount of the note. If you've put a "0" in A above, then you'll put the purchase price here, otherwise deduct the down payment from the purchase price.

C. In this spot you'll put the sales price.

Paragraph #4: The first blank will have the number of years the loan will run. Most loans are made for 30 years, so you'll write "30."

On the second blank, insert the number of days from the contract date the buyer will take to go for financing. Generally, 5 or 10 days is enough. You certainly don't want them to delay in going for a loan.

Paragraph #5: Take as much earnest money as possible; 1% of the sales price, or at least $500, should be the minimum. Put the amount in the first blank. On the second blank indicate who will hold the earnest money. Depending on your state, it could be a title or escrow company, an attorney, or a broker. Write your name if you'll hold the earnest money yourself.

If there will be additional earnest money at a future date before the closing, then indicate the date and the amount of the additional funds on the remaining blanks.

Paragraph #6: Check box A if you'll furnish a title insurance policy, and indicate the name of the company that will issue the policy. Check box B if you'll provide an abstract of title, and indicate the abstractor or abstract company that will provide it.

Paragraph #7: You'll check box A if the property is being sold "as is" except for any repairs that may be required by a lender, or other conditions you'll indicate in the blank in the first paragraph.

Box B will be checked if the buyer will be allowed to inspect the property before closing. If you check this box, then you will include a Property Condition Addendum form (Appendix L).

Paragraph #8: If one or more brokers are to receive a commission, this paragraph will be used. In most situations you'll place "N/A" in each of these blanks, because if brokers are involved, they'll want to use their own contract forms.

Paragraph #9: Fill in the closing date. Make sure you give yourself enough time to find financing for the buyer. Check with several mortgage companies to see how long to allow. If you run out of time and the buyer has not been approved for a loan, this contract will become null and void and the buyer could back out on the transaction.

Paragraph #10: Indicate when the buyer will take possession. If you put in an exact date predicated on the closing date and you don't make the closing date, then you'll have confusion. Rather, indicate whether possession will be "on date of closing," "three days after closing," or other such date that is agreeable to both you and the buyer.

Paragraph #11: Include here any special provisions that are important to your agreement with the buyer. For example, include any personal property that's included with the property, such as "Refrigerator and all window treatments to remain with property." Any personal property that looks like it is attached to the property, but which you will take with you, should be included here.

You can also show other terms of purchase or financing that don't fit anywhere else, such as "First five payments on owner financing to be made in the amount of $250.00, to cover principal only. Interest to begin on the sixth month."

Paragraph #12:

_A._ The loan appraisal fees are often paid by the seller, since you'll want to keep the appraisal if the buyer doesn't get financing. Insert "buyer" or "seller" in this space.

_B.(1)_ On this line you want to limit your discount points. Check with the lenders and see what is a reasonable number of points you must pay. Three or four should generally be sufficient.

Paragraph #21: There are two spaces at the end of this paragraph to include the name of the buyer's and seller's attorneys. Write in the names if attorneys will represent either party. Often, on simple transactions, attorneys will not be used and you'll mark out these lines.

On the blanks that ask for the date, fill in the effective date of the contract, which is when all parties have affixed their signatures.

VA GUARANTEED LOAN — RESIDENTIAL EARNEST MONEY CONTRACT (RESALE)

1. PARTIES: *DARRELL D. DYKES AND WIFE LINDA L. DYKES* (Seller) agrees to sell and convey to *SID T. SIMONS AND BROTHER JULES SIMONS* (Buyer) and Buyer agrees to buy from Seller the following property situated in *DALLAS* County, Texas, known as *8300 CENTER ST. GARLAND, TX 88888* (Address).

2. PROPERTY: Lot *GR*, Block *12*, *HAY FIELD* *#3* Addition, City of *GARLAND*, or as described on attached exhibit, together with the following fixtures, if any: curtain rods, drapery rods, venetian blinds, window shades, screens and shutters, awnings, wall-to-wall carpeting, mirrors fixed in place, attic fans, permanently installed heating and air conditioning units and equipment, lighting and plumbing fixtures, TV antennas, mail boxes, water softeners, shrubbery and all other property owned by Seller and attached to the above described real property. All property sold by this contract is called "Property".

3. CONTRACT SALES PRICE:
   A. Cash down payment payable at closing .... $ ~0~
   B. Note described in 4 below (the Note) in the amount of .... $ 50,000.00
   C. Sales Price payable to Seller on Loan funding after closing (Sum of A and B) .... $ 50,000.00

4. FINANCING CONDITIONS: This contract is subject to approval for Buyer of a VA loan (the Loan) of not less than the amount of the Note, amortizable monthly for not less than *30* years, with interest at maximum rate allowable at time of Loan funding. Buyer shall apply for the Loan within *10* days from the effective date of this contract and shall make every reasonable effort to obtain approval. If the Loan has not been approved by the Closing Date, this contract shall terminate and the Earnest Money shall be refunded to Buyer without delay. VA NOTICE TO BUYER: "It is expressly agreed that, notwithstanding any other provisions of this contract, the Buyer shall not incur any penalty by forfeiture of earnest money or otherwise or be obligated to complete the purchase of the Property described herein, if the contract purchase price or cost exceeds the reasonable value of the Property established by the Veterans Administration. The Buyer shall, however, have the privilege and option of proceeding with the consummation of this contract without regard to the amount of the reasonable value established by the Veterans Administration." Buyer agrees that should Buyer elect to complete the purchase at an amount in excess of the reasonable value established by VA, Buyer shall pay such excess amount in cash from a source which Buyer agrees to disclose to the VA and which Buyer represents will not be from borrowed funds except as approved by VA. If VA reasonable value of the Property is less than the Sales Price (3C above), Seller may reduce the Sales Price to an amount equal to the VA reasonable value and both parties agree to close the sale at such lower Sales Price with appropriate adjustments to 3A and 3B above.

5. EARNEST MONEY: $ *500* is herewith tendered and is to be deposited as Earnest Money with *ABC TITLE COMPANY*, as Escrow Agent, upon execution of the contract by both parties. Additional Earnest Money, if any, shall be deposited with the Escrow Agent on or before _____, 19____, in the amount of $_____.

6. TITLE: Seller at Seller's expense shall furnish either:
   X A. Owner's Policy of Title Insurance (the Title Policy) issued by *ABC TITLE CO.* in the amount of the Sales Price and dated at or after closing: OR
   ☐ B. Complete Abstract of Title (the Abstract) certified by _____ to current date.
   NOTICE TO BUYER: AS REQUIRED BY LAW, Broker advises that YOU should have the Abstract covering the Property examined by an attorney of YOUR selection, or YOU should be furnished with or obtain a Title Policy.

7. PROPERTY CONDITION (Check "A" or "B"):
   ☐ A. Buyer accepts the Property in its present condition, subject only to VA required repairs and _____.

   X B. Buyer requires inspections and repairs required by the Property Condition Addendum (the Addendum) and those required by VA. Upon Seller's receipt of the Loan approval and inspection reports Seller shall commence and complete prior to closing all required repairs at Seller's expense.

   All inspections, reports and repairs required of Seller by this contract and the Addendum shall not exceed $_____. If Seller fails to complete such requirements, Buyer may do so and Seller shall be liable up to the amount specified and the same paid from the proceeds of the sale. If such expenditures exceed the stated amount and Seller refuses to pay such excess, Buyer may pay the additional cost or accept the Property with the limited repairs and this sale shall be closed as scheduled, or Buyer may terminate this contract and the Earnest Money shall be refunded to Buyer. Broker and sales associates have no responsibility or liability for repair or replacement of any of the Property.

8. BROKER'S FEE: *N/A* Listing Broker (____%) and _____ _____ Co-Broker (____%), as Real Estate Broker (the Broker), has negotiated this sale and Seller agrees to pay Broker in _____ County, Texas, on consummation of this sale or on Seller's default (unless otherwise provided herein) a total cash fee of _____ of the total Sales Price, which Escrow Agent may pay from the sale proceeds.

9. CLOSING: The closing of the sale (the Closing Date) shall be on or before *JULY 30*, 19*88*, or within 7 days after objections to title have been cured, whichever date is later; however, if necessary to complete Loan requirements, the Closing Date shall be extended daily up to 15 days.

10. POSSESSION: The possession of the Property shall be delivered to Buyer on *3 DAYS AFTER CLOSING* in its present or required improved condition, ordinary wear and tear excepted. Any possession by Buyer prior to or by Seller after Closing Date shall establish a landlord-tenant at sufferance relationship between the parties.

11. SPECIAL PROVISIONS:

    ALL WINDOW TREATMENTS TO REMAIN WITH THE PROPERTY.

(Insert terms and conditions of a factual nature applicable to this sale, e.g., prior purchase or sale of other property, lessee's surrender of possession, and the like.)

Nº 65

12. SALES EXPENSES TO BE PAID IN CASH AT OR PRIOR TO CLOSING:
   A. Loan appraisal fees shall be paid by _SELLER_
   B. Seller's Expenses:
      (1) Seller's Loan discount points not exceeding _2% OF LOAN AMOUNT_ and in the Addendum.
      (2) VA required repairs and any other inspections, reports and repairs required of Seller herein, and in the Addendum.
      (3) Releases of existing loans, including prepayment penalties and recordation; escrow fee; tax statements; preparation of Deed, Note and Deed of Trust; expenses VA prohibits Buyer to pay, (e.g., copies of restrictions, photos, excess cost of survey of Property); other expenses stipulated to be paid by Seller under other provisions of this contract.
   C. Buyer's Expenses: Expenses incident to Loan (e.g., credit reports; recording fees; Mortgagee's Title Policy; Loan origination fee; that portion of survey cost Buyer can pay by VA regulation; Loan related inspection fees; premiums for 1 year's hazard insurance and any flood insurance; required reserve deposits for insurance premiums, ad valorem taxes and special assessments; interest from date of disbursement to 1 month prior to date of first monthly payment on the Note); premiums on non-required insurance; expenses stipulated to be paid by Buyer under other provisions of this contract.
   D. If any sales expenses exceed the maximum amount herein stipulated to be paid by either party, either party may terminate this contract unless the other party agrees to pay such excess. In no event shall Buyer pay charges and fees other than those expressly permitted by VA Regulations.

13. PRORATIONS: Insurance (at Buyer's option), taxes and any rents and maintenance fees shall be prorated to the Closing Date.

14. TITLE APPROVAL: If Abstract is furnished, Seller shall deliver same to Buyer within 20 days from the effective date hereof. Buyer shall have 20 days from date of receipt of Abstract to deliver a copy of the title opinion to Seller, stating any objections to title, and only objections so stated shall be considered. If Title Policy is furnished, the Title Policy shall guarantee Buyer's title to be good and indefeasible subject only to (i) restrictive covenants affecting the Property (ii) any discrepancies, conflicts or shortages in area or boundary lines or any encroachments, or any overlapping of improvements (iii) all taxes for the current and subsequent years (iv) any existing building and zoning ordinances (v) rights of parties in possession (vi) any liens created as security for the sale consideration and (vii) any reservations or exceptions contained in the Deed. In either instance, if title objections are disclosed, Seller shall have 30 days to cure the same. Exceptions permitted in the Deed and zoning ordinances shall not be valid objections to title. Seller shall furnish at Seller's expense tax statements showing no delinquent taxes and a General Warranty Deed conveying title subject only to liens securing debt created as part of the consideration, taxes for the current year, usual restrictive covenants and utility easements common to the platted subdivision of which the Property is a part and any other reservations or exceptions acceptable to Buyer. The Note shall be secured by Vendor's and Deed of Trust liens. In case of dispute as to the form of Deed, such shall be upon a form prepared by the State Bar of Texas.

15. CASUALTY LOSS: If any part of Property is damaged or destroyed by fire or other casualty loss, Seller shall restore the same to its previous condition as soon as reasonably possible, but in any event by Closing Date; and if Seller is unable to do so without fault, this contract shall terminate and Earnest Money shall be refunded with no Broker's fee due.

16. DEFAULT: If Buyer fails to comply herewith, Seller may either enforce specific performance or terminate this contract and receive the Earnest Money as liquidated damages, one-half of which (but not exceeding the herein recited Broker's fee) shall be paid by Seller to Broker in full payment for Broker's services. If Seller is unable without fault to deliver Abstract or Title Policy or to make any non-casualty repairs required herein within the time herein specified, Buyer may either terminate this contract and receive the Earnest Money as the sole remedy, and no Broker's fee shall be earned, or extend the time up to 30 days. If Seller fails to comply herewith for any other reason, Buyer may (i) terminate this contract and receive the Earnest Money, thereby releasing Seller from this contract (ii) enforce specific performance hereof or (iii) seek such other relief as may be provided by law. If completion of sale is prevented by Buyer's default, and Seller elects to enforce specific performance, the Broker's fee is payable only if and when Seller collects damages for such default by suit, compromise, settlement or otherwise, and after first deducting the expenses of collection, and then only in an amount equal to one-half of that portion collected, but not exceeding the amount of Broker's fee.

17. ATTORNEY'S FEES: Any signatory to this contract who is the prevailing party in any legal proceeding against any other signatory brought under or with relation to this contract or transaction shall be additionally entitled to recover court costs and reasonable attorney fees from the non-prevailing party.

   ESCROW: Earnest Money is deposited with Escrow Agent with the understanding that Escrow Agent (i) does not assume or have any liability for performance or nonperformance of any party (ii) has the right to require the receipt, release and authorization in writing of all parties before paying the deposit to any party and (iii) is not liable for interest or other charge on the funds held. If any party unreasonably fails to agree in writing to an appropriate release of Earnest Money, then such party shall be liable to the other parties to the extent provided in paragraph 17. At closing, Earnest Money shall be applied to any cash down payment required, next to Buyer's closing costs and any excess refunded to Buyer. Before Buyer shall be entitled to refund of Earnest Money, any actual and VA allowable expenses incurred or paid on Buyer's behalf shall be deducted therefrom and paid to the creditors entitled thereto.

19. REPRESENTATIONS: Seller represents that there will be no Title I liens, unrecorded liens or Uniform Commercial Code liens against any of the Property on Closing Date. If any representation above is untrue this contract may be terminated by Buyer and the Earnest Money shall be refunded without delay. Representations shall survive closing.

20. AGREEMENT OF PARTIES: This contract contains the entire agreement of the parties and cannot be changed except by their written consent.

21. CONSULT YOUR ATTORNEY: This is intended to be a legally binding contract. READ IT CAREFULLY. If you do not understand the effect of any part, consult your attorney BEFORE signing. The Broker cannot give you legal advice — only factual and business details concerning land and improvements. Attorneys to represent parties may be designated below, and, so employment may be accepted, Broker shall promptly deliver a copy of this contract to such attorneys.

Seller's Atty: _____N/A_____   Buyer's Atty: _____N/A_____

EXECUTED in multiple originals effective the _39th_ day of _MAY_, 19 _88_   (BROKER FILL IN THE DATE LAST PARTY SIGNS).

Listing Broker _____ License No. _____

By _____

Co-Broker _____ License No. _____

By _____

Receipt of $ _500_ Earnest Money is acknowledged in the form

of _CHECK_

ABC TITLE CO.   _5/30/88_
Escrow Agent   Date

By _[signature]_

Darrell D. Dykes
Seller

Linda L Dykes
Seller

8300 CENTER, GARLAND   _222-2222_ Tel.
Seller's Address

Sid T. Simons
Buyer

Jules Simons
Buyer

287 S.W. 5TH, DALLAS   _666-2354_ Tel.
Buyer's Address

VA GUARANTEED LOAN — RESIDENTIAL EARNEST MONEY CONTRACT (RESALE)

1. PARTIES: _____ (Seller) agrees
   to sell and convey to _____ (Buyer)
   and Buyer agrees to buy from Seller the following property situated in _____ County,
   known as _____ (Address).

2. PROPERTY: Lot _____, Block _____, _____
   _____ Addition, City of _____, or as described on attached exhibit,
   together with the following fixtures, if any: curtain rods, drapery rods, venetian blinds, window shades, screens and shutters, awnings, wall-to-
   wall carpeting, mirrors fixed in place, attic fans, permanently installed heating and air conditioning units and equipment, lighting and plumbing
   fixtures, TV antennas, mail boxes, water softeners, shrubbery and all other property owned by Seller and attached to the above described real
   property. All property sold by this contract is called "Property".

3. CONTRACT SALES PRICE:
   A. Cash down payment payable at closing . . . . $ _____

   B. Note described in 4 below (the Note) in the amount of . . . . $ _____

   C. Sales Price payable to Seller on Loan funding after closing (Sum of A and B) . . . . $ _____

4. FINANCING CONDITIONS: This contract is subject to approval for Buyer of a VA loan (the Loan) of not less than the amount of the Note,
   amortizable monthly for not less than _____ years, with interest at maximum rate allowable at time of Loan funding. Buyer shall apply
   for the Loan within _____ days from the effective date of this contract and shall make every reasonable effort to obtain approval. If the
   Loan has not been approved by the Closing Date, this contract shall terminate and the Earnest Money shall be refunded to Buyer without delay.
   VA NOTICE TO BUYER: "It is expressly agreed that, notwithstanding any other provisions of this contract, the Buyer shall not incur any
   penalty by forfeiture of earnest money or otherwise or be obligated to complete the purchase of the Property described herein, if the contract
   purchase price or cost exceeds the reasonable value of the Property established by the Veterans Administration. The Buyer shall, however, have
   the privilege and option of proceeding with the consummation of this contract without regard to the amount of the reasonable value established
   by the Veterans Administration." Buyer agrees that should Buyer elect to complete the purchase at an amount in excess of the reasonable value
   established by VA, Buyer shall pay such excess amount in cash from a source which Buyer agrees to disclose to the VA and which Buyer
   represents will not be from borrowed funds except as approved by VA. If VA reasonable value of the Property is less than the Sales Price (3C
   above), Seller may reduce the Sales Price to an amount equal to the VA reasonable value and both parties agree to close the sale at such lower
   Sales Price with appropriate adjustments to 3A and 3B above.

5. EARNEST MONEY: $_____ is herewith tendered and is to be deposited as Earnest Money with _____
   _____, as Escrow Agent, upon execution of the contract by both parties. Additional Earnest
   Money, if any, shall be deposited with the Escrow Agent on or before _____, 19 ____, in the amount of $_____.

6. TITLE: Seller at Seller's expense shall furnish either:
   ☐ A. Owner's Policy of Title Insurance (the Title Policy) issued by _____
   in the amount of the Sales Price and dated at or after closing: OR
   ☐ B. Complete Abstract of Title (the Abstract) certified by _____ to current date.
   NOTICE TO BUYER: AS REQUIRED BY LAW. Broker advises that YOU should have the Abstract covering the Property examined by an
   attorney of YOUR selection, or YOU should be furnished with or obtain a Title Policy.

7. PROPERTY CONDITION (Check "A" or "B"):
   ☐ A. Buyer accepts the Property in its present condition, subject only to VA required repairs and _____
   _____

   ☐ B. Buyer requires inspections and repairs required by the Property Condition Addendum (the Addendum) and those required by VA.
   Upon Seller's receipt of the Loan approval and inspection reports Seller shall commence and complete prior to closing all required repairs at
   Seller's expense.

   All inspections, reports and repairs required of Seller by this contract and the Addendum shall not exceed $_____. If Seller fails to com-
   plete such requirements, Buyer may do so and Seller shall be liable up to the amount specified and the same paid from the proceeds of the sale.
   If such expenditures exceed the stated amount and Seller refuses to pay such excess, Buyer may pay the additional cost or accept the Property
   with the limited repairs and this sale shall be closed as scheduled, or Buyer may terminate this contract and the Earnest Money shall be refunded
   to Buyer. Broker and sales associates have no responsibility or liability for repair or replacement of any of the Property.

8. BROKER'S FEE: _____ Listing Broker (_____%) and _____
   _____ Co-Broker (_____%), as Real Estate Broker (the Broker), has negotiated this sale and Seller
   agrees to pay Broker in _____ County, on consummation of this sale or on Seller's default (unless
   otherwise provided herein) a total cash fee of _____ of the total Sales Price, which Escrow Agent may pay from the sale proceeds.

9. CLOSING: The closing of the sale (the Closing Date) shall be on or before _____, 19 ____, or within 7 days after objections to title have been cured, whichever date is later; however, if necessary to complete Loan requirements, the Closing Date shall be extended
   daily up to 15 days.

10. POSSESSION: The possession of the Property shall be delivered to Buyer on _____ in its present or required
    improved condition, ordinary wear and tear excepted. Any possession by Buyer prior to or by Seller after Closing Date shall establish a landlord-
    tenant at sufferance relationship between the parties.

11. SPECIAL PROVISIONS:

(Insert terms and conditions of a factual nature applicable to this sale, e.g., prior purchase or sale of other property, lessee's surrender of possession, and the like.)

12. SALES EXPENSES TO BE PAID IN CASH AT OR PRIOR TO CLOSING:
   A. Loan appraisal fees shall be paid by _____.
   B. Seller's Expenses:
      (1) Seller's Loan discount points not exceeding _____
      (2) VA required repairs and any other inspections, reports and repairs required of Seller herein, and in the Addendum.
      (3) Releases of existing loans, including prepayment penalties and recordation: escrow fee; tax statements; preparation of Deed, Note and Deed of Trust; expenses VA prohibits Buyer to pay, (e.g., copies of restrictions, photos, excess cost of survey of Property); other expenses stipulated to be paid by Seller under other provisions of this contract.
   C. Buyer's Expenses: Expenses incident to Loan (e.g., credit reports; recording fees; Mortgagee's Title Policy; Loan origination fee; that portion of survey cost Buyer can pay by VA regulation; Loan related inspection fees; premiums for 1 year's hazard insurance and any flood insurance; required reserve deposits for insurance premiums, ad valorem taxes and special assessments; interest from date of disbursement to 1 month prior to date of first monthly payment on the Note); premiums on non-required insurance; expenses stipulated to be paid by Buyer under other provisions of this contract.
   D. If any sales expenses exceed the maximum amount herein stipulated to be paid by either party, either party may terminate this contract unless the other party agrees to pay such excess. In no event shall Buyer pay charges and fees other than those expressly permitted by VA Regulations.
13. PRORATIONS: Insurance (at Buyer's option), taxes and any rents and maintenance fees shall be prorated to the Closing Date.
14. TITLE APPROVAL: If Abstract is furnished, Seller shall deliver same to Buyer within 20 days from the effective date hereof. Buyer shall have 20 days from date of receipt of Abstract to deliver a copy of the title opinion to Seller, stating any objections to title, and only objections so stated shall be considered. If Title Policy is furnished, the Title Policy shall guarantee Buyer's title to be good and indefeasible subject only to (i) restrictive covenants affecting the Property (ii) any discrepancies, conflicts or shortages in area or boundary lines or any encroachments, or any overlapping of improvements (iii) all taxes for the current and subsequent years (iv) any existing building and zoning ordinances (v) rights of parties in possession (vi) any liens created as security for the sale consideration and (vii) any reservations or exceptions contained in the Deed. In either instance, if title objections are disclosed, Seller shall have 30 days to cure the same. Exceptions permitted in the Deed and zoning ordinances shall not be valid objections to title. Seller shall furnish at Seller's expense tax statements showing no delinquent taxes and a General Warranty Deed conveying title subject only to liens securing debt created as part of the consideration, taxes for the current year, usual restrictive covenants and utility easements common to the platted subdivision of which the Property is a part and any other reservations or exceptions acceptable to Buyer. The Note shall be secured by Vendor's and Deed of Trust liens. In case of dispute as to the form of Deed, such shall be upon a form prepared by the State Bar of
15. CASUALTY LOSS: If any part of Property is damaged or destroyed by fire or other casualty loss, Seller shall restore the same to its previous condition as soon as reasonably possible, but in any event by Closing Date; and if Seller is unable to do so without fault, this contract shall terminate and Earnest Money shall be refunded with no Broker's fee due.
16. DEFAULT: If Buyer fails to comply herewith, Seller may either enforce specific performance or terminate this contract and receive the Earnest Money as liquidated damages, one-half of which (but not exceeding the herein recited Broker's fee) shall be paid by Seller to Broker in full payment for Broker's services. If Seller is unable without fault to deliver Abstract or Title Policy or to make any non-casualty repairs required herein within the time herein specified, Buyer may either terminate this contract and receive the Earnest Money as the sole remedy, and no Broker's fee shall be earned, or extend the time up to 30 days. If Seller fails to comply herewith for any other reason, Buyer may (i) terminate this contract and receive the Earnest Money, thereby releasing Seller from this contract (ii) enforce specific performance hereof or (iii) seek such other relief as may be provided by law. If completion of sale is prevented by Buyer's default, and Seller elects to enforce specific performance, the Broker's fee is payable only if and when Seller collects damages for such default by suit, compromise, settlement or otherwise, and after first deducting the expenses of collection, and then only in an amount equal to one-half of that portion collected, but not exceeding the amount of Broker's fee.
17. ATTORNEY'S FEES: Any signatory to this contract who is the prevailing party in any legal proceeding against any other signatory brought under or with relation to this contract or transaction shall be additionally entitled to recover court costs and reasonable attorney fees from the non-prevailing party.

   ESCROW: Earnest Money is deposited with Escrow Agent with the understanding that Escrow Agent (i) does not assume or have any liability for performance or nonperformance of any party (ii) has the right to require the receipt, release and authorization in writing of all parties before paying the deposit to any party and (iii) is not liable for interest or other charge on the funds held. If any party unreasonably fails to agree in writing to an appropriate release of Earnest Money, then such party shall be liable to the other parties to the extent provided in paragraph 17. At closing, Earnest Money shall be applied to any cash down payment required, next to Buyer's closing costs and any excess refunded to Buyer. Before Buyer shall be entitled to refund of Earnest Money, any actual and VA allowable expenses incurred or paid on Buyer's behalf shall be deducted therefrom and paid to the creditors entitled thereto.
19. REPRESENTATIONS: Seller represents that there will be no Title I liens, unrecorded liens or Uniform Commercial Code liens against any of the Property on Closing Date. If any representation above is untrue this contract may be terminated by Buyer and the Earnest Money shall be refunded without delay. Representations shall survive closing.
20. AGREEMENT OF PARTIES: This contract contains the entire agreement of the parties and cannot be changed except by their written consent.
21. CONSULT YOUR ATTORNEY: This is intended to be a legally binding contract. READ IT CAREFULLY. If you do not understand the effect of any part, consult your attorney BEFORE signing. The Broker cannot give you legal advice — only factual and business details concerning land and improvements. Attorneys to represent parties may be designated below, and, so employment may be accepted, Broker shall promptly deliver a copy of this contract to such attorneys.

Seller's Atty: _____ Buyer's Atty: _____

EXECUTED in multiple originals effective the _____ day of _____, 19 _____. (BROKER FILL IN THE DATE LAST PARTY SIGNS).

Listing Broker _____ License No. _____   Seller _____

By _____   Seller _____

Co-Broker _____ License No. _____   Seller's Address _____ Tel. ____

By _____   Buyer _____

Receipt of $ _____ Earnest Money is acknowledged in the form   Buyer _____

of _____.   Buyer's Address _____ Tel. ____

Escrow Agent _____ Date _____

By _____

Appendix G
FHA Contract Form

USE THIS CONTRACT FOR A SALE USING AN FHA-INSURED LOAN.

Paragraph #1: Write your legal name(s) on the first line, as sellers, and the legal names of the buyers on the next line. Remember to note the marital status of all parties. For example:

- If one of the parties is a married couple, you would write "John M. Doe and wife Mary M. Doe."

- For a single person, you can simply write "John M. Doe," or you can write "John M. Doe, a single person."

- For a divorced person, write "John M. Doe, a divorced person since May 23, 1985."

- For a widower, write "John M. Doe, a widower since May 23, 1985."

- For a corporation, you would write "JMD Industries, Inc., a Texas corporation."

- For a Partnership, you would write "Doe Properties, a Texas General Partnership," or "Doe Properties, a Texas Limited Partnership."

- For a pension and profit-sharing plan, you would write "JMD Industries, Inc., Pension & Profit-Sharing Trust."

- For two individuals not related or married, you would write "John M. Doe and John R. Smith, in indiscriminate interest."

The next blank asks for the name of the county in which the real estate is located, then place the two letter code for the state after the word "County."

The last blank requests the address of the property.

Paragraph #2: This paragraph asks for the legal description of the property. You'll find this information in your copies of your original closing papers. Make *certain* you have the correct description. Write the lot number, the block number, then the name of the addition in the first three blanks. On the fourth blank insert the city in which the property is located.

Paragraph #3: On an FHA loan, if the sales price is $50,000 or higher, the required down payment is 3% of the first $25,000, and 5% of everything above that. If the sales price is under $50,000, then the down payment is only 3% of the total purchase price. Let's look at some examples:

- Sales price of $47,000. The down payment is $1,410 (3% of that amount). The loans are made in $50 increments, so you would round up to $1,450. In A you would enter $1,450. In B you would enter $45,550, and in C you would enter the sales price, $47,000.

- Sales price of $82,000. The down payment is 3% of the first $25,000 ($750) and 5% of the $57,000 balance ($2,850). The total down payment is $3,600. There is an easy way to figure this without much confusion: On any house that's under $50,000, simply figure 3%. On any house over $50,000, figure 5% of the sales price and deduct $500. So on the $82,000 example above, you would figure $82,000 × 5% = $4,100. Then deduct $500 from that and you would come up with $3,600.

Paragraph #4:

A. In the first blank, most of the time you'll put in "203b." Most FHA programs are the 203b type. If you're working a 245 program, then you'd use that number. The second blank will more than likely be "30." Most loans are written for 30 years. On the third blank, put in anywhere between 5 and 10. You want the buyer to apply for a loan as soon as possible.

B. In this blank, fill in the purchase price.

Paragraph #5: Take as much earnest money as possible; 1% of the sales price, or at least $500, should be the minimum. Put the amount in the first blank. On the second blank indicate who will hold the earnest money. Depending on your state, it could be a title or escrow company, an attorney, or a broker. Write your name if you'll hold the earnest money yourself.

If there will be additional earnest money at a future date before the closing, then indicate the date and the amount of the additional funds on the remaining blanks.

Paragraph #6: Check box A if you'll furnish a title insurance policy, and indicate the name of the company that will issue the policy. Check box B if you'll provide an abstract of title, and indicate the abstractor or abstract company that will provide it.

Paragraph #7: You'll check box A if the property is being sold "as is" except for any repairs that may be required by a lender, or other conditions you'll indicate in the blank in the first paragraph.

Box B will be checked if the buyer will be allowed to inspect the property before closing. If you check this box, then you will include a Property Condition Addendum form (Appendix L).

Paragraph #8: If one or more brokers are to receive a commission, this paragraph will be used. In most situations you'll place "N/A" in each of these blanks, because if brokers are involved, they'll want to use their own contract forms.

Paragraph #9: Fill in the closing date. Make sure you give yourself enough time to find financing for the buyer. Check with several mortgage companies to see how long to allow. If you run out of time and the buyer has not been approved for a loan, this contract will become null and void and the buyer could back out on the transaction.

Paragraph #10: Indicate when the buyer will take possession. If you put in an exact date predicated on the closing date and you don't make the closing date, then you'll have confusion. Rather, indicate whether possession will be "on date of closing," "three days after closing," or other such date that is agreeable to both you and the buyer.

Paragraph #11: Include here any special provisions that are important to your agreement with the buyer. For example, include any personal property that's included with the property, such as "Refrigerator and all window treatments to remain with property." Any personal property that looks like it is attached to the property, but which you will take with you, should be included here.

You can also show other terms of purchase or financing that don't fit anywhere else, such as "First five payments on owner financing to be made in the amount of $250.00, to cover principal only. Interest to begin on the sixth month."

Paragraph #12:

A. Most of the time, the loan appraisal fees are paid by the seller. Sometimes they are paid by the buyer. You need to state "buyer" or "seller" here. Of course, if you've already got an appraisal, you'll indicate "seller."

B. In the blank fill in a percentage, not a dollar amount, of the number of points you are willing to pay for the buyer to obtain his loan. Normally, two to three points is sufficient for a loan, unless you are going to do a deep buydown.

Paragraph #21: There are two spaces at the end of this paragraph to include the name of the buyer's and seller's attorneys. Write in the names if attorneys will represent either party. Often, on simple transactions, attorneys will not be used and you'll mark out these lines.

On the blanks that ask for the date, fill in the effective date of the contract, which is when all parties have affixed their signatures.

FHA INSURED LOAN — RESIDENTIAL EARNEST MONEY CONTRACT (RESALE)

1. PARTIES: _JOE J. DOE AND WIFE MARY B. DOE_ (Seller) agrees to sell and convey to _EDDIE E. EDWARDS, AND WIFE JO EDWARDS_ (Buyer) and Buyer agrees to buy from Seller the following property situated in _TARRANT_ County, Texas, known as _1807 MESQUITE LN, ARLINGTON, TX 33333_ (Address).

2. PROPERTY: Lot _106_, Block _77_, _McBRIDE OAKS_ Addition, City of _ARLINGTON_, or as described on attached exhibit, together with the following fixtures, if any: curtain rods, drapery rods, venetian blinds, window shades, screens and shutters, awnings, wall-to-wall carpeting, mirrors fixed in place, attic fans, permanently installed heating and air conditioning units and equipment, lighting and plumbing fixtures, TV antennas, mail boxes, water softeners, shrubbery and all other property owned by Seller and attached to the above described real property. All property sold by this contract is called "Property".

3. CONTRACT SALES PRICE:
   A. Cash down payment payable at closing .... $ _3,500.00_
   B. Amount of Note (the Note) described in 4-A below .... $ _76,500.00_
   C. Sales Price payable to Seller on Loan funding after closing (Sum of A plus B) .... $ _80,000.00_

4. FINANCING CONDITIONS:
   A. This contract is subject to approval for Buyer of a Section _203 B_ FHA Insured Loan (the Loan) of not less than the amount of the Note, amortizable monthly for not less than _30_ years, with interest at maximum rate allowable at time of Loan funding. Buyer shall apply for the Loan within _10_ days from the effective date of this contract and shall make every reasonable effort to obtain approval of the Loan. If the Loan has not been approved by the Closing Date, this contract shall terminate and Earnest Money shall be refunded to Buyer without delay.
   B. As required by HUD-FHA regulation, if FHA valuation is unknown, "It is expressly agreed that, notwithstanding any other provisions of this contract, the Purchaser (Buyer) shall not be obligated to complete the purchase of the Property described herein or to incur any penalty by forfeiture of Earnest Money deposits or otherwise unless the Seller has delivered to the Purchaser (Buyer) a written statement issued by the Federal Housing Commissioner setting forth the appraised value of the Property (excluding closing costs) of not less than $ _80,000_, which statement the Seller hereby agrees to deliver to the Purchaser (Buyer) promptly after such appraised value statement is made available to the Seller. The Purchaser (Buyer) shall, however, have the privilege and option of proceeding with the consummation of this contract without regard to the amount of the appraised valuation made by the Federal Housing Commissioner. The appraised valuation is arrived at to determine the maximum mortgage the Department of Housing and Urban Development will insure. HUD does not warrant the value or the condition of the property. The purchaser should satisfy himself/herself that the price and the condition of the property are acceptable."

5. EARNEST MONEY: $ _500_ is herewith tendered and is to be deposited as Earnest Money with _LIBERTY TITLE CO._, as Escrow Agent, upon execution of the contract by both parties. Additional Earnest Money, if any, shall be deposited with the Escrow Agent on or before _N/A_, 19 ____, in the amount of $ _____.

6. TITLE: Seller at Seller's expense shall furnish either:
   ☒ A. Owner's Policy of Title Insurance (the Title Policy) issued by _LIBERTY TITLE CO._ in the amount of the Sales Price and dated at or after closing: OR
   ☐ B. Complete Abstract of Title (the Abstract) certified by _____ to current date.
   NOTICE TO BUYER: AS REQUIRED BY LAW, Broker advises that YOU should have the Abstract covering the Property examined by an attorney of YOUR selection, or YOU should be furnished with or obtain a Title Policy.

7. PROPERTY CONDITION (Check "A" or "B"):
   ☒ A. Buyer accepts the Property in its present condition, subject only to FHA required repairs and _____

   ☐ B. Buyer requires inspections and repairs required by the Property Condition Addendum (the Addendum) and those required by FHA. Upon Seller's receipt of the Loan approval and inspection reports Seller shall commence and complete prior to closing all required repairs at Seller's expense.
   All inspections, reports and repairs required of Seller by this contract and the Addendum shall not exceed $ _500_. If Seller fails to complete such requirements, Buyer may do so and Seller shall be liable up to the amount specified and the same paid from the proceeds of the sale. If such expenditures exceed the stated amount and Seller refuses to pay such excess, Buyer may pay the additional cost or accept the Property with the limited repairs and this sale shall be closed as scheduled, or Buyer may terminate this contract and the Earnest Money shall be refunded to Buyer. Broker and sales associates have no responsibility or liability for repair or replacement of any of the Property.

8. BROKER'S FEE: _N/A_ Listing Broker (____%) and _____ Co-Broker (____%), as Real Estate Broker (the Broker), has negotiated this sale and Seller agrees to pay Broker in _____ County, Texas, on consummation of this sale or on Seller's default (unless otherwise provided herein) a total cash fee of _____ of the total Sales Price, which Escrow Agent may pay from the sale proceeds.

9. CLOSING: The closing of the sale (the Closing Date) shall be on or before _3/30_, 19 _88_, or within 7 days after objections to title have been cured, whichever date is later; however, if necessary to complete Loan requirements, the Closing Date shall be extended daily up to 15 days.

10. POSSESSION: The possession of the Property shall be delivered to Buyer on _DATE OF CLOSING_ in its present or required improved condition, ordinary wear and tear excepted. Any possession by Buyer prior to or by Seller after Closing Date shall establish a landlord-tenant at sufferance relationship between the parties.

11. SPECIAL PROVISIONS:

    ANTIQUE FAN IN LIVING ROOM WILL NOT REMAIN WITH PROPERTY. SELLER TO INSTALL NEW FAN OF EQUAL SIZE AND SIMILAR DESIGN.

№ 65

(Insert terms and conditions of a factual nature applicable to this sale, e.g., prior purchase or sale of other property, lessee's surrender of possession, and the like.)

12. SALES EXPENSES TO BE PAID IN CASH AT OR PRIOR TO CLOSING:
   A. Loan appraisal fee (FHA application fee) shall be paid by _BUYER_
   B. Seller's Expenses:
      (1) Seller's Loan discount points not exceeding _$2,300.00_
      (2) FHA required repairs and any other inspections, reports and repairs required of Seller herein, and in the Addendum.
      (3) Expenses incident to Loan (e.g., preparation of Loan documents, survey, recording fees, copies of restrictions and easements, amortization schedule, Mortgagee's Title Policy, Loan origination fee, credit reports, photographs).
      (4) Releases of existing loans, including prepayment penalties and recordation; tax statements; preparation of Deed; escrow fee; and other expenses stipulated to be paid by Seller under other provisions of this contract.
   C. Buyer's Expenses: All prepaid items required by applicable HUD-FHA or other regulations (e.g., required premiums for flood and hazard insurance; required reserve deposits for FHA and other insurance, ad valorem taxes and special assessments); interest on the Note from date of disbursement to one month prior to date of first monthly payment; expenses stipulated to be paid by Buyer under other provisions of this contract.
   D. If any sales expenses exceed the maximum amount herein stipulated to be paid by either party, either party may terminate this Contract unless other party agrees to pay such excess. In no event shall Buyer pay charges and fees other than those expressly permitted by FHA regulation.

13. PRORATIONS: Insurance (at Buyer's option), taxes, and any rents and maintenance fees shall be prorated to the Closing Date.

14. TITLE APPROVAL: If Abstract is furnished, Seller shall deliver same to Buyer within 20 days from the effective date hereof. Buyer shall have 20 days from date of receipt of Abstract to deliver a copy of the title opinion to Seller, stating any objections to title, and only objections so stated shall be considered. If Title Policy is furnished, the Title Policy shall guarantee Buyer's title to be good and indefeasible subject only to (i) restrictive covenants affecting the Property (ii) any discrepancies, conflicts or shortages in area or boundary lines or any encroachments, or any overlapping of improvements (iii) all taxes for the current and subsequent years (iv) any existing building and zoning ordinances (v) rights of parties in possession (vi) any liens created as security for the sale consideration and (vii) any reservations or exceptions contained in the Deed. In either instance, if title objections are disclosed, Seller shall have 30 days to cure the same. Exceptions permitted in the Deed and zoning ordinances shall not be valid objections to title. Seller shall furnish at Seller's expense tax statements showing no delinquent taxes and a General Warranty Deed conveying title subject only to liens securing debt created as part of the consideration, taxes for the current year, usual restrictive covenants and utility easements common to the platted subdivision of which the Property is a part and any other reservations or exceptions acceptable to Buyer. The Note shall be secured by Vendor's and Deed of Trust liens. In case of dispute as to the form of Deed, such shall be upon a form prepared by the State Bar of Texas.

15. CASUALTY LOSS: If any part of Property is damaged or destroyed by fire or other casualty loss, Seller shall restore the same to its previous condition as soon as reasonably possible, but in any event by Closing Date; and if Seller is unable to do so without fault, this contract shall terminate and Earnest Money shall be refunded with no Broker's fee due.

16. DEFAULT: If Buyer fails to comply herewith, Seller may either enforce specific performance or terminate this contract and receive the Earnest Money as liquidated damages, one-half of which (but not exceeding the herein recited Broker's fee) shall be paid by Seller to Broker in full payment for Broker's services. If Seller is unable without fault to deliver Abstract or Title Policy or to make any non-casualty repairs required herein within the time herein specified, Buyer may either terminate this contract and receive the Earnest Money as the sole remedy, and no Broker's fee shall be earned, or extend the time up to 30 days. If Seller fails to comply herewith for any other reason, Buyer may (i) terminate this contract and receive the Earnest Money, thereby releasing Seller from this contract (ii) enforce specific performance hereof or (iii) seek such other relief as may be provided by law. If completion of sale is prevented by Buyer's default, and Seller elects to enforce specific performance, the Broker's fee is payable only if and when Seller collects damages for such default by suit, compromise, settlement or otherwise, and after first deducting the expenses of collection, and then only in an amount equal to one-half of that portion collected, but not exceeding the amount of Broker's fee.

17. ATTORNEY'S FEES: Any signatory to this contract who is the prevailing party in any legal proceeding against any other signatory brought under or with relation to this contract or transaction shall be additionally entitled to recover court costs and reasonable attorney fees from the non-prevailing party.

18. ESCROW: Earnest Money is deposited with Escrow Agent with the understanding that Escrow Agent (i) does not assume or have any liability for performance or nonperformance of any party (ii) has the right to require the receipt, release and authorization in writing of all parties before paying the deposit to any party and (iii) is not liable for interest or other charge on the funds held. If any party unreasonably fails to agree in writing to an appropriate release of Earnest Money, then such party shall be liable to the other parties to the extent provided in paragraph 17. At closing, Earnest Money shall be applied to Buyer's cash down payment required, next to Buyer's closing costs and any excess refunded to Buyer. Before Buyer shall be entitled to refund of Earnest Money, any actual and FHA allowable expenses incurred or paid on Buyer's behalf shall be deducted therefrom and paid to the creditors entitled thereto.

19. REPRESENTATIONS: Seller represents that there will be no Title I liens, unrecorded liens or Uniform Commercial Code liens against any of the Property on Closing Date. If any representation above is untrue this contract may be terminated by Buyer and the Earnest Money shall be refunded without delay. Representations shall survive closing.

20. AGREEMENT OF PARTIES: This contract contains the entire agreement of the parties and cannot be changed except by their written consent.

21. CONSULT YOUR ATTORNEY: This is intended to be a legally binding contract. READ IT CAREFULLY. If you do not understand the effect of any part, consult your attorney BEFORE signing. The Broker cannot give you legal advice — only factual and business details concerning land and improvements. Attorneys to represent parties may be designated below, and, so employment may be accepted, Broker shall promptly deliver a copy of this contract to such attorneys.

Seller's Atty: _____N/A_____   Buyer's Atty: _____N/A_____

EXECUTED in multiple originals effective the _1st_ day of _JAN_, 19 _88_   (BROKER FILL IN THE DATE LAST PARTY SIGNS).

Listing Broker	License No.	Seller _Joe J. Doe_
By _____		Seller _Mary B. Doe_
		2600 MESQUITE LN., ARLINGTON
Co-Broker	License No.	Seller's Address _555-2345_ Tel.
By _____		Buyer _Eddie E. Edwards_
Receipt of $ _500_ Earnest Money is acknowledged in the form		Buyer _X Edwards_
of _CHECK_		_2607 B MAIN ST., FT. WORTH_
LIBERTY TITLE CO. _1/15/88_		Buyer's Address _123-4567_ Tel.
Escrow Agent Date		
By _Harry Vernon_		

FHA INSURED LOAN — RESIDENTIAL EARNEST MONEY CONTRACT (RESALE)

1. PARTIES: _____ (Seller) agrees
   to sell and convey to _____ (Buyer)
   and Buyer agrees to buy from Seller the following property situated in _____ County,
   known as _____ (Address).

2. PROPERTY: Lot _____, Block _____, _____
   _____ Addition, City of _____, or as described on attached exhibit, together
   with the following fixtures, if any: curtain rods, drapery rods, venetian blinds, window shades, screens and shutters, awnings, wall-to-wall
   carpeting, mirrors fixed in place, attic fans, permanently installed heating and air conditioning units and equipment, lighting and plumbing fixtures, TV antennas, mail boxes, water softeners, shrubbery and all other property owned by Seller and attached to the above described real property. All property sold by this contract is called "Property".

3. CONTRACT SALES PRICE:
   A. Cash down payment payable at closing .... $_____

   B. Amount of Note (the Note) described in 4-A below.................................... $_____

   C. Sales Price payable to Seller on Loan funding after closing (Sum of A plus B) .... $_____

4. FINANCING CONDITIONS:
   A. This contract is subject to approval for Buyer of a Section _____ FHA Insured Loan (the Loan) of not less
      than the amount of the Note, amortizable monthly for not less than _____ years, with interest at maximum rate allowable at time of
      Loan funding. Buyer shall apply for the Loan within _____ days from the effective date of this contract and shall make every
      reasonable effort to obtain approval of the Loan. If the Loan has not been approved by the Closing Date, this contract shall terminate and
      Earnest Money shall be refunded to Buyer without delay.
   B. As required by HUD-FHA regulation, if FHA valuation is unknown, "It is expressly agreed that, notwithstanding any other provisions of
      this contract, the Purchaser (Buyer) shall not be obligated to complete the purchase of the Property described herein or to incur any penalty
      by forfeiture of Earnest Money deposits or otherwise unless the Seller has delivered to the Purchaser (Buyer) a written statement issued by
      the Federal Housing Commissioner setting forth the appraised value of the Property (excluding closing costs) of not less than
      $ _____ , which statement the Seller hereby agrees to deliver to the Purchaser (Buyer) promptly after such appraised value statement
      is made available to the Seller. The Purchaser (Buyer) shall, however, have the privilege and option of proceeding with the consummation
      of this contract without regard to the amount of the appraised valuation made by the Federal Housing Commissioner. The appraised valu-
      ation is arrived at to determine the maximum mortgage the Department of Housing and Urban Development will insure. HUD does not
      warrant the value or the condition of the property. The purchaser should satisfy himself/herself that the price and the condition of the pro-
      perty are acceptable."

5. EARNEST MONEY: $_____ is herewith tendered and is to be deposited as Earnest Money with _____
   _____, as Escrow Agent, upon execution of the contract by both parties. Additional Earnest
   Money, if any, shall be deposited with the Escrow Agent on or before _____, 19 ____, in the amount of $_____ .

6. TITLE: Seller at Seller's expense shall furnish either:
   ☐ A. Owner's Policy of Title Insurance (the Title Policy) issued by _____
       in the amount of the Sales Price and dated at or after closing: OR
   ☐ B. Complete Abstract of Title (the Abstract) certified by _____ to current date.
   NOTICE TO BUYER: AS REQUIRED BY LAW, Broker advises that YOU should have the Abstract covering the Property examined by an
   attorney of YOUR selection, or YOU should be furnished with or obtain a Title Policy.

7. PROPERTY CONDITION (Check "A" or "B"):
   ☐ A. Buyer accepts the Property in its present condition, subject only to FHA required repairs and _____
   _____ .
   ☐ B. Buyer requires inspections and repairs required by the Property Condition Addendum (the Addendum) and those required by FHA.
   Upon Seller's receipt of the Loan approval and inspection reports Seller shall commence and complete prior to closing all required repairs at
   Seller's expense.
   All inspections, reports and repairs required of Seller by this contract and the Addendum shall not exceed $_____ . If Seller fails to com-
   plete such requirements, Buyer may do so and Seller shall be liable up to the amount specified and the same paid from the proceeds of the sale.
   If such expenditures exceed the stated amount and Seller refuses to pay such excess, Buyer may pay the additional cost or accept the Property
   with the limited repairs and this sale shall be closed as scheduled, or Buyer may terminate this contract and the Earnest Money shall be refunded
   to Buyer. Broker and sales associates have no responsibility or liability for repair or replacement of any of the Property.

8. BROKER'S FEE: _____ Listing Broker (____%) and _____
   _____ Co-Broker (____%), as Real Estate Broker (the Broker), has negotiated this sale and Seller
   agrees to pay Broker in _____ County, on consummation of this sale or on Seller's default (unless
   otherwise provided herein) a total cash fee of _____ of the total Sales Price, which Escrow Agent may pay from the sale proceeds.

9. CLOSING: The closing of the sale (the Closing Date) shall be on or before _____, 19 ____, or within 7 days after objections to title have been cured, whichever date is later; however, if necessary to complete Loan requirements, the Closing Date shall be extended
   daily up to 15 days.

10. POSSESSION: The possession of the Property shall be delivered to Buyer on _____ in its present or required
    improved condition, ordinary wear and tear excepted. Any possession by Buyer prior to or by Seller after Closing Date shall establish a landlord-
    tenant at sufferance relationship between the parties.

11. SPECIAL PROVISIONS:

(Insert terms and conditions of a factual nature applicable to this sale, e.g., prior purchase or sale of other property, lessee's surrender of possession, and the like.)

12. SALES EXPENSES TO BE PAID IN CASH AT OR PRIOR TO CLOSING:
    A.   Loan appraisal fee (FHA application fee) shall be paid by _____.
    B.   Seller's Expenses:
        (1) Seller's Loan discount points not exceeding _____.
        (2) FHA required repairs and any other inspections, reports and repairs required of Seller herein, and in the Addendum.
        (3) Expenses incident to Loan (e.g., preparation of Loan documents, survey, recording fees, copies of restrictions and easements, amortization schedule, Mortgagee's Title Policy, Loan origination fee, credit reports, photographs).
        (4) Releases of existing loans, including prepayment penalties and recordation; tax statements; preparation of Deed; escrow fee; and other expenses stipulated to be paid by Seller under other provisions of this contract.
    C.   Buyer's Expenses: All prepaid items required by applicable HUD-FHA or other regulations (e.g., required premiums for flood and hazard insurance; required reserve deposits for FHA and other insurance, ad valorem taxes and special assessments); interest on the Note from date of disbursement to one month prior to date of first monthly payment; expenses stipulated to be paid by Buyer under other provisions of this contract.
    D   If any sales expenses exceed the maximum amount herein stipulated to be paid by either party, either party may terminate this Contract unless other party agrees to pay such excess. In no event shall Buyer pay charges and fees other than those expressly permitted by FHA regulation.

13. PRORATIONS: Insurance (at Buyer's option), taxes, and any rents and maintenance fees shall be prorated to the Closing Date.

14. TITLE APPROVAL: If Abstract is furnished, Seller shall deliver same to Buyer within 20 days from the effective date hereof. Buyer shall have 20 days from date of receipt of Abstract to deliver a copy of the title opinion to Seller, stating any objections to title, and only objections so stated shall be considered. If Title Policy is furnished, the Title Policy shall guarantee Buyer's title to be good and indefeasible subject only to (i) restrictive covenants affecting the Property (ii) any discrepancies, conflicts or shortages in area or boundary lines or any encroachments, or any overlapping of improvements (iii) all taxes for the current and subsequent years (iv) any existing building and zoning ordinances (v) rights of parties in possession (vi) any liens created as security for the sale consideration and (vii) any reservations or exceptions contained in the Deed. In either instance, if title objections are disclosed, Seller shall have 30 days to cure the same. Exceptions permitted in the Deed and zoning ordinances shall not be valid objections to title. Seller shall furnish at Seller's expense tax statements showing no delinquent taxes and a General Warranty Deed conveying title subject only to liens securing debt created as part of the consideration, taxes for the current year, usual restrictive covenants and utility easements common to the platted subdivision of which the Property is a part and any other reservations or exceptions acceptable to Buyer. The Note shall be secured by Vendor's and Deed of Trust liens. In case of dispute as to the form of Deed, such shall be upon a form prepared by the State Bar of

15. CASUALTY LOSS: If any part of Property is damaged or destroyed by fire or other casualty loss, Seller shall restore the same to its previous condition as soon as reasonably possible, but in any event by Closing Date; and if Seller is unable to do so without fault, this contract shall terminate and Earnest Money shall be refunded with no Broker's fee due.

16. DEFAULT: If Buyer fails to comply herewith, Seller may either enforce specific performance or terminate this contract and receive the Earnest Money, one-half of which (but not exceeding the herein recited Broker's fee) shall be paid by Seller to Broker in full payment for Broker's services. If Seller is unable without fault to deliver Abstract or Title Policy or to make any non-casualty repairs required herein within the time herein specified, Buyer may either terminate this contract and receive the Earnest Money as the sole remedy, and no Broker's fee shall be earned, or extend the time up to 30 days. If Seller fails to comply herewith for any other reason, Buyer may (i) terminate this contract and receive the Earnest Money, thereby releasing Seller from this contract (ii) enforce specific performance hereof or (iii) seek such other relief as may be provided by law. If completion of sale is prevented by Buyer's default, and Seller elects to enforce specific performance, the Broker's fee is payable only if and when Seller collects damages for such default by suit, compromise, settlement or otherwise, and after first deducting the expenses of collection, and then only in an amount equal to one-half of that portion collected, but not exceeding the amount of Broker's fee.

17. ATTORNEY'S FEES: Any signatory to this contract who is the prevailing party in any legal proceeding against any other signatory brought under or with relation to this contract or transaction shall be additionally entitled to recover court costs and reasonable attorney fees from the non-prevailing party.

18. ESCROW: Earnest Money is deposited with Escrow Agent with the understanding that Escrow Agent (i) does not assume or have any liability for performance or nonperformance of any party (ii) has the right to require the receipt, release and authorization in writing of all parties before paying the deposit to any party and (iii) is not liable for interest or other charge on the funds held. If any party unreasonably fails to agree in writing to an appropriate release of Earnest Money, then such party shall be liable to the other parties to the extent provided in paragraph 17. At closing, Earnest Money shall be applied to any cash down payment required, next to Buyer's closing costs and any excess refunded to Buyer. Before Buyer shall be entitled to refund of Earnest Money, any actual and FHA allowable expenses incurred or paid on Buyer's behalf shall be deducted therefrom and paid to the creditors entitled thereto.

19. REPRESENTATIONS: Seller represents that there will be no Title I liens, unrecorded liens or Uniform Commercial Code liens against any of the Property on Closing Date. If any representation above is untrue this contract may be terminated by Buyer and the Earnest Money shall be refunded without delay. Representations shall survive closing.

20. AGREEMENT OF PARTIES: This contract contains the entire agreement of the parties and cannot be changed except by their written consent.

21. CONSULT YOUR ATTORNEY: This is intended to be a legally binding contract. READ IT CAREFULLY. If you do not understand the effect of any part, consult your attorney BEFORE signing. The Broker cannot give you legal advice — only factual and business details concerning land and improvements. Attorneys to represent parties may be designated below, and, so employment may be accepted, Broker shall promptly deliver a copy of this contract to such attorneys.

Seller's Atty: _____   Buyer's Atty: _____

EXECUTED in multiple originals effective the _____ day of _____, 19 _____.   (BROKER FILL IN THE DATE LAST PARTY SIGNS).

Listing Broker License No.	Seller
By _____	Seller
Co-Broker License No.	Seller's Address Tel.
By _____	Buyer
Receipt of $_____ Earnest Money is acknowledged in the form	Buyer
of _____	Buyer's Address Tel.
Escrow Agent Date	
By _____	

Appendix H
Conventional Loan Contract Form

USE THIS CONTRACT WHEN YOU HAVE A CASH BUYER, OR WHEN YOU ARE DOING OWNER FINANCING WITH no third party financing.

Paragraph #1: Write your legal name(s) on the first line, as sellers, and the legal names of the buyers on the next line. Remember to note the marital status of all parties. For example:

- If one of the parties is a married couple, you would write "John M. Doe and wife Mary M. Doe."

- For a single person, you can simply write "John M. Doe," or you can write "John M. Doe, a single person."

- For a divorced person, write "John M. Doe, a divorced person since May 23, 1985."

- For a widower, write "John M. Doe, a widower since May 23, 1985."

- For a corporation, you would write "JMD Industries, Inc., a Texas corporation."

- For a Partnership, you would write "Doe Properties, a Texas General Partnership," or "Doe Properties, a Texas Limited Partnership."

- For a pension and profit-sharing plan, you would write "JMD Industries, Inc., Pension & Profit-Sharing Trust."

- For two individuals not related or married, you would write "John M. Doe and John R. Smith, in indiscriminate interest."

The next blank asks for the name of the county in which the real estate is located, then place the two letter code for the state after the word "County."

The last blank requests the address of the property.

Paragraph #2: This paragraph asks for the legal description of the property. You'll find this information in your copies of your original closing papers. Make *certain* you have the correct description. Write the lot number, the block number, then the name of the addition in the first three blanks. On the fourth blank insert the city in which the property is located.

Paragraph #3:

A. Insert the cash down payment the buyer will pay, at least 5% of the sales price.

B. Write the amount of the first lien the buyer will obtain from the mortgage company.

C. Check the first box (1) if you will be carrying a second lien. Then on the first blank show the interest rate. Check the next box if the second lien will be paid in a lump sum, and indicate the date the lump sum is due. Normally though, you'll check the box indicating payments will be made in installments. On the first blank include the amount of each installment, on the second blank you'll more than likely want to write "monthly," and on the last blank show when the first installment will be made.

Check the "Third Party" box (2) if there will be a second lien provided by a commercial lien lender, and in the first blank indicate what the maximum monthly payment the buyer is willing to pay for the second lien. On the second blank, show the amount of the second lien.

D. On the blank indicate the total of all the liens and the down payment, for the final sales price.

Paragraph #4: Check the first box if the first lien will be for 80% or less of the sales price. Check the second box if the first lien will be for 81% or more of the sales price, in which case there will be private mortgage insurance (PMI). On the first blank indicate the number of years of the first lien, and on the second blank show the maximum interest rate your buyer is willing to pay. If it looks like rates are climbing, you might try to talk the buyer into showing a rate ¼% to ½% above the existing rate at the time you sign the contract.

On the third blank, insert anywhere from "5" to "10." Don't allow the buyer to hold up the transaction by not going for a loan application soon after the contract date.

On the last blank, put in a realistic figure for financing approval. Generally 60 days should be enough. But keep in mind that if approval doesn't come within that time period, your buyers may back out and get their earnest money back.

Paragraph #5: Take as much earnest money as possible; 1% of the sales price, or at least $500, should be the minimum. Put the amount in the first blank. On the second blank indicate who will hold the earnest money. Depending on your state, it could be a title or escrow company, an attorney, or a broker. Write your name if you'll hold the earnest money yourself.

If there will be additional earnest money at a future date before the closing, then indicate the date and the amount of the additional funds on the remaining blanks.

Paragraph #6: Check box A if you'll furnish a title insurance policy, and indicate the name of the company that will issue the policy. Check box B if you'll provide an abstract of title, and indicate the abstractor or abstract company that will provide it.

Paragraph #7: You'll check box A if the property is being sold "as is" except for any repairs that may be required by a lender, or other conditions you'll indicate in the blank in the first paragraph.

Box B will be checked if the buyer will be allowed to inspect the property before closing. If you check this box, then you will include a Property Condition Addendum form (Appendix L).

Paragraph #8: If one or more brokers are to receive a commission, this paragraph will be used. In most situations you'll place "N/A" in each of these blanks, because if brokers are involved, they'll want to use their own contract forms.

Paragraph #9: Fill in the closing date. Make sure you give yourself enough time to find financing for the buyer. Check with several mortgage companies to see how long to allow. If you run out of time and the buyer has not been approved for a loan, this contract will become null and void and the buyer could back out on the transaction.

Paragraph #10: Indicate when the buyer will take possession. If you put in an exact date predicated on the closing date and you don't make the closing date, then you'll have confusion. Rather, indicate whether possession will be "on date of closing," "three days after closing," or other such date that is agreeable to both you and the buyer.

Paragraph #11: Include here any special provisions that are important to your agreement with the buyer. For example, include any personal property that's included with the property, such as "Refrigerator and all window treatments to remain with property." Any personal property that looks like it is attached to the property, but which you will take with you, should be included here. You can also show other terms of purchase or financing that don't fit anywhere else, such as "First five payments on owner financing to be made in the amount of $250.00, to cover principal only. Interest to begin on the sixth month."

Paragraph #12:

A. Most of the time, the loan appraisal fees are paid by the seller. Sometimes they are paid by the buyer. You need to state "buyer" or "seller" here. Of course, if you've already got an appraisal, you'll indicate "seller."

B (1). In the blank fill in a percentage, not a dollar amount, of the number of points you are willing to pay for the buyer to obtain his loan. Normally, two to three points is sufficient for a loan, unless you are going to do a deep buydown.

C. You should have checked with a mortgage company to see what is normal for buyer's expenses, then include in this blank an amount of a couple of hundred dollars more.

Paragraph #21: There are two spaces at the end of this paragraph to include the name of the buyer's and seller's attorneys. Write in the names if attorneys will represent either party. Often, on simple transactions, attorneys will not be used and you'll mark out these lines.

On the blanks that ask for the date, fill in the effective date of the contract, which is when all parties have affixed their signatures.

CONVENTIONAL LOAN — RESIDENTIAL EARNEST MONEY CONTRACT (RESALE)

1. PARTIES: JACK B. NIMBLE AND WIFE, SANDY W. NIMBLE _____ (Seller) agrees
to sell and convey to LADY N. SHOE, A SINGLE WOMAN _____ (Buyer)
and Buyer agrees to buy from Seller the following property situated in TARRANT _____ County, Texas,
known as 1717 WILSON LANE, FOREST HILL, TX 66666 (Address).

2. PROPERTY: Lot 75 _____, Block N _____, SUNNY
HILLS _____ Addition, City of FOREST HILL _____, or as described on attached exhibit,
together with the following fixtures, if any: curtain rods, drapery rods, venetian blinds, window shades, screens and shutters, awnings, wall-to-wall carpeting, mirrors fixed in place, attic fans, permanently installed heating and air conditioning units and equipment, lighting and plumbing fixtures, TV antennas, mail boxes, water softeners, shrubbery and all other property owned by Seller and attached to the above described real property. All property sold by this contract is called "Property".

3. CONTRACT SALES PRICE:
   A. Cash down payment payable at closing . . . . $ 50,000.00
   B. Note described in 4 below (the Note) in the amount of . . . . $ 200,000.00
   C. Any balance of Sales Price to be evidenced by a second lien note (the Second Note)payable to [check (1) or (2) below]:
      ☐ (1) Seller, bearing interest at the rate of _____ % per annum, in
         ☐ lump sum on or before _____ .
         ☐ principal and interest installments of $_____, or more per _____,
         with first installment payable on _____
      ☐ (2) Third Party in principal and interest installments not in excess of $_____ per month
      in the principal amount of . . . . $ _____
   D. Sales Price payable to Seller on Loan funding after closing (Sum of A, B & C) . . . . $ 250,000.00

4. FINANCING CONDITIONS: This contract is subject to approval for Buyer of a ☒ Conventional or ☐ Conventional private mortgage insured third party loan (the Loan) of not less than the amount of the Note, amortizable monthly for not less than 20 years, with interest not to exceed 10 percent per annum, and approval of any third party Second Note. Buyer shall apply for all financing within 5 days from the effective date of this contract and shall make every reasonable effort to obtain approval. If all financing cannot be approved within 60 days from effective date of this contract, this contract shall terminate and Earnest Money shall be refunded to Buyer without delay.

5. EARNEST MONEY: $ 2,500 is herewith tendered and is to be deposited as Earnest Money with FRIENDLY TITLE COMPANY _____, as Escrow Agent, upon execution of the contract by both parties. Additional Earnest Money, if any, shall be deposited with the Escrow Agent on or before N/A _____, 19____, in the amount of $_____.

6. TITLE: Seller at Seller's expense shall furnish either:
   ☒ A. Owner's Policy of Title Insurance (the Title Policy) issued by FRIENDLY TITLE CO.
   in the amount of the Sales Price and dated at or after closing: OR
   ☐ B. Complete Abstract of Title (the Abstract) certified by _____ to current date.
   NOTICE TO BUYER: AS REQUIRED BY LAW, Broker advises that YOU should have the Abstract covering the Property examined by an attorney of YOUR selection, or YOU should be furnished with or obtain a Title Policy.

7. PROPERTY CONDITION (Check "A" or "B"):
   ☒ A. Buyer accepts the Property in its present condition, subject only to lender required repairs and INSTALLATION OF NEW #1 CEDAR SHINGLE ROOF _____
   ☐ B. Buyer requires inspections and repairs required by the Property Condition Addendum (the Addendum) and any lender.
   Upon Seller's receipt of all loan approvals and inspection reports Seller shall commence and complete prior to closing all required repairs at Seller's expense.
   All inspections, reports and repairs required of Seller by this contract and the Addendum shall not exceed $ 1,000. If Seller fails to complete such requirements, Buyer may do so and Seller shall be liable up to the amount specified and the same paid from the proceeds of the sale. If such expenditures exceed the stated amount and Seller refuses to pay such excess, Buyer may pay the additional cost or accept the Property with the limited amount and this sale shall be closed as scheduled, or Buyer may terminate this contract and the Earnest Money shall be refunded to Buyer. Broker and sales associates have no responsibility or liability for repair or replacement of any of the Property.

8. BROKER'S FEE: N/A _____ Listing Broker (____%) and _____
   _____ Co-Broker (____%), as Real Estate Broker (the Broker), has negotiated this sale and Seller
   agrees to pay Broker in _____ County, Texas, on consummation of this sale or on Seller's default (unless otherwise provided herein) a total cash fee of _____ of the total Sales Price, which Escrow Agent may pay from the sale proceeds.

9. CLOSING: The closing of the sale (the Closing Date) shall be on or before 3/15 _____, 19 88, or within 7 days after objections to title have been cured, whichever date is later; however, if necessary to complete Loan requirements, the Closing Date shall be extended daily up to 15 days.

10. POSSESSION: The possession of the Property shall be delivered to Buyer on 3 DAYS AFTER CLOSING in its present or required improved condition, ordinary wear and tear excepted. Any possession by Buyer prior to or by Seller after Closing Date shall establish a landlord-tenant at sufferance relationship between the parties.

11. SPECIAL PROVISIONS:

ALL WINDOW TREATMENTS TO REMAIN
WITH THE PROPERTY

(Insert terms and conditions of a factual nature applicable to this sale, e.g., personal property included in sale [curtains, draperies, valances, etc.], prior purchase or sale of other property, lessee's surrender of possession, and the like.)

Nᵒ 65

12. SALES EXPENSES TO BE PAID IN CASH AT OR PRIOR TO CLOSING:
   A. Loan appraisal fees shall be paid by _SELLER_
   B. Seller's Expenses:
      (1) Seller's loan discount points not exceeding _2% OF LOAN AMOUNT_
      (2) Lender required repairs and any other inspections, reports and repairs required of Seller herein and in the Addendum.
      (3) Prepayment penalties on any existing loans, plus cost of releasing such loans and recording releases; tax statements; 1/2 of any escrow fee; preparation of Deed; other expenses stipulated to be paid by Seller under other provisions of this contract.
   C. Buyer's Expenses:
      (1) Fees for loans (e.g., any private mortgage insurance premiums; loan and mortgage application, origination and commitment fees; Buyer's loan discount points) not exceeding $ _4,000.00_
      (2) Expenses incident to loan(s) (e.g., preparation of any Note, Deed of Trust and other loan documents, survey, recording fees, copies of restrictions and easements, Mortgagee's Title Policies, credit reports, photos); 1/2 of any escrow fee; any required premiums for flood and hazard insurance; any required reserve deposits for insurance premiums, ad valorem taxes and special assessments; interest on all monthly installment payment notes from date of disbursements to 1 month prior to dates of first monthly payments; expenses stipulated to be paid by Buyer under other provisions of this contract.
   D. If any sales expenses exceed the maximum amount herein stipulated to be paid by either party, either party may terminate this contract unless the other party agrees to pay such excess.

13. PRORATIONS: Insurance (at Buyer's option), taxes and any rents and maintenance fees shall be prorated to the Closing Date.

14. TITLE APPROVAL: If Abstract is furnished, Seller shall deliver same to Buyer within 20 days from the effective date hereof. Buyer shall have 20 days from date of receipt of Abstract to deliver a copy of the title opinion to Seller, stating any objections to title, and only objections so stated shall be considered. If Title Policy is furnished, the Title Policy shall guarantee Buyer's title to be good and indefeasible subject only to (i) restrictive covenants affecting the Property (ii) any discrepancies, conflicts or shortages in area or boundary lines or any encroachments, or any overlapping of improvements (iii) all taxes for the current and subsequent years (iv) any existing building and zoning ordinances (v) rights of parties in possession (vi) any liens created as security for the sale consideration and (vii) any reservations or exceptions contained in the Deed. In either instance, if title objections are disclosed, Seller shall have 30 days to cure the same. Exceptions permitted in the Deed and zoning ordinances shall not be valid objections to title. Seller shall furnish at Seller's expense tax statements showing no delinquent taxes and a General Warranty Deed conveying title subject only to liens securing debt created as part of the consideration, taxes for the current year, usual restrictive covenants and utility easements common to the platted subdivision of which the Property is a part and any other reservations or exceptions acceptable to Buyer. Each note herein provided shall be secured by Vendor's and Deed of Trust liens. In case of dispute as to the form of Deed, Note(s) or Deed(s) of Trust, such shall be upon a form prepared by the State Bar of Texas.

15. CASUALTY LOSS: If any part of Property is damaged or destroyed by fire or other casualty loss, Seller shall restore the same to its previous condition as soon as reasonably possible, but in any event by Closing Date; and if Seller is unable to do so without fault, this contract shall terminate and Earnest Money shall be refunded with no Broker's fee due.

16. DEFAULT: If Buyer fails to comply herewith, Seller may either enforce specific performance or terminate this contract and receive the Earnest Money as liquidated damages, one-half of which (but not exceeding the herein recited Broker's fee) shall be paid by Seller to Broker in full payment for Broker's services. If Seller is unable without fault to deliver Abstract or Title Policy or to make any non-casualty repairs required herein within the time herein specified, Buyer may either terminate this contract and receive the Earnest Money as the sole remedy, and no Broker's fee shall be earned, or extend the time up to 30 days. If Seller fails to comply herewith for any other reason, Buyer may (i) terminate this contract and receive the Earnest Money, thereby releasing Seller from this contract (ii) enforce specific performance hereof or (iii) seek such other relief as may be provided by law. If completion of sale is prevented by Buyer's default, and Seller elects to enforce specific performance, the Broker's fee is payable only if and when Seller collects damages for such default by suit, compromise, settlement or otherwise, and after first deducting the expenses of collection, and then only in an amount equal to one-half of that portion collected, but not exceeding the amount of Broker's fee.

17. ATTORNEY'S FEES: Any signatory to this contract who is the prevailing party in any legal proceeding against any other signatory brought under or with relation to this contract or transaction shall be additionally entitled to recover court costs and reasonable attorney fees from the non-prevailing party.

18. ESCROW: Earnest Money is deposited with Escrow Agent with the understanding that Escrow Agent (i) does not assume or have any liability for performance or nonperformance of any party (ii) has the right to require the receipt, release and authorization in writing of all parties before paying the deposit to any party and (iii) is not liable for interest or other charge on the funds held. If any party unreasonably fails to agree in writing to an appropriate release of Earnest Money, then such party shall be liable to the other parties to the extent provided in paragraph 17. At closing, Earnest Money shall be applied to any cash down payment required, next to Buyer's closing costs and any excess refunded to Buyer. Before Buyer shall be entitled to refund of Earnest Money, any actual expenses incurred or paid on Buyer's behalf shall be deducted therefrom and paid to the creditors entitled thereto.

19. REPRESENTATIONS: Seller represents that unless securing payment of the Note there will be no Title I liens, unrecorded liens or Uniform Commercial Code liens against any of the Property on Closing Date. If any representation above is untrue this contract may be terminated by Buyer and the Earnest Money shall be refunded without delay. Representations shall survive closing.

20. AGREEMENT OF PARTIES: This contract contains the entire agreement of the parties and cannot be changed except by their written consent.

21. CONSULT YOUR ATTORNEY: This is intended to be a legally binding contract. READ IT CAREFULLY. If you do not understand the effect of any part, consult your attorney BEFORE signing. The Broker cannot give you legal advice — only factual and business details concerning land and improvements. Attorneys to represent parties may be designated below, and, so employment may be accepted, Broker shall promptly deliver a copy of this contract to such attorneys.

Seller's Atty: _N/A_   Buyer's Atty: _N/A_

EXECUTED in multiple originals effective the _10TH_ day of _JAN_, 19 _88_.   **(BROKER FILL IN THE DATE LAST PARTY SIGNS).**

Listing Broker	License No.	_Jack B. Nimble_ Seller
By _____		_Sandy W. Nimble_ Seller
Co-Broker	License No.	_1717 WILSON LN., FOREST HILL_ Seller's Address _666-7777_ Tel.
By _____		_Lady N. Shoe_ Buyer
Receipt of $ _2,500_ Earnest Money is acknowledged in the form		Buyer
of _CASH_		_666 HIGH HILL, FT. WORTH_ Buyer's Address _222-7676_ Tel.
FRIENDLY TITLE CO. 1/11/88 Escrow Agent Date		
By _____		

CONVENTIONAL LOAN — RESIDENTIAL EARNEST MONEY CONTRACT (RESALE)

1. PARTIES: _____ (Seller) agrees
to sell and convey to _____ (Buyer)
and Buyer agrees to buy from Seller the following property situated in _____ County,
known as _____ (Address).

2. PROPERTY: Lot _____, Block _____, _____
_____ Addition, City of _____, or as described on attached exhibit,
together with the following fixtures, if any: curtain rods, drapery rods, venetian blinds, window shades, screens and shutters, awnings, wall-to-wall carpeting, mirrors fixed in place, attic fans, permanently installed heating and air conditioning units and equipment, lighting and plumbing fixtures, TV antennas, mail boxes, water softeners, shrubbery and all other property owned by Seller and attached to the above described real property. All property sold by this contract is called "Property".

3. CONTRACT SALES PRICE:
A. Cash down payment payable at closing.. $ _____
B. Note described in 4 below (the Note) in the amount of .... $ _____
C. Any balance of Sales Price to be evidenced by a second lien note (the Second Note)payable to [check (1) or (2) below]:
☐ (1) Seller, bearing interest at the rate of _____ % per annum, in
☐ lump sum on or before _____.
☐ principal and interest installments of $_____, or more per _____,
with first installment payable on _____
☐ (2) Third Party in principal and interest installments not in excess of $ _____ per month
in the principal amount of.. $ _____
D. Sales Price payable to Seller on Loan funding after closing (Sum of A, B & C) .... $ _____

4. FINANCING CONDITIONS: This contract is subject to approval for Buyer of a ☐ Conventional or ☐ Conventional private mortgage insured third party loan (the Loan) of not less than the amount of the Note, amortizable monthly for not less than _____ years, with interest not to exceed _____ percent per annum, and approval of any third party Second Note. Buyer shall apply for all financing within _____ days from the effective date of this contract and shall make every reasonable effort to obtain approval. If all financing cannot be approved within _____ days from effective date of this contract, this contract shall terminate and Earnest Money shall be refunded to Buyer without delay.

5. EARNEST MONEY: $_____ is herewith tendered and is to be deposited as Earnest Money with _____ , as Escrow Agent, upon execution of the contract by both parties. Additional Earnest Money, if any, shall be deposited with the Escrow Agent on or before _____ , 19 ____, in the amount of $_____.

6. TITLE: Seller at Seller's expense shall furnish either:
☐ A. Owner's Policy of Title Insurance (the Title Policy) issued by _____
in the amount of the Sales Price and dated at or after closing: OR
☐ B. Complete Abstract of Title (the Abstract) certified by _____ to current date.
NOTICE TO BUYER: AS REQUIRED BY LAW, Broker advises that YOU should have the Abstract covering the Property examined by an attorney of YOUR selection, or YOU should be furnished with or obtain a Title Policy.

7. PROPERTY CONDITION (Check "A" or "B"):
☐ A. Buyer accepts the Property in its present condition, subject only to lender required repairs and _____
_____
☐ B. Buyer requires inspections and repairs required by the Property Condition Addendum (the Addendum) and any lender.
Upon Seller's receipt of all loan approvals and inspection reports Seller shall commence and complete prior to closing all required repairs at Seller's expense.
All inspections, reports and repairs required of Seller by this contract and the Addendum shall not exceed $_____. If Seller fails to complete such requirements, Buyer may do so and Seller shall be liable up to the amount specified and the same paid from the proceeds of the sale. If such expenditures exceed the stated amount and Seller refuses to pay such excess, Buyer may pay the additional cost or accept the Property with the limited repairs and this sale shall be closed as scheduled, or Buyer may terminate this contract and the Earnest Money shall be refunded to Buyer. Broker and sales associates have no responsibility or liability for repair or replacement of any of the Property.

8. BROKER'S FEE: _____ Listing Broker (____%) and _____
_____ Co-Broker (____%), as Real Estate Broker (the Broker), has negotiated this sale and Seller agrees to pay Broker in _____ County, on consummation of this sale or on Seller's default (unless otherwise provided herein) a total cash fee of _____ of the total Sales Price, which Escrow Agent may pay from the sale proceeds.

9. CLOSING: The closing of the sale (the Closing Date) shall be on or before _____ , 19____ , or within 7 days after objections to title have been cured, whichever date is later; however, if necessary to complete Loan requirements, the Closing Date shall be extended daily up to 15 days.

10. POSSESSION: The possession of the Property shall be delivered to Buyer on _____ in its present or required improved condition, ordinary wear and tear excepted. Any possession by Buyer prior to or by Seller after Closing Date shall establish a landlord-tenant at sufferance relationship between the parties.

11. SPECIAL PROVISIONS:

(Insert terms and conditions of a factual nature applicable to this sale, e.g., personal property included in sale [curtains, draperies, valances, etc.], prior purchase or sale of other property, lessee's surrender of possession, and the like.)

12. SALES EXPENSES TO BE PAID IN CASH AT OR PRIOR TO CLOSING:
    A. Loan appraisal fees shall be paid by _____
    B. Seller's Expenses:
       (1) Seller's loan discount points not exceeding _____
       (2) Lender required repairs and any other inspections, reports and repairs required of Seller herein and in the Addendum.
       (3) Prepayment penalties on any existing loans, plus cost of releasing such loans and recording releases; tax statements; 1/2 of any escrow fee; preparation of Deed; other expenses stipulated to be paid by Seller under other provisions of this contract.
    C. Buyer's Expenses:
       (1) Fees for loans (e.g., any private mortgage insurance premiums; loan and mortgage application, origination and commitment fees; Buyer's loan discount points) not exceeding $_____
       (2) Expenses incident to loan(s) (e.g., preparation of any Note, Deed of Trust and other loan documents, survey, recording fees, copies of restrictions and easements, Mortgagee's Title Policies, credit reports, photos); 1/2 of any escrow fee; any required premiums for flood and hazard insurance; any required reserve deposits for insurance premiums, ad valorem taxes and special assessments; interest on all monthly installment payment notes from date of disbursements to 1 month prior to dates of first monthly payments; expenses stipulated to be paid by Buyer under other provisions of this contract.
    D. If any sales expenses exceed the maximum amount herein stipulated to be paid by either party, either party may terminate this contract unless the other party agrees to pay such excess.

13. PRORATIONS: Insurance (at Buyer's option), taxes and any rents and maintenance fees shall be prorated to the Closing Date.

14. TITLE APPROVAL: If Abstract is furnished, Seller shall deliver same to Buyer within 20 days from the effective date hereof. Buyer shall have 20 days from date of receipt of Abstract to deliver a copy of the title opinion to Seller, stating any objections to title, and only objections so stated shall be considered. If Title Policy is furnished, the Title Policy shall guarantee Buyer's title to be good and indefeasible subject only to (i) restrictive covenants affecting the Property (ii) any discrepancies, conflicts or shortages in area or boundary lines or any encroachments, or any overlapping of improvements (iii) all taxes for the current and subsequent years (iv) any existing building and zoning ordinances (v) rights of parties in possession (vi) any liens created as security for the sale consideration and (vii) any reservations or exceptions contained in the Deed. In either instance, if title objections are disclosed, Seller shall have 30 days to cure the same. Exceptions permitted in the Deed and zoning ordinances shall not be valid objections to title. Seller shall furnish at Seller's expense tax statements showing no delinquent taxes and a General Warranty Deed conveying title subject only to liens securing debt created as part of the consideration, taxes for the current year, usual restrictive covenants and utility easements common to the platted subdivision of which the Property is a part and any other reservations or exceptions acceptable to Buyer. Each note herein provided shall be secured by Vendor's and Deed of Trust liens. In case of dispute as to the form of Deed, Note(s) or Deed(s) of Trust, such shall be upon a form prepared by the State Bar of

15. CASUALTY LOSS: If any part of Property is damaged or destroyed by fire or other casualty loss, Seller shall restore the same to its previous condition as soon as reasonably possible, but in any event by Closing Date; and if Seller is unable to do so without fault, this contract shall terminate and Earnest Money shall be refunded with no Broker's fee due.

16. DEFAULT: If Buyer fails to comply herewith, Seller may either enforce specific performance or terminate this contract and receive the Earnest Money as liquidated damages, one-half of which (but not exceeding the herein recited Broker's fee) shall be paid by Seller to Broker in full payment for Broker's services. If Seller is unable without fault to deliver Abstract or Title Policy or to make any non-casualty repairs required herein within the time herein specified, Buyer may either terminate this contract and receive the Earnest Money as the sole remedy, and no Broker's fee shall be earned, or extend the time up to 30 days. If Seller fails to comply herewith for any other reason, Buyer may (i) terminate this contract and receive the Earnest Money, thereby releasing Seller from this contract (ii) enforce specific performance hereof or (iii) seek such other relief as may be provided by law. If completion of sale is prevented by Buyer's default, and Seller elects to enforce specific performance, the Broker's fee is payable only if and when Seller collects damages for such default by suit, compromise, settlement or otherwise, and after first deducting the expenses of collection, and then only in an amount equal to one-half of that portion collected, but not exceeding the amount of Broker's fee.

17. ATTORNEY'S FEES: Any signatory to this contract who is the prevailing party in any legal proceeding against any other signatory brought under or with relation to this contract or transaction shall be additionally entitled to recover court costs and reasonable attorney fees from the non-prevailing party.

18. ESCROW: Earnest Money is deposited with Escrow Agent with the understanding that Escrow Agent (i) does not assume or have any liability for performance or nonperformance of any party (ii) has the right to require the receipt, release and authorization in writing of all parties before paying the deposit to any party and (iii) is not liable for interest or other charge on the funds held. If any party unreasonably fails to agree in writing to an appropriate release of Earnest Money, then such party shall be liable to the other parties to the extent provided in paragraph 17. At closing, Earnest Money shall be applied to any cash down payment required, next to Buyer's closing costs and any excess refunded to Buyer. Before Buyer shall be entitled to refund of Earnest Money, any actual expenses incurred or paid on Buyer's behalf shall be deducted therefrom and paid to the creditors entitled thereto.

19. REPRESENTATIONS: Seller represents that unless securing payment of the Note there will be no Title I liens, unrecorded liens or Uniform Commercial Code liens against any of the Property on Closing Date. If any representation above is untrue this contract may be terminated by Buyer and the Earnest Money shall be refunded without delay. Representations shall survive closing.

20. AGREEMENT OF PARTIES: This contract contains the entire agreement of the parties and cannot be changed except by their written consent.

21. CONSULT YOUR ATTORNEY: This is intended to be a legally binding contract. READ IT CAREFULLY. If you do not understand the effect of any part, consult your attorney BEFORE signing. The Broker cannot give you legal advice — only factual and business details concerning land and improvements. Attorneys to represent parties may be designated below, and, so employment may be accepted, Broker shall promptly deliver a copy of this contract to such attorneys.

Seller's Atty: _____   Buyer's Atty: _____

EXECUTED in multiple originals effective the _____ day of _____, 19 _____.   **(BROKER FILL IN THE DATE LAST PARTY SIGNS).**

Listing Broker License No.	Seller	
By _____	Seller	
Co-Broker License No.	Seller's Address Tel.	
By _____	Buyer	
Receipt of $ _____ Earnest Money is acknowledged in the form	Buyer	
of _____	Buyer's Address Tel.	
Escrow Agent Date		
By _____		

Appendix I
Cash or Owner-Financed Contract Form

USE THIS CONTRACT WHEN YOU HAVE A CASH BUYER, OR WHEN YOU ARE DOING OWNER FINANCING WITH no third party financing.

Paragraph #1: Write your legal name(s) on the first line, as sellers, and the legal names of the buyers on the next line. Remember to note the marital status of all parties. For example:

- If one of the parties is a married couple, you would write "John M. Doe and wife Mary M. Doe."

- For a single person, you can simply write "John M. Doe," or you can write "John M. Doe, a single person."

- For a divorced person, write "John M. Doe, a divorced person since May 23, 1985."

- For a widower, write "John M. Doe, a widower since May 23, 1985."

- For a corporation, you would write "JMD Industries, Inc., a Texas corporation."

- For a Partnership, you would write "Doe Properties, a Texas General Partnership," or "Doe Properties, a Texas Limited Partnership."

- For a pension and profit-sharing plan, you would write "JMD Industries, Inc., Pension & Profit-Sharing Trust."

- For two individuals not related or married, you would write "John M. Doe and John R. Smith, in indiscriminate interest."

The next blank asks for the name of the county in which the real estate is located, then place the two letter code for the state after the word "County."

The last blank requests the address of the property.

Paragraph #2: This paragraph asks for the legal description of the property. You'll find this information in your copies of your original closing papers. Make *certain* you have the correct description. Write the lot number, the block number, then the name of the addition in the first three blanks. On the fourth blank insert the city in which the property is located.

Paragraph #3:

A. In this blank write the amount of the down payment.

B. Here write the amount of the note you will be carrying.

C. This is the sum of the two above, and the final sales price.

Paragraph #4:

A. Check this box if the deal is all cash.

B. Check this box if you will be doing owner financing. On the first blank insert the interest rate. Check box (1) if the payments will be made in installments. If they're monthly, indicate so in the first blank, showing the amount of each payment on the second blank. On the last blank, you can indicate a date, or write something like 30 days after closing, or whenever you want the first payment to start after the closing date. Then check box "a" if the payments will continue for the entire term of the loan—20 to 30 years, or whatever you've negotiated with the buyer. You would check box "b" if you want them to make regular payments for several months or years, then have a balloon due on a certain date, which you would show on the blanks.

Check box (2) if there will only be one lump sum due at a future date, which you will specify in the blank.

C. Always check this box. Even if you're getting a substantial down payment, you should run a credit check to see what the buyer looks like.

Paragraph #5: Take as much earnest money as possible; 1% of the sales price, or at least $500, should be the minimum. Put the amount in the first blank. On the second blank indicate who will hold the earnest money. Depending on your state, it could be a title or escrow company, an attorney, or a broker. Write your name if you'll hold the earnest money yourself.

If there will be additional earnest money at a future date before the closing, then indicate the date and the amount of the additional funds on the remaining blanks.

Paragraph #6: Check box A if you'll furnish a title insurance policy, and indicate the name of the company that will issue the policy. Check box B if you'll provide an abstract of title, and indicate the abstractor or abstract company that will provide it.

Paragraph #7: You'll check box A if the property is being sold "as is" except for any repairs that may be required, or other conditions you'll indicate in the blank in the first paragraph.

Box B will be checked if the buyer will be allowed to inspect the property before closing. If you check this box, then you will include a Property Condition Addendum form (Appendix L).

Paragraph #8: If one or more brokers are to receive a commission, this paragraph will be used. In most situations you'll place "N/A" in each of these blanks, because if brokers are involved, they'll want to use their own contract forms.

Paragraph #9: Fill in the closing date.

Paragraph #10: Indicate when the buyer will take possession. If you put in an exact date predicated on the closing date and you don't make the closing date, then you'll have confusion. Rather, indicate whether possession will be "on date of closing," "three days after closing," or other such date that is agreeable to both you and the buyer.

Paragraph #11: Include here any special provisions that are important to your agreement with the buyer. For example, include any personal property that's included with the property, such as "Refrigerator and all window treatments to remain with property." Any personal property that looks like it is attached to the property, but which you will take with you, should be included here.

You can also show other terms of purchase or financing that don't fit anywhere else, such as "First five payments on owner financing to be made in the amount of $250.00, to cover principal only. Interest to begin on the sixth month."

Paragraph #21: There are two spaces at the end of this paragraph to include the name of the buyer's and seller's attorneys. Write in the names if attorneys will represent either party. Often, on simple transactions, attorneys will not be used and you'll mark out these lines.

On the blanks that ask for the date, fill in the effective date of the contract, which is when all parties have affixed their signatures.

ALL CASH OR OWNER FINANCED — RESIDENTIAL EARNEST MONEY CONTRACT (RESALE)

1. PARTIES: _JACK B. NIMBLE AND WIFE, SANDY W. NIMBLE_ (Seller) agrees
to sell and convey to _LADY N. SHOE, A SINGLE WOMAN_ (Buyer)
and Buyer agrees to buy from Seller the following property situated in _DALLAS_ County, Texas,
known as _123 CANDLESTICK LANE, DALLAS, TX 77777_ (Address).

2. PROPERTY: Lot _2_, Block _7/1653_, _FOREST
PARK_ Addition, City of _DALLAS_, or as described on attached exhibit, together
with the following fixtures, if any: curtain rods, drapery rods, venetian blinds, window shades, screens and shutters, awnings, wall-to-wall
carpeting, mirrors fixed in place, attic fans, permanently installed heating and air conditioning units and equipment, lighting and plumbing fixtures, TV antennas, mail boxes, water softeners, shrubbery and all other property owned by Seller and attached to the above described real property. All property sold by this contract is called "Property".

3. CONTRACT SALES PRICE:
   A. Cash payment payable at closing .... $ _10,000.00_
   B. Note described in 4 B below (the Note) .... $ _90,000.00_
   C. Sales Price payable to Seller (Sum of A and B) .... $ _100,000.00_

4. FINANCING CONDITIONS:
   ☐ A. This is an all cash sale; no financing is involved.
   ☒ B. The Note in the principal sum shown in 3 B above, dated as of the Closing Date, to be executed and delivered by Buyer and payable to
   the order of Seller, bearing interest at the rate of _9½_ percent per annum from date thereof until maturity, matured unpaid
   principal and interest to bear interest at the rate of 10% per annum, principal and interest to be due and payable
      ☒ (1) In _MONTHLY_ installments of $ _756.77_ or more each, beginning on or before _2/1/88_
      after date of the Note, and (Check "a" or "b")
         ☒ a. continuing regularly and at the same intervals thereafter until fully paid.
         ☐ b. continuing regularly and at the same intervals thereafter until _____, 19 _____, when the entire balance
         of principal and accrued interest shall be due and payable.
      ☐ (2) In a lump sum on or before _____ after date of the Note,
   ☒ C. This contract is subject to Buyer furnishing Seller evidence that Buyer has a history of good credit.

5. EARNEST MONEY: $ _1,000_ is herewith tendered and is to be deposited as Earnest Money with _ABC TITLE
COMPANY_, as Escrow Agent, upon execution of the contract by both parties. Additional Earnest
Money, if any, shall be deposited with the Escrow Agent on or before _N/A_, 19 ____, in the amount of $ _____.

6. TITLE: Seller at Seller's expense shall furnish either:
   ☒ A. Owner's Policy of Title Insurance (the Title Policy) issued by _ABC TITLE COMPANY_
   in the amount of the Sales Price and dated at or after closing; OR
   ☐ B. Complete Abstract of Title (the Abstract) certified by _____ to current date.
   NOTICE TO BUYER: AS REQUIRED BY LAW, Broker advises that YOU should have the Abstract covering the Property examined by an
   attorney of YOUR selection, or YOU should be furnished with or obtain a Title Policy.

7. PROPERTY CONDITION (Check "A" or "B"):
   ☐ A. Buyer accepts the Property in its present condition, subject only to _____
   _____
   ☒ B. Buyer requires inspections and repairs required by the Property Condition Addendum (the Addendum).
   Seller shall commence and complete prior to closing all required repairs at Seller's expense.
   All inspections, reports and repairs required of Seller by this contract and the Addendum shall not exceed $ _____. If Seller fails to complete
   such requirements, Buyer may do so and Seller shall be liable up to the amount specified and the same paid from the proceeds of the sale.
   If such expenditures exceed the stated amount and Seller refuses to pay such excess, Buyer may pay the additional cost or accept the Property
   with the limited repairs and this sale shall be closed as scheduled, or Buyer may terminate this contract and the Earnest Money shall be refunded
   to Buyer. Broker and sales associates have no responsibility or liability for repair or replacement of any of the Property.

8. BROKER'S FEE: _N/A_ Listing Broker (____%) and _____
   _____ Co-Broker (____%), as Real Estate Broker (the Broker), has negotiated this sale and Seller
   agrees to pay Broker in _____ County, Texas, on consummation of this sale or on Seller's default (unless
   otherwise provided herein) a total cash fee of _____ of the total Sales Price, which Escrow Agent may pay from the sale proceeds.

9. CLOSING: The closing of the sale (the Closing Date) shall be on or before _12/30_, 19 _87_, or within 7 days after objections
   to title have been cured, whichever date is later.

10. POSSESSION: The possession of the Property shall be delivered to Buyer on _DATE OF CLOSING_ in its present or required
    improved condition, ordinary wear and tear excepted. Any possession by Buyer prior to or by Seller after Closing Date shall establish a landlord-
    tenant at sufferance relationship between the parties.

11. SPECIAL PROVISIONS:

    _CHEST FREEZER IN GARAGE AND POOL TABLE
    IN GAME ROOM WILL REMAIN WITH THE
    PROPERTY._

(Insert terms and conditions of a factual nature applicable to this sale, e.g., personal property included in sale [curtains, draperies, valances, etc.]
prior purchase or sale of other property, lessee's surrender of possession, and the like.)

N° 65

12. **SALES EXPENSES TO BE PAID IN CASH AT OR PRIOR TO CLOSING:**
    A. Seller's Expenses:
       (1) Any inspections, reports and repairs required of Seller herein, and in the Addendum.
       (2) All cost of releasing existing loans and recording the releases; tax statements; 1/2 of any escrow fee; preparation of Deed; copies of restrictions and easements; other expenses stipulated to be paid by Seller under other provisions of this contract.
    B. Buyer's Expenses: All expenses incident to any loan (e.g., preparation of Note, Deed of Trust and other loan documents; recording fees, Mortgagee's Title Policy, credit reports); 1/2 of any escrow fee; one year premium for hazard insurance unless insurance is prorated; and expenses stipulated to be paid by Buyer under other provisions of this contract.
    C. If any sales expenses exceed the maximum amount herein stipulated to be paid by either party, either party may terminate this contract unless the other party agrees to pay such excess.

13. **PRORATIONS:** Insurance (at Buyer's option), taxes and any rents and maintenance fees, shall be prorated to the Closing Date.

14. **TITLE APPROVAL:** If Abstract is furnished, Seller shall deliver same to Buyer within 20 days from the effective date hereof. Buyer shall have 20 days from date of receipt of Abstract to deliver a copy of the title opinion to Seller, stating any objections to title, and only objections so stated shall be considered. If Title Policy is furnished, the Title Policy shall guarantee Buyer's title to be good and indefeasible subject only to (i) restrictive covenants affecting the Property (ii) any discrepancies, conflicts or shortages in area or boundary lines or any encroachments, or any overlapping of improvements (iii) all taxes for the current and subsequent years (iv) any existing building and zoning ordinances (v) rights of parties in possession (vi) any liens created as security for the sale consideration and (vii) any reservations or exceptions contained in the Deed. In either instance, if title objections are disclosed, Seller shall have 30 days to cure the same. Exceptions permitted in the Deed and zoning ordinances shall not be valid objections to title. Seller shall furnish at Seller's expense tax statements showing no delinquent taxes and a General Warranty Deed conveying title subject only to liens securing debt created as part of the consideration, taxes for the current year, usual restrictive covenants and utility easements common to the platted subdivision of which the Property is a part and any other reservations or exceptions acceptable to Buyer. The Note shall be secured by Vendor's and Deed of Trust liens. In case of dispute as to the form of Deed, Deed of Trust or Note, such shall be upon a form prepared by the State Bar of Texas.

15. **CASUALTY LOSS:** If any part of Property is damaged or destroyed by fire or other casualty loss, Seller shall restore the same to its previous condition as soon as reasonably possible, but in any event by Closing Date; and if Seller is unable to do so without fault, this contract shall terminate and Earnest Money shall be refunded with no Broker's fee due.

16. **DEFAULT:** If Buyer fails to comply herewith, Seller may either enforce specific performance or terminate this contract and receive the Earnest Money as liquidated damages, one-half of which (but not exceeding the herein recited Broker's fee) shall be paid by Seller to Broker in full payment for Broker's services. If Seller is unable without fault to deliver Abstract or Title Policy or to make any non-casualty repairs required herein within the time herein specified, Buyer may either terminate this contract and receive the Earnest Money as the sole remedy, and no Broker's fee shall be earned, or extend the time up to 30 days. If Seller fails to comply herewith for any other reason, Buyer may (i) terminate this contract and receive the Earnest Money, thereby releasing Seller from this contract (ii) enforce specific performance hereof or (iii) seek such other relief as may be provided by law. If completion of sale is prevented by Buyer's default, and Seller elects to enforce specific performance, the Broker's fee is payable only if and when Seller collects damages for such default by suit, compromise, settlement or otherwise, and after first deducting the expenses of collection, and then only in an amount equal to one-half of that portion collected, but not exceeding the amount of Broker's fee.

17. **ATTORNEY'S FEES:** Any signatory to this contract who is the prevailing party in any legal proceeding against any other signatory brought under or with relation to this contract or transaction shall be additionally entitled to recover court costs and reasonable attorney fees from the non-prevailing party.

18. **ESCROW:** Earnest Money is deposited with Escrow Agent with the understanding that Escrow Agent (i) does not assume or have any liability for performance or nonperformance of any party (ii) has the right to require the receipt, release and authorization in writing of all parties before paying the deposit to any party and (iii) is not liable for interest or other charge on the funds held. If any party unreasonably fails to agree in writing to an appropriate release of Earnest Money, then such party shall be liable to the other parties to the extent provided in paragraph 17. At closing, Earnest Money shall be applied to any cash down payment required, next to Buyer's closing costs and any excess refunded to Buyer. Before Buyer shall be entitled to refund of Earnest Money, any actual expenses incurred or paid on Buyer's behalf shall be deducted therefrom and paid to the creditors entitled thereto.

19. **REPRESENTATIONS:** Seller represents that there will be no Title I liens, unrecorded liens or Uniform Commercial Code liens against any of the Property on Closing Date. If any representation above is untrue this contract may be terminated by Buyer and the Earnest Money shall be refunded without delay. Representations shall survive closing.

20. **AGREEMENT OF PARTIES:** This contract contains the entire agreement of the parties and cannot be changed except by their written consent.

21. **CONSULT YOUR ATTORNEY:** This is intended to be a legally binding contract. READ IT CAREFULLY. If you do not understand the effect of any part, consult your attorney BEFORE signing. The Broker cannot give you legal advice — only factual and business details concerning land and improvements. Attorneys to represent parties may be designated below, and, so employment may be accepted, Broker shall promptly deliver a copy of this contract to such attorneys.

Seller's Atty: _EDWARD BARRISTER_   Buyer's Atty: _JOHNNY JOHNS_

EXECUTED in multiple originals effective the _23rd_ day of _NOV._, 19 _87_   **(BROKER FILL IN THE DATE LAST PARTY SIGNS).**

Listing Broker	License No.	_Jack B Nimble_ — Seller
By _____		_Sandy W. Nimble_ — Seller
		25 CEDAR LN., DALLAS 123-4444 — Seller's Address / Tel.
Co-Broker	License No.	_Jady N. Shae_ — Buyer
By _____		
Receipt of $_1,000_ Earnest Money is acknowledged in the form		Buyer
of _CHECK_		_1000 PINECREST, KELLER 333-5555_ — Buyer's Address / Tel.
ABC TITLE CO. _11/23/87_		
Escrow Agent Date		
By _____		

ALL CASH OR OWNER FINANCED — RESIDENTIAL EARNEST MONEY CONTRACT (RESALE)

1. PARTIES: _____ (Seller) agrees
   to sell and convey to _____ (Buyer)
   and Buyer agrees to buy from Seller the following property situated in _____ County,
   known as _____ (Address).

2. PROPERTY: Lot _____, Block _____, _____
   _____ Addition, City of _____, or as described on attached exhibit, together
   with the following fixtures, if any: curtain rods, drapery rods, venetian blinds, window shades, screens and shutters, awnings, wall-to-wall
   carpeting, mirrors fixed in place, attic fans, permanently installed heating and air conditioning units and equipment, lighting and plumbing fixtures, TV antennas, mail boxes, water softeners, shrubbery and all other property owned by Seller and attached to the above described real property. All property sold by this contract is called "Property".

3. CONTRACT SALES PRICE:
   A. Cash payment payable at closing . . . . $_____

   B. Note described in 4 B below (the Note) . . . . $_____

   C. Sales Price payable to Seller (Sum of A and B) . . . . $_____

4. FINANCING CONDITIONS:
   ☐ A. This is an all cash sale; no financing is involved.
   ☐ B. The Note in the principal sum shown in 3 B above, dated as of the Closing Date, to be executed and delivered by Buyer and payable to
          the order of Seller, bearing interest at the rate of _____ percent per annum from date thereof until maturity, matured unpaid
          principal and interest to bear interest at the rate of 10% per annum, principal and interest to be due and payable
          ☐ (1) In _____ installments of $_____ or more each, beginning on or before _____
                 after date of the Note, and (Check "a" or "b")
                 ☐ a. continuing regularly and at the same intervals thereafter until fully paid.
                 ☐ b. continuing regularly and at the same intervals thereafter until _____, 19 _____, when the entire balance
                        of principal and accrued interest shall be due and payable.
          ☐ (2) In a lump sum on or before _____ after date of the Note,
   ☐ C. This contract is subject to Buyer furnishing Seller evidence that Buyer has a history of good credit.

5. EARNEST MONEY: $_____ is herewith tendered and is to be deposited as Earnest Money with _____
   _____, as Escrow Agent, upon execution of the contract by both parties. Additional Earnest
   Money, if any, shall be deposited with the Escrow Agent on or before _____, 19 _____, in the amount of $_____.

6. TITLE: Seller at Seller's expense shall furnish either:
   ☐ A. Owner's Policy of Title Insurance (the Title Policy) issued by _____
          in the amount of the Sales Price and dated at or after closing: OR
   ☐ B. Complete Abstract of Title (the Abstract) certified by _____ to current date.
   NOTICE TO BUYER: AS REQUIRED BY LAW, Broker advises that YOU should have the Abstract covering the Property examined by an
   attorney of YOUR selection, or YOU should be furnished with or obtain a Title Policy.

7. PROPERTY CONDITION (Check "A" or "B"):
   ☐ A. Buyer accepts the Property in its present condition, subject only to _____
          _____.
   ☐ B. Buyer requires inspections and repairs required by the Property Condition Addendum (the Addendum).
   Seller shall commence and complete prior to closing all required repairs at Seller's expense.

   All inspections, reports and repairs required of Seller by this contract and the Addendum shall not exceed $_____. If Seller fails to complete
   such requirements, Buyer may do so and Seller shall be liable up to the amount specified and the same paid from the proceeds of the sale.
   If such expenditures exceed the stated amount and Seller refuses to pay such excess, Buyer may pay the additional cost or accept the Property
   with the limited repairs and this sale shall be closed as scheduled, or Buyer may terminate this contract and the Earnest Money shall be refunded
   to Buyer. Broker and sales associates have no responsibility or liability for repair or replacement of any of the Property.

8. BROKER'S FEE: _____ Listing Broker (_____%) and _____
   _____ Co-Broker (_____%), as Real Estate Broker (the Broker), has negotiated this sale and Seller
   agrees to pay Broker in _____ County, on consummation of this sale or on Seller's default (unless
   otherwise provided herein) a total cash fee of _____ of the total Sales Price, which Escrow Agent may pay from the sale proceeds.

9. CLOSING: The closing of the sale (the Closing Date) shall be on or before _____, 19 _____, or within 7 days after objections
   to title have been cured, whichever date is later.

10. POSSESSION: The possession of the Property shall be delivered to Buyer on _____ in its present or required
    improved condition, ordinary wear and tear excepted. Any possession by Buyer prior to or by Seller after Closing Date shall establish a landlord-
    tenant at sufferance relationship between the parties.

11. SPECIAL PROVISIONS:

    (Insert terms and conditions of a factual nature applicable to this sale, e.g., personal property included in sale [curtains, draperies, valances, etc.],
    prior purchase or sale of other property, lessee's surrender of possession, and the like.)

12. SALES EXPENSES TO BE PAID IN CASH AT OR PRIOR TO CLOSING:

    A. Seller's Expenses:
        (1) Any inspections, reports and repairs required of Seller herein, and in the Addendum.
        (2) All cost of releasing existing loans and recording the releases; tax statements; 1/2 of any escrow fee; preparation of Deed; copies of restrictions and easements; other expenses stipulated to be paid by Seller under other provisions of this contract.
    B. Buyer's Expenses: All expenses incident to any loan (e.g., preparation of Note, Deed of Trust and other loan documents, recording fees, Mortgagee's Title Policy, credit reports); 1/2 of any escrow fee; one year premium for hazard insurance unless insurance is prorated; and expenses stipulated to be paid by Buyer under other provisions of this contract.
    C. If any sales expenses exceed the maximum amount herein stipulated to be paid by either party, either party may terminate this contract unless the other party agrees to pay such excess.

13. PRORATIONS: Insurance (at Buyer's option), taxes and any rents and maintenance fees, shall be prorated to the Closing Date.

14. TITLE APPROVAL: If Abstract is furnished, Seller shall deliver same to Buyer within 20 days from the effective date hereof. Buyer shall have 20 days from date of receipt of Abstract to deliver a copy of the title opinion to Seller, stating any objections to title, and only objections so stated shall be considered. If Title Policy is furnished, the Title Policy shall guarantee Buyer's title to be good and indefeasible subject only to (i) restrictive covenants affecting the Property (ii) any discrepancies, conflicts or shortages in area or boundary lines or any encroachments, or any overlapping of improvements (iii) all taxes for the current and subsequent years (iv) any existing building and zoning ordinances (v) rights of parties in possession (vi) any liens created as security for the sale consideration and (vii) any reservations or exceptions contained in the Deed. In either instance, if title objections are disclosed, Seller shall have 30 days to cure the same. Exceptions permitted in the Deed and zoning ordinances shall not be valid objections to title. Seller shall furnish at Seller's expense tax statements showing no delinquent taxes and a General Warranty Deed conveying title subject only to liens securing debt created as part of the consideration, taxes for the current year, usual restrictive covenants and utility easements common to the platted subdivision of which the Property is a part and any other reservations or exceptions acceptable to Buyer. The Note shall be secured by Vendor's and Deed of Trust liens. In case of dispute as to the form of Deed, Deed of Trust or Note, such shall be upon a form prepared by the State Bar of

15. CASUALTY LOSS: If any part of Property is damaged or destroyed by fire or other casualty loss, Seller shall restore the same to its previous condition as soon as reasonably possible, but in any event by Closing Date; and if Seller is unable to do so without fault, this contract shall terminate and Earnest Money shall be refunded with no Broker's fee due.

16. DEFAULT: If Buyer fails to comply herewith, Seller may either enforce specific performance or terminate this contract and receive the Earnest Money as liquidated damages, one-half of which (but not exceeding the herein recited Broker's fee) shall be paid by Seller to Broker in full payment for Broker's services. If Seller is unable without fault to deliver Abstract or Title Policy or to make any non-casualty repairs required herein within the time herein specified, Buyer may either terminate this contract and receive the Earnest Money as the sole remedy, and no Broker's fee shall be earned, or extend the time up to 30 days. If Seller fails to comply herewith for any other reason, Buyer may (i) terminate this contract and receive the Earnest Money, thereby releasing Seller from this contract (ii) enforce specific performance hereof or (iii) seek such other relief as may be provided by law. If completion of sale is prevented by Buyer's default, and Seller elects to enforce specific performance, the Broker's fee is payable only if and when Seller collects damages for such default by suit, compromise, settlement or otherwise, and after first deducting the expenses of collection, and then only in an amount equal to one-half of that portion collected, but not exceeding the amount of Broker's fee.

17. ATTORNEY'S FEES: Any signatory to this contract who is the prevailing party in any legal proceeding against any other signatory brought under or with relation to this contract or transaction shall be additionally entitled to recover court costs and reasonable attorney fees from the non-prevailing party.

18. ESCROW: Earnest Money is deposited with Escrow Agent with the understanding that Escrow Agent (i) does not assume or have any liability for performance or nonperformance of any party (ii) has the right to require the receipt, release and authorization in writing of all parties before paying the deposit to any party and (iii) is not liable for interest or other charge on the funds held. If any party unreasonably fails to agree in writing to an appropriate release of Earnest Money, then such party shall be liable to the other parties to the extent provided in paragraph 17. At closing, Earnest Money shall be applied to any cash down payment required, next to Buyer's closing costs and any excess refunded to Buyer. Before Buyer shall be entitled to refund of Earnest Money, any actual expenses incurred or paid on Buyer's behalf shall be deducted therefrom and paid to the creditors entitled thereto.

19. REPRESENTATIONS: Seller represents that there will be no Title I liens, unrecorded liens or Uniform Commercial Code liens against any of the Property on Closing Date. If any representation above is untrue this contract may be terminated by Buyer and the Earnest Money shall be refunded without delay. Representations shall survive closing.

20. AGREEMENT OF PARTIES: This contract contains the entire agreement of the parties and cannot be changed except by their written consent.

21. CONSULT YOUR ATTORNEY: This is intended to be a legally binding contract. READ IT CAREFULLY. If you do not understand the effect of any part, consult your attorney BEFORE signing. The Broker cannot give you legal advice — only factual and business details concerning land and improvements. Attorneys to represent parties may be designated below, and, so employment may be accepted, Broker shall promptly deliver a copy of this contract to such attorneys.

Seller's Atty: _____   Buyer's Atty: _____

EXECUTED in multiple originals effective the _____ day of _____, 19 _____. **(BROKER FILL IN THE DATE LAST PARTY SIGNS).**

Listing Broker _____ License No.   Seller _____

By _____   Seller _____

Co-Broker _____ License No.   Seller's Address _____ Tel. _____

By _____   Buyer _____

Receipt of $_____ Earnest Money is acknowledged in the form

of _____.   Buyer _____

     Buyer's Address _____ Tel. _____

Escrow Agent _____ Date _____

By _____

Appendix J
Assumption-of-Loan Contract Form

USE THIS CONTRACT FOR A SALE TO A BUYER WHO IS TO ASSUME YOUR EXISTING LOAN.

Paragraph #1: Write your legal name(s) on the first line, as sellers, and the legal names of the buyers on the next line. Remember to note the marital status of all parties. For example:

- If one of the parties is a married couple, you would write "John M. Doe and wife Mary M. Doe."

- For a single person, you can simply write "John M. Doe," or you can write "John M. Doe, a single person."

- For a divorced person, write "John M. Doe, a divorced person since May 23, 1985."

- For a widower, write "John M. Doe, a widower since May 23, 1985."

- For a corporation, you would write "JMD Industries, Inc., a Texas corporation."

- For a Partnership, you would write "Doe Properties, a Texas General Partnership," or "Doe Properties, a Texas Limited Partnership."

- For a pension and profit-sharing plan, you would write "JMD Industries, Inc., Pension & Profit-Sharing Trust."

- For two individuals not related or married, you would write "John M. Doe and John R. Smith, in indiscriminate interest."

The next blank asks for the name of the county in which the real estate is located, then place the two letter code for the state after the word "County."

The last blank requests the address of the property.

Paragraph #2: This paragraph asks for the legal description of the property. You'll find this information in your copies of your original closing papers. Make *certain* you have the correct description. Write the lot number, the block number, then the name of the addition in the first three blanks. On the fourth blank insert the city in which the property is located.

Paragraph #3:

A. If you check the first box "Exact," then you will have to check the "Approximate" box in D below, and vice-versa. The reason for this is that you won't know the exact balance *to the day of closing* on the existing loan that the buyer is assuming from you; therefore, if you want the amount of the down payment to be exact, the final sales price will have to be approximate, and if you want the sales price to be exact, the amount of the down payment will have to vary (up to $250 as is stated at the end of B). Check the appropriate box, and insert the amount of down payment the buyer will pay out of his own funds.

B. On the first blank, include your total payment for principal, interest, taxes, and insurance. On the second blank include the name of your mortgage company. On the next two blanks is the date the new owner will make his first payment. Remember that all payments are made in arrears. If you close at the end of August, the payment due September first is the payment for the month of August. To be fair, the payment due September first should be your responsibility. On the other hand, if the buyer has been severe with you in the negotiation, this is where you can catch up one payment's worth.

If you are doing any owner financing—such as a second or third lien—you can also catch up a little more (up to the $250) by indicating on the last blank a figure that's $250 less than what you know your mortgage balance is, and checking the "Exact" box in A and D. At closing the true sales price will be increased by $250, to be shown as an increase on your owner financing.

C. Check box (1) if you will be carrying a second lien, then on the first blank show the interest rate. Check the lump sum box if the second lien will be paid in a lump sum, and indicate the date the lump sum is due. Normally you'll check the next box when payments are made in installments. On the first blank include the amount of each installment, on the second blank you'll more than likely want to write "monthly," and on the last blank show when the first installment will be made.

Check the second box if there will be a second lien provided by a commercial lien lender, and in the first blank indicate what the maximum monthly payment the buyer is willing to pay for the second lien. See the instructions for Paragraph #3A to determine if you will check the "Exact" box or the "Approximate" box.

D. See above to determine which box will be checked here.

Paragraph #4: On the first blank you need to check $50. The cost to transfer a loan is generally $50 if it is a non-qualifying, fully-assumable loan. If it is a conventional assumable loan, then you'll need to check with the lender to see what he'll require for your buyer to assume it. On the second blank, insert the existing interest rate if the loan is a non-qualifying, fully-assumable loan. If it is a conventional loan, check with the lender to make sure the rate won't change. If it will change, then write in the new rate.

Paragraph #5: Take as much earnest money as possible; 1% of the sales price, or at least $500, should be the minimum. Put the amount in the first blank. On the second blank indicate who will hold the earnest money. Depending on your state, it could be a title or escrow company, an attorney, or a broker. Write your name if you'll hold the earnest money yourself.

If there will be additional earnest money at a future date before the closing, then indicate the date and the amount of the additional funds on the remaining blanks.

Paragraph #6: Check box A if you'll furnish a title insurance policy, and indicate the name of the company that will issue the policy. Check box B if you'll provide an abstract of title, and indicate the abstractor or abstract company that will provide it.

Paragraph #7: You'll check box A if the property is being sold "as is" except for any repairs that may be required by a lender, or other conditions you'll indicate in the blank in the first paragraph.

Box B will be checked if the buyer will be allowed to inspect the property before closing. If you check this box, then you will include a Property Condition Addendum form (Appendix L).

Paragraph #8: If one or more brokers are to receive a commission, this paragraph will be used. In most situations you'll place "N/A" in each of these blanks, because if brokers are involved, they'll want to use their own contract forms.

Paragraph #9: Fill in the closing date. Make sure you give yourself enough time to find financing for the buyer if a second lien is needed. Check with several mortgage companies to see how long to allow. If you run out of time and the buyer has not been approved for a loan, this contract will become null and void and the buyer could back out on the transaction.

Paragraph #10: Indicate when the buyer will take possession. If you put in an exact date predicated on the closing date and you don't make the closing date, then you'll have confusion. Rather, indicate whether possession will be "on date of closing," "three days after closing," or other such date that is agreeable to both you and the buyer.

Paragraph #11: Include here any special provisions that are important to your agreement with the buyer. For example, include any personal property that's included with the property, such as "Refrigerator and all window treatments to remain with property." Any personal property that looks like it is attached to the property, but which you will take with you, should be included here.

You can also show other terms of purchase or financing that don't fit anywhere else, such as "First five payments on owner financing to be made in the amount of $250.00, to cover principal only. Interest to begin on the sixth month."

Paragraph #12: To know which box to check here, you need to know the status of your escrow account. If you know there is an excess of funds in it and you are due a refund, then you want to check the first box. That way, you'll receive a refund of the excess at closing. If the funds in the account are about what's needed, then check the second box. If there's a shortage, you can check the second box, but more than likely the escrow agent will require that you make up the difference at closing. So before you put the house up for sale, get the information on your escrow account from your mortgage company so you know where you stand.

Paragraph #21: There are two spaces at the end of this paragraph to include the name of the buyer's and seller's attorneys. Write in the names if attorneys will represent either party. Often, on simple transactions, attorneys will not be used and you'll mark out these lines.

On the blanks that ask for the date, fill in the effective date of the contract, which is when all parties have affixed their signatures.

ASSUMPTION OF LOAN — RESIDENTIAL EARNEST MONEY CONTRACT

1. PARTIES: _BOBBY McGEE AND WIFE LEA E. McGEE_ (Seller) agrees
to sell and convey to _SMITH ENTERPRISES, INC., A TEXAS CORP._ (Buyer)
and Buyer agrees to buy from Seller the following property situated in _DALLAS_ County, Texas,
known as _8543 AVENUE C, DUNCANVILLE, TX 55555_ (Address).

2. PROPERTY: Lot _111_, Block _24_, _CEDAR_
TREES Addition, City of _DUNCANVILLE_, or as described on attached exhibit,
together with the following fixtures, if any: curtain rods, drapery rods, venetian blinds, window shades, screens and shutters, awnings, wall-to-
wall carpeting, mirrors fixed in place, attic fans, permanently installed heating and air conditioning units and equipment, lighting and plumbing
fixtures, TV antennas, mail boxes, water softeners, shrubbery and all other property owned by Seller and attached to the above described real
property. All property sold by this contract is called "Property".

3. CONTRACT SALES PRICE:
   A. The ☒ Exact ☐ Approximate   Cash down payment payable at closing .... $ _5,000.00_
   B. Buyer's assumption of the unpaid balance of a promissory note (the Note) payable in present monthly installments of $ _237.55_, including principal and interest and any reserve deposits, with Buyer's first
   installment payable to _MAURY MORTGAGE CO._
   on _JUNE 1_, 19 _88_, the assumed principal balance of which at closing
   (allowing for an agreed $250 variance) will be .... $ _22,600.00_
   C. Any balance of Sales Price to be evidenced by a second lien note payable to [check (1) or (2) below]:
      ☒ (1) Seller, bearing interest at the rate of _9_ % per annum, in
         ☐ lump sum on or before _____
         ☒ principal and interest installments of $ _126.68_, or more per _MONTH_,
         with first installment payable on _JUNE 1, 1988_
      ☐ (2) Third Party in principal and interest installments not in excess of $ _____ per month
      and in the ☐ Exact ☐ Approximate (check "Approximate" only if A above and D below are "Exact")
      amount of .... $ _10,000.00_

   D. The ☒ Exact ☐ Approximate total Sales Price of (Sum of A, B and C above) .... $ _37,600.00_

4. FINANCING CONDITIONS: If a Noteholder on assumption (i) requires Buyer to pay an assumption fee in excess of $ _50.00_
and Seller declines to pay such excess (ii) raises the existing interest rate above _8_ % or (iii) requires approval of Buyer or can accelerate the Note and Buyer does not receive from the Noteholder written approval and acceleration waiver prior to the Closing Date, Buyer
may terminate this contract and the Earnest Money shall be refunded. Buyer shall apply for the approval and waiver under (iii) above within 7
days from the effective date hereof and shall make every reasonable effort to obtain the same.

5. EARNEST MONEY: $ _500_ is herewith tendered and is to be deposited as Earnest Money with _FRIENDLY_
TITLE CO., as Escrow Agent, upon execution of the contract by both parties. Additional Earnest
Money, if any, shall be deposited with the Escrow Agent on or before _APRIL 15_, 19 _88_, in the amount of $ _500_.

6. TITLE: Seller at Seller's expense shall furnish either:
   ☒ A. Owner's Policy of Title Insurance (the Title Policy) issued by _FRIENDLY TITLE CO._
   in the amount of the Sales Price and dated at or after closing: OR
   ☐ B. Complete Abstract of Title (the Abstract) certified by _____ to current date.
NOTICE TO BUYER: AS REQUIRED BY LAW, Broker advises that YOU should have the Abstract covering the Property examined by an
attorney of YOUR selection, or YOU should be furnished with or obtain a Title Policy.

7. PROPERTY CONDITION (Check "A" or "B"):
   ☐ A. Buyer accepts the Property in its present condition, subject only to _____
   ☒ B. Buyer requires inspections and repairs required by the Property Condition Addendum (the Addendum).
Upon Seller's receipt of all loan approvals and inspection reports Seller shall commence and complete prior to closing all required repairs at
Seller's expense.
All inspections, reports and repairs required of Seller by this contract and the Addendum shall not exceed $_____. If Seller fails to com-
plete such requirements, Buyer may do so and Seller shall be liable up to the amount specified and the same paid from the proceeds of the sale.
If such expenditures exceed the stated amount and Seller refuses to pay such excess, Buyer may pay the additional cost or accept the Property
with the limited repairs and this sale shall be closed as scheduled, or Buyer may terminate this contract and the Earnest Money shall be refunded
to Buyer. Broker and sales associates have no responsibility or liability for repair or replacement of any of the Property.

8. BROKER'S FEE: _N/A_ Listing Broker (____%) and
_____ Co-Broker (____%), as Real Estate Broker (the Broker), has negotiated this sale and Seller
agrees to pay Broker in _____ County, Texas, on consummation of this sale or on Seller's default (unless
otherwise provided herein) a total cash fee of _____ of the total Sales Price, which Escrow Agent may pay from the sale proceeds.

9. CLOSING: The closing of the sale (the Closing Date) shall be on or before _APRIL 30_, 19 _88_, or within 7 days after objections to title have been cured, whichever date is later.

10. POSSESSION: The possession of the Property shall be delivered to Buyer on _DATE OF CLOSING_ in its present or required
improved condition, ordinary wear and tear excepted. Any possession by Buyer prior to or by Seller after Closing Date shall establish a landlord-
tenant at sufferance relationship between the parties.

11. SPECIAL PROVISIONS:

PAYMENT IN #3C ABOVE WILL VARY DEPENDING
ON FINAL AMOUNT OF SECOND LIEN NOTE.

(Insert terms and conditions of a factual nature applicable to this sale, e.g., personal property included in sale [curtains, draperies, valances, etc.],
prior purchase or sale of other property, lessee's surrender of possession, and the like.)

Nọ 315

12. PRORATION: Taxes, insurance, rents, interest and maintenance fees, if any, ☐ SHALL ☐ SHALL NOT be prorated to the Closing Date. If these are not prorated, all funds held in reserve for payment of taxes, maintenance fees and insurance and the insurance policy shall be transferred to the Buyer by Seller without cost to Buyer.

13. SALES EXPENSES TO BE PAID IN CASH AT OR PRIOR TO CLOSING: Preparing Deed, preparing and recording Deed of Trust to Secure Assumption, all inspections, reports and repairs required of Seller herein and in the Addendum and 1/2 of escrow fee shall be Seller's expense. All other costs and expenses incurred in connection with this contract which are not recited herein to be the obligation of Seller, shall be the obligation of Buyer. Unless otherwise paid, before Buyer shall be entitled to refund of Earnest Money, any such costs and expenses shall be deducted therefrom and paid to the creditors entitled thereto. If any sales expenses exceed the maximum amount herein stipulated to be paid by either party, either party may terminate this contract unless the other party agrees to pay such excess.

14. TITLE APPROVAL: If Abstract is furnished, Seller shall deliver same to Buyer within 20 days from the effective date hereof. Buyer shall have 20 days from date of receipt of Abstract to deliver a copy of the title opinion to Seller, stating any objections to title, and only objections so stated shall be considered. If Title Policy is furnished, the Title Policy shall guarantee Buyer's title to be good and indefeasible subject only to (i) restrictive covenants affecting the Property (ii) any discrepancies, conflicts or shortages in area or boundary lines or any encroachments, or any overlapping of improvements (iii) all taxes for the current and subsequent years (iv) any existing building and zoning ordinances (v) rights of parties in possession (vi) any liens assumed or created as security for the sale consideration and (vii) any reservations or exceptions contained in the Deed. In either instance, if title objections are disclosed, Seller shall have 30 days to cure the same. Exceptions permitted in the Deed and zoning ordinances shall not be valid objections to title. Seller shall furnish at Seller's expense tax statements showing no delinquent taxes and a General Warranty Deed conveying title subject only to liens securing debt created or assumed as part of the consideration, taxes for the current year, usual restrictive covenants and utility easements common to the platted subdivision of which the Property is a part and any other reservations or exceptions acceptable to Buyer. Each note herein provided shall be secured by Vendor's and Deed of Trust liens. A Vendor's lien shall be retained and a Deed of Trust to Secure Assumption required, which shall be automatically released on execution and delivery of a release by noteholder. In the case of dispute as to the form of Deed, Note(s) or Deed(s) of Trust, such shall be upon a form prepared by the State Bar of Texas.

15. CASUALTY LOSS: If any part of Property is damaged or destroyed by fire or other casualty loss, Seller shall restore the same to its previous condition as soon as reasonably possible, but in any event by Closing Date; and if Seller is unable to do so without fault, this contract shall terminate and Earnest Money shall be refunded with no Broker's fee due.

16. DEFAULT: If Buyer fails to comply herewith, Seller may either enforce specific performance or terminate this contract and receive the Earnest Money as liquidated damages, one-half of which (but not exceeding the herein recited Broker's fee) shall be paid by Seller to Broker in full payment for Broker's services. If Seller is unable without fault to deliver Abstract or Title Policy or to make any non-casualty repairs required herein within the time herein specified, Buyer may either terminate this contract and receive the Earnest Money as the sole remedy, and no Broker's fee shall be earned, or extend the time up to 30 days. If Seller fails to comply herewith for any other reason, Buyer may (i) terminate this contract and receive the Earnest Money, thereby releasing Seller from this contract (ii) enforce specific performance hereof or (iii) seek such other relief as may be provided by law. If completion of sale is prevented by Buyer's default, and Seller elects to enforce specific performance, the Broker's fee is payable only if and when Seller collects damages for such default by suit, compromise, settlement or otherwise, and after first deducting the expenses of collection, and then only in an amount equal to one-half of that portion collected, but not exceeding the amount of Broker's fee.

17. ATTORNEY'S FEES: Any signatory to this contract who is the prevailing party in any legal proceeding against any other signatory brought under or with relation to this contract or transaction shall be additionally entitled to recover court costs and reasonable attorney fees from the non-prevailing party.

18. ESCROW: Earnest Money is deposited with Escrow Agent with the understanding that Escrow Agent (i) does not assume or have any liability for performance or nonperformance of any party (ii) has the right to require the receipt, release and authorization in writing of all parties before paying the deposit to any party and (iii) is not liable for interest or other charge on the funds held. If any party unreasonably fails to agree in writing to an appropriate release of Earnest Money, then such party shall be liable to the other parties to the extent provided in paragraph 17. At closing, Earnest Money shall be applied to any cash down payment required, next to Buyer's closing costs and any excess refunded to Buyer. Before Buyer shall be entitled to refund of Earnest Money, any actual expenses incurred or paid on Buyer's behalf shall be deducted therefrom and paid to the creditors entitled thereto.

19. REPRESENTATIONS: Seller represents that unless securing payment of the Note there will be no Title I liens, unrecorded liens or Uniform Commerical Code liens against any of the Property on Closing Date, that loan(s) will be without default, and reserve deposits will not be deficient. If any representation above is untrue this contract may be terminated by Buyer and the Earnest Money refunded without delay. Representations shall survive closing.

20. THIRD PARTY FINANCING: If financing by Third Party under 3C(2) above is required herein, Buyer shall have 15 days from effective date hereof to obtain the same, and failure to secure the same after reasonable effort shall render this contract null and void, and the Earnest Money refunded without delay.

21. AGREEMENT OF PARTIES: This contract contains the entire agreement of the parties and cannot be changed except by their written consent.

22. CONSULT YOUR ATTORNEY: This is intended to be a legally binding contract. READ IT CAREFULLY. If you do not understand the effect of any part, consult your attorney BEFORE signing. The Broker cannot give you legal advice — only factual and business details concerning land and improvements. Attorneys to represent parties may be designated below, and, so employment may be accepted, Broker shall promptly deliver a copy of this contract to such attorneys.

Seller's Atty: _____N/A_____   Buyer's Atty: _____N/A_____

EXECUTED in multiple originals effective the 1ST day of _APRIL_, 19 88 (BROKER FILL IN THE DATE LAST PARTY SIGNS).

Listing Broker _____ License No. _____

By _____

Co-Broker _____ License No. _____

By _____

Receipt of $ 500 Earnest Money is acknowledged in the form

of _CHECK_____

FRIENDLY TITLE CO. 4/1/88
Escrow Agent   Date

By _____

Seller _Molly M. Lee_

Seller _Lea E. M. Lee_

12345 AUDELIA, DALLAS 77777
Seller's Address   222-3333 Tel.

Ted Armstrong PRES.
Buyer

Buyer _____

6704 ABRAMS, SUITE 210
Buyer's Address   Tel.
DALLAS 77777   666-7777

ASSUMPTION OF LOAN — RESIDENTIAL EARNEST MONEY CONTRACT

1. PARTIES: _____ (Seller) agrees
   to sell and convey to _____ (Buyer)
   and Buyer agrees to buy from Seller the following property situated in _____ County,
   known as _____ (Address).

2. PROPERTY: Lot _____, Block _____, _____
   _____ Addition, City of _____, or as described on attached exhibit,
   together with the following fixtures, if any: curtain rods, drapery rods, venetian blinds, window shades, screens and shutters, awnings, wall-to-
   wall carpeting, mirrors fixed in place, attic fans, permanently installed heating and air conditioning units and equipment, lighting and plumbing
   fixtures, TV antennas, mail boxes, water softeners, shrubbery and all other property owned by Seller and attached to the above described real
   property. All property sold by this contract is called "Property".

3. CONTRACT SALES PRICE:
   A. The ☐ Exact ☐ Approximate   Cash down payment payable at closing .... $ _____
   B. Buyer's assumption of the unpaid balance of a promissory note (the Note) payable in present monthly instal-
      lments of $ _____, including principal and interest and any reserve deposits, with Buyer's first
      installment payable to _____
      on _____, 19 _____, the assumed principal balance of which at closing
      (allowing for an agreed $250 variance) will be .... $ _____
   C. Any balance of Sales Price to be evidenced by a second lien note payable to [check (1) or (2) below]:
      ☐ (1) Seller, bearing interest at the rate of _____ % per annum, in
         ☐ lump sum on or before _____
         ☐ principal and interest installments of $ _____, or more per _____,
         with first installment payable on _____.
      ☐ (2) Third Party in principal and interest installments not in excess of $ _____ per month
      and in the ☐ Exact ☐ Approximate (check "Approximate" only if A above and D below are "Exact")
      amount of .... $ _____

   D. The ☐ Exact ☐ Approximate total Sales Price of (Sum of A, B and C above) .... $ _____

4. FINANCING CONDITIONS: If a Noteholder on assumption (i) requires Buyer to pay an assumption fee in excess of $ _____
   and Seller declines to pay such excess (ii) raises the existing interest rate above _____ % or (iii) requires approval of Buyer or can accelerate the Note and Buyer does not receive from the Noteholder written approval and acceleration waiver prior to the Closing Date, Buyer
   may terminate this contract and the Earnest Money shall be refunded. Buyer shall apply for the approval and waiver under (iii) above within 7
   days from the effective date hereof and shall make every reasonable effort to obtain the same.

5. EARNEST MONEY: $ _____ is herewith tendered and is to be deposited as Earnest Money with _____
   _____, as Escrow Agent, upon execution of the contract by both parties. Additional Earnest
   Money, if any, shall be deposited with the Escrow Agent on or before _____, 19 _____, in the amount of $ _____.

6. TITLE: Seller at Seller's expense shall furnish either:
   ☐ A. Owner's Policy of Title Insurance (the Title Policy) issued by _____
      in the amount of the Sales Price and dated at or after closing: OR
   ☐ B. Complete Abstract of Title (the Abstract) certified by _____ to current date.
   NOTICE TO BUYER: AS REQUIRED BY LAW, Broker advises that YOU should have the Abstract covering the Property examined by an
   attorney of YOUR selection, or YOU should be furnished with or obtain a Title Policy.

7. PROPERTY CONDITION (Check "A" or "B"):
   ☐ A. Buyer accepts the Property in its present condition, subject only to _____
      _____.
   ☐ B. Buyer requires inspections and repairs required by the Property Condition Addendum (the Addendum).
   Upon Seller's receipt of all loan approvals and inspection reports Seller shall commence and complete prior to closing all required repairs at
   Seller's expense.

   All inspections, reports and repairs required of Seller by this contract and the Addendum shall not exceed $ _____. If Seller fails to com-
   plete such requirements, Buyer may do so and Seller shall be liable up to the amount specified and the same paid from the proceeds of the sale.
   If such expenditures exceed the stated amount and Seller refuses to pay such excess, Buyer may pay the additional cost or accept the Property
   with the limited repairs and this sale shall be closed as scheduled, or Buyer may terminate this contract and the Earnest Money shall be refunded
   to Buyer. Broker and sales associates have no responsibility or liability for repair or replacement of any of the Property.

8. BROKER'S FEE: _____ Listing Broker (_____ %) and _____
   _____ Co-Broker (_____ %), as Real Estate Broker (the Broker), has negotiated this sale and Seller
   agrees to pay Broker in _____ County, on consummation of this sale or on Seller's default (unless
   otherwise provided herein) a total cash fee of _____ of the total Sales Price, which Escrow Agent may pay from the sale proceeds.

9. CLOSING: The closing of the sale (the Closing Date) shall be on or before _____, 19 _____, or within 7 days after objections to title have been cured, whichever date is later.

10. POSSESSION: The possession of the Property shall be delivered to Buyer on _____ in its present or required
   improved condition, ordinary wear and tear excepted. Any possession by Buyer prior to or by Seller after Closing Date shall establish a landlord-
   tenant at sufferance relationship between the parties.

11. SPECIAL PROVISIONS:

   (Insert terms and conditions of a factual nature applicable to this sale, e.g., personal property included in sale [curtains, draperies, valances, etc.],
   prior purchase or sale of other property, lessee's surrender of possession, and the like.)

12. PRORATION: Taxes, insurance, rents, interest and maintenance fees, if any, ☐ SHALL ☐ SHALL NOT be prorated to the Closing Date. If these are not prorated, all funds held in reserve for payment of taxes, maintenance fees and insurance and the insurance policy shall be transferred to the Buyer by Seller without cost to Buyer.

13. SALES EXPENSES TO BE PAID IN CASH AT OR PRIOR TO CLOSING: Preparing Deed, preparing and recording Deed of Trust to Secure Assumption, all inspections, reports and repairs required of Seller herein and in the Addendum and 1/2 of escrow fee shall be Seller's expense. All other costs and expenses incurred in connection with this contract which are not recited herein to be the obligation of Seller, shall be the obligation of Buyer. Unless otherwise paid, before Buyer shall be entitled to refund of Earnest Money, any such costs and expenses shall be deducted therefrom and paid to the creditors entitled thereto. If any sales expenses exceed the maximum amount herein stipulated to be paid by either party, either party may terminate this contract unless the other party agrees to pay such excess.

14. TITLE APPROVAL: If Abstract is furnished, Seller shall deliver same to Buyer within 20 days from the effective date hereof. Buyer shall have 20 days from date of receipt of Abstract to deliver a copy of the title opinion to Seller, stating any objections to title, and only objections so stated shall be considered. If Title Policy is furnished, the Title Policy shall guarantee Buyer's title to be good and indefeasible subject only to (i) restrictive covenants affecting the Property (ii) any discrepancies, conflicts or shortages in area or boundary lines or any encroachments, or any overlapping of improvements (iii) all taxes for the current and subsequent years (iv) any existing building and zoning ordinances (v) rights of parties in possession (vi) any liens assumed or created as security for the sale consideration and (vii) any reservations or exceptions contai~ ed in the Deed. In either instance, if title objections are disclosed, Seller shall have 30 days to cure the same. Exceptions permitted in the Deed and zoning ordinances shall not be valid objections to title. Seller shall furnish at Seller's expense tax statements showing no delinquent taxes and a General Warranty Deed conveying title subject only to liens securing debt created or assumed as part of the consideration, taxes for the current year, usual restrictive covenants and utility easements common to the platted subdivision of which the Property is a part and any other reservations or exceptions acceptable to Buyer. Each note herein provided shall be secured by Vendor's and Deed of Trust liens. A Vendor's lien shall be retained and a Deed of Trust to Secure Assumption required, which shall be automatically released on execution and delivery of a release by noteholder. In the case of dispute as to the form of Deed, Note(s) or Deed(s) of Trust, such shall be upon a form prepared by the State Bar of

15. CASUALTY LOSS: If any part of Property is damaged or destroyed by fire or other casualty loss, Seller shall restore the same to its previous condition as soon as reasonably possible, but in any event by Closing Date; and if Seller is unable to do so without fault, this contract shall terminate and Earnest Money shall be refunded with no Broker's fee due.

16. DEFAULT: If Buyer fails to comply herewith, Seller may either enforce specific performance or terminate this contract and receive the Earnest Money as liquidated damages, one-half of which (but not exceeding the herein recited Broker's fee) shall be paid by Seller to Broker in full payment for Broker's services. If Seller is unable without fault to deliver Abstract or Title Policy or to make any non-casualty repairs required herein within the time herein specified, Buyer may either terminate this contract and receive the Earnest Money as the sole remedy, and no Broker's fee shall be earned, or extend the time up to 30 days. If Seller fails to comply herewith for any other reason, Buyer may (i) terminate this contract and receive the Earnest Money, thereby releasing Seller from this contract (ii) enforce specific performance hereof or (iii) seek such other relief as may be provided by law. If completion of sale is prevented by Buyer's default, and Seller elects to enforce specific performance, the Broker's fee is payable only if and when Seller collects damages for such default by suit, compromise, settlement or otherwise, and after first deducting the expenses of collection, and then only in an amount equal to one-half of that portion collected, but not exceeding the amount of Broker's fee.

17. ATTORNEY'S FEES: Any signatory to this contract who is the prevailing party in any legal proceeding against any other signatory brought under or with relation to this contract or transaction shall be additionally entitled to recover court costs and reasonable attorney fees from the non-prevailing party.

18. ESCROW: Earnest Money is deposited with Escrow Agent with the understanding that Escrow Agent (i) does not assume or have any liability for performance or nonperformance of any party (ii) has the right to require the receipt, release and authorization in writing of all parties before paying the deposit to any party and (iii) is not liable for interest or other charge on the funds held. If any party unreasonably fails to agree in writing to an appropriate release of Earnest Money, then such party shall be liable to the other parties to the extent provided in paragraph 17. At closing, Earnest Money shall be applied to any cash down payment required, next to Buyer's closing costs and any excess refunded to Buyer. Before Buyer shall be entitled to refund of Earnest Money, any actual expenses incurred or paid on Buyer's behalf shall be deducted therefrom and paid to the creditors entitled thereto.

19. REPRESENTATIONS: Seller represents that unless securing payment of the Note there will be no Title I liens, unrecorded liens or Uniform Commercial Code liens against any of the Property on Closing Date, that loan(s) will be without default, and reserve deposits will not be deficient. If any representation above is untrue this contract may be terminated by Buyer and the Earnest Money shall be refunded without delay. Representations shall survive closing.

20. THIRD PARTY FINANCING: If financing by Third Party under 3C(2) above is required herein, Buyer shall have 15 days from effective date hereof to obtain the same, and failure to secure the same after reasonable effort shall render this contract null and void, and the Earnest Money refunded without delay.

21. AGREEMENT OF PARTIES: This contract contains the entire agreement of the parties and cannot be changed except by their written consent.

22. CONSULT YOUR ATTORNEY: This is intended to be a legally binding contract. READ IT CAREFULLY. If you do not understand the effect of any part, consult your attorney BEFORE signing. The Broker cannot give you legal advice — only factual and business details concerning land and improvements. Attorneys to represent parties may be designated below, and, so employment may be accepted, Broker shall promptly deliver a copy of this contract to such attorneys.

Seller's Atty: _____ Buyer's Atty: _____

EXECUTED in multiple originals effective the _____ day of _____, 19 _____. **(BROKER FILL IN THE DATE LAST PARTY SIGNS).**

Listing Broker	License No.	Seller
By _____		Seller
Co-Broker	License No.	Seller's Address _____ Tel.
By _____		Buyer
Receipt of $ _____ Earnest Money is acknowledged in the form		Buyer
of _____		Buyer's Address _____ Tel.
Escrow Agent	Date	
By _____		

Appendix K

CREDIT APPLICATION

BORROWER INFORMATION

Name		Date of birth		Social security number	
Home phone (give area code)	His work phone Her work phone		Present address (include zip code)		
Name and address of present landlord or agent		Present rent		Length at present address	
Previous address (include zip code)		Previous rent		Length at previous address	
Employer (name and address)		Employment length	Monthly income		
Position held		Marital status		Number of dependents	
Previous employer		Employment length	Monthly income		
Other income source		Type	Monthly income		

CO-BORROWER INFORMATION

Name		Date of birth		Social security number	
Employer (name and address)		Employment length	Monthly income		
Position held		Marital status		Number of dependents	
Previous employer		Employment length	Monthly income		
Other income source		Type	Monthly income		

Names of nearest relatives not living with you

Name	Address	Telephone number (area code)
Name	Address	Telephone number (area code)
Name	Address	Telephone number (area code)

Bank		Checking account #	Savings account #

Cash in bank	Furniture and household goods		Other assets

Location and type of real estate owned	Value of property	Name of mortgagee	Unpaid balance	Monthly payment

Value of automobiles

Make	Year	Model	Value	Lender	Unpaid balance	Monthly payment
Make	Year	Model	Value	Lender	Unpaid balance	Monthly payment
Make	Year	Model	Value	Lender	Unpaid balance	Monthly payment

Name of creditor	Original debt	Unpaid balance	Monthly payment	Amount past due (if any)
Name of creditor	Original debt	Unpaid balance	Monthly payment	Amount past due (if any)
Name of creditor	Original debt	Unpaid balance	Monthly payment	Amount past due (if any)
Name of creditor	Original debt	Unpaid balance	Monthly payment	Amount past due (if any)
Name of creditor	Original debt	Unpaid balance	Monthly payment	Amount past due (if any)
Name of creditor	Original debt	Unpaid balance	Monthly payment	Amount past due (if any)
Name of creditor	Original debt	Unpaid balance	Monthly payment	Amount past due (if any)

Child support obligation	Job related expenses

I hereby certify that all statements are true and complete to the best of my knowledge and are made for the purpose of obtaining credit. I authorize you to obtain such information as you may require concerning the statements made in this application and agree that the application shall remain your property whether the loan is granted or not.

Borrower's signature	Co-borrower's signature
Date	Date

Appendix L
Property Condition Addendum Form

THE PROPERTY CONDITION ADDENDUM FORM ALLOWS THE BUYER THE RIGHT TO INSPECT THE PROPERTY. Make sure you write the address of the property on the first blank to tie this form in with the main contract.

If you are selling a marginal property, in an "as is" condition at a substantial discount, then don't use this form. On the other hand, if you know your house is in tip-top condition, then use this form and *check all the boxes*, whether they apply to your property or not.

By checking all the boxes you are allowing the buyer to inspect the house and are more or less relieving yourself of liability in case there are problems once he moves in and he didn't do an inspection. Of course, if you've hidden structural or mechanical defects, you could end up with a lawsuit later on even if he doesn't have the property professionally inspected.

This form is self-explanatory. If you are selling the property in good condition, with exceptions for known defects, then you should leave blank those items that pertain to the problems, and *make a note of the problems* on one of the blank lines, stating that the buyer acknowledges existence of the problem and is buying the house "as is" with respect to that problem.

Under C, if you are going to do repairs, make sure you state specifically what you will repair, or put a limit on the amount to be spent on repairs. Generally, it is better just to give the buyer credit in a lump sum so you don't have problems with cost overruns on repairs the buyer may force you to make. This won't work with some lenders, though. Often, if there are problems, the lender wants the problems corrected before he funds a loan. For example, if the roof leaks, the lender or the FHA or VA will want the roof replaced or fixed before closing. It's smart business on their part. Otherwise, if it never gets done, and they have to foreclose, they'll have to do the repairs themselves.

PROPERTY CONDITION ADDENDUM

ADDENDUM TO EARNEST MONEY CONTRACT BETWEEN THE UNDERSIGNED PARTIES
CONCERNING THE PROPERTY AT _1237 MAIN ST, DALLAS_

(Street Address and City)

CHECK APPLICABLE BOXES:

☒ A. TERMITES: Buyer, at Buyer's expense (except at Seller's expense in VA transactions), may have the Property inspected by a Structural Pest Control Business Licensee to determine whether or not there is visible evidence of active termite infestation or visible termite damage to the improvements. If termite treatment or repairs are required, Buyer will furnish a written report to Seller from such Licensee within _30_ days from the effective date of this Contract, but no treatment or repairs will be required for fences, trees or shrubs. Buyer's failure to furnish such report to Seller within the time specified shall constitute a waiver of Buyer's right to any treatment and repairs.

☒ B. INSPECTIONS: Buyer, at Buyer's expense, may have any of the items designated below inspected by inspectors of Buyer's choice. Repairs will only be required of items designated by this Contract for inspection and reported to be in need of immediate repair or which are not performing the function for which intended. Failure of Buyer to furnish written inspection reports and to designate the repairs to which Buyer is entitled by this Contract within the times specified below shall be deemed a waiver of Buyer's repair rights.

STRUCTURAL: Buyer requires inspections of the following: (check applicable boxes)

☒ foundation, ☒ roof, ☒ load bearing walls, ☒ ceilings, ☐ basement, ☒ water penetration, ☒ fireplace and chimney, ☒ floors,
☒ and _STORAGE BUILDING_

Within _30_ days from the effective date of this Contract, Buyer will furnish Seller written inspection reports with a designation of repairs if repairs are required.

EQUIPMENT AND SYSTEMS: Buyer requires inspections of the following: (check applicable boxes)

☒ plumbing system (including any water heater, wells and septic system), ☒ electrical system, ☒ all heating and cooling units and systems,
☒ any built-in range, oven, dishwasher, disposer, exhaust fans, trash compactor, ☒ swimming pool and related mechanical equipment, ☒ sprinkler systems,
☐ gas lines (inspection by private inspector) ☐ gas lines (inspection by gas supplier) ☐ and _____

Within _____ days from the effective date of this Contract, Buyer will furnish Seller written inspection reports with a designation of repairs if repairs are required.

☒ C. OTHER REPAIRS: Seller shall make the following repairs in addition to those required above: _REPLACE BROKEN OVERHEAD GARAGE DOOR_

All inspections shall be by persons who regularly provide such service and who are either registered as inspectors with the Texas Real Estate Commission or otherwise permitted by law to perform inspections. Repairs shall be by trained and qualified persons who are, whenever possible, manufacturer-approved service persons and who are licensed or bonded whenever such license or bond is required by law. Seller shall permit access to the Property at any reasonable time for inspection or repairs and for reinspection after repairs have been completed. Seller shall only be responsible for termite treatment and repairs to termite damage, repairs to items specifically designated above for inspection, and repairs specifically described in Paragraph C, subject to the provisions of Paragraph 7 of this Contract. Broker and sales associates shall not be liable or responsible for any inspections or repairs pursuant to this Contract and Addendum.

SELLER _____   BUYER _____

SELLER _____   BUYER _____

PROPERTY CONDITION ADDENDUM

ADDENDUM TO EARNEST MONEY CONTRACT BETWEEN THE UNDERSIGNED PARTIES CONCERNING THE PROPERTY AT _____

(Street Address and City)

CHECK APPLICABLE BOXES:

☐ A. TERMITES: Buyer, at Buyer's expense (except at Seller's expense in VA transactions), may have the Property inspected by a Structural Pest Control Business Licensee to determine whether or not there is visible evidence of active termite infestation or visible termite damage to the improvements. If termite treatment

or repairs are required, Buyer will furnish a written report to Seller from such Licensee within _____days from the effective date of this Contract, but no treatment or repairs will be required for fences, trees or shrubs. Buyer's failure to furnish such report to Seller within the time specified shall constitute a waiver of Buyer's right to any treatment and repairs.

☐ B. INSPECTIONS: Buyer, at Buyer's expense, may have any of the items designated below inspected by inspectors of Buyer's choice. Repairs will only be required of items designated by this Contract for inspection and reported to be in need of immediate repair or which are not performing the function for which intended. Failure of Buyer to furnish written inspection reports and to designate the repairs to which Buyer is entitled by this Contract within the times specified below shall be deemed a waiver of Buyer's repair rights.

STRUCTURAL: Buyer requires inspections of the following: (check applicable boxes)

☐ foundation, ☐ roof, ☐ load bearing walls, ☐ ceilings, ☐ basement, ☐ water penetration, ☐ fireplace and chimney, ☐ floors.
☐ and _____
_____

Within _____days from the effective date of this Contract, Buyer will furnish Seller written inspection reports with a designation of repairs if repairs are required.

EQUIPMENT AND SYSTEMS: Buyer requires inspections of the following: (check applicable boxes)

☐ plumbing system (including any water heater, wells and septic system), ☐ electrical system, ☐ all heating and cooling units and systems,
☐ any built-in range, oven, dishwasher, disposer, exhaust fans, trash compactor, ☐ swimming pool and related mechanical equipment, ☐ sprinkler systems,
☐ gas lines (inspection by private inspector) ☐ gas lines (inspection by gas supplier) ☐ and _____
_____

Within _____days from the effective date of this Contract, Buyer will furnish Seller written inspection reports with a designation of repairs if repairs are required.

☐ C. OTHER REPAIRS: Seller shall make the following repairs in addition to those required above: _____
_____
_____

All inspections shall be by persons who regularly provide such service and who are either registered as inspectors with the   Real Estate Commission or otherwise permitted by law to perform inspections. Repairs shall be by trained and qualified persons who are, whenever possible, manufacturer-approved service persons and who are licensed or bonded whenever such license or bond is required by law. Seller shall permit access to the Property at any reasonable time for inspection or repairs and for reinspection after repairs have been completed. Seller shall only be responsible for termite treatment and repairs to termite damage, repairs to items specifically designated above for inspection, and repairs specifically described in Paragraph C, subject to the provisions of Paragraph 7 of this Contract. Broker and sales associates shall not be liable or responsible for any inspections or repairs pursuant to this Contract and Addendum.

_____   _____
SELLER   BUYER

_____   _____
SELLER   BUYER

Appendix M

WARRANTY DEED
(LONG FORM)

THE STATE OF   Texas

COUNTY OF   Dallas   }   KNOW ALL MEN BY THESE PRESENTS:

That Jack B. Nimble and wife, Sandy W. Nimble

(hereinafter called Grantor(s),

of the County of   Dallas   and State of   Texas   for and in

consideration of the sum of   ten and 00/100 ($10.00)----------------------- DOLLARS

and other valuable consideration to the undersigned paid by the grantee s   herein named, the receipt of which

is hereby acknowledged, and for the further consideration that the Grantee(s) hereby assume(s) and promise(s) to pay,

according to the terms thereof, all principal and interest now remaining unpaid on that one certain promissory note in the

original principal sum of $90,000.00   payable to the order of   Olive Oil's
Investment Company

and secured by a vendor's lien

retained in Deed of even date therewith recorded in Volume   388-456   Page(s)   197

of the Deed Records of the hereinbelow stated County, Texas, and additionally secured by a Deed of Trust of even date therewith

to   John Smith

Trustee, recorded in

Volume   397-455   Page(s)   216   of the Deed of Trust Records of said County, Tex, and

Grantee(s) assume(s) and promise(s) to keep and perform all of the covenants and obligations of the Grantor(s) named in

said Deed of Trust;

have GRANTED, SOLD AND CONVEYED, and by these presents do GRANT, SELL AND CONVEY unto

Lady N. Shoe, a single woman

of the County of   Dallas   and State of   Texas   , all of

the following described real property in   Dallas   County, Tex, to-wit:

All that certain lot, tract or parcel of land, described as follows: Being Lot 5, Block 9 of Forest
Park, an Addition to the City of Dallas, Texas, according to the Map
thereof recorded in Volume 188, Page 2179, Map Records of Dallas
County, Texas.

TO HAVE AND TO HOLD the above described premises, together with all and singular the rights and appurtenances thereto in anywise belonging, unto the said grantee her heirs and assigns forever; and we do hereby bind ourselves, our heirs, executors and administrators to WARRANT AND FOREVER DEFEND all and singular the said premises unto the said grantee her heirs and assigns, against every person whomsoever lawfully claiming or to claim the same or any part thereof.

BUT IT IS EXPRESSLY AGREED that the Grantor(s) herein expressly reserve for themselves, their heirs and assigns, the Vendor's Lien as well as the Superior Title in and to the above described property, premises and improvements, until the note and indebtedness herein assumed by the Grantee(s) has been fully paid according to the face, tenor, effect and reading thereof, when this Deed shall become absolute, and to additionally secure the Grantor(s) herein in the payment of the note and indebtedness so assumed, the Grantee(s) ha executed and delivered a Deed of Trust to Secure Assumption of even date herewith conveying the herein described property.

EXECUTED this   12th   day of   November   , A. D. 19 87

Jack B. Nimble
_____

Sandy W. Nimble
_____

(Acknowledgment)

STATE OF TEXAS
COUNTY OF DALLAS

This instrument was acknowledged before me on the 12th day of   November   , 19 87
by Jack B. Nimble and wife Sandy W. Nimble
My commission expires: 4/30/91

Jack S. Doe, Notary Public
_____

WARRANTY DEED
(LONG FORM)

THE STATE OF

COUNTY OF

} KNOW ALL MEN BY THESE PRESENTS:

That

(hereinafter called Grantor(s),

of the County of   and State of   for and in

consideration of the sum of   DOLLARS

and other valuable consideration to the undersigned paid by the grantee s   herein named, the receipt of which

is hereby acknowledged, and for the further consideration that the Grantee(s) hereby assume(s) and promise(s) to pay,

according to the terms thereof, all principal and interest now remaining unpaid on that one certain promissory note in the

original principal sum of   payable to the order of

and secured by a vendor's lien

retained in Deed of even date therewith recorded in Volume   Page(s)

of the Deed Records of the hereinbelow stated County,   , and additionally secured by a Deed of Trust of even date therewith

to   Trustee, recorded in

Volume   Page(s)   of the Deed of Trust Records of said County,   , and

Grantee(s) assume(s) and promise(s) to keep and perform all of the covenants and obligations of the Grantor(s) named in

said Deed of Trust;

have GRANTED, SOLD AND CONVEYED, and by these presents do GRANT, SELL AND CONVEY unto

of the County of   and State of   , all of

the following described real property in   County,   , to-wit:

All that certain lot, tract or parcel of land, described as follows:

TO HAVE AND TO HOLD the above described premises, together with all and singular the rights and appurtenances thereto in anywise belonging, unto the said grantee   heirs and assigns forever; and   do hereby bind   heirs, executors and administrators to WARRANT AND FOREVER DEFEND all and singular the said premises unto the said grantee

heirs and assigns, against every person whomsoever lawfully claiming or to claim the same or any part thereof.

BUT IT IS EXPRESSLY AGREED that the Grantor(s) herein expressly reserve for themselves, their heirs and assigns, the Vendor's Lien as well as the Superior Title in and to the above described property, premises and improvements, until the note and indebtedness herein assumed by the Grantee(s) has been fully paid according to the face, tenor, effect and reading thereof, when this Deed shall become absolute, and to additionally secure the Grantor(s) herein in the payment of the note and indebtedness so assumed, the Grantee(s) ha   executed and delivered a Deed of Trust to Secure Assumption of even date herewith conveying the herein described property.

EXECUTED this   day of   , A. D. 19

_____

_____

(Acknowledgment)

STATE OF

COUNTY OF

This instrument was acknowledged before me on the   day of   , 19

by

My commission expires:

_____

Appendix N

OPEN LISTING AGREEMENT

This agreement authorizes _____ agent, to show to prospective buyers (a phone appointment must be made before showing the property), my property located at:

_____

_____

If the property is sold, traded, exchanged or otherwise disposed of by me, at the amount stated below, or any sum that I may accept, to any purchaser with whom the agent has had negotiations and to whom the agent has shown the property, and whose name has been furnished by the agent to me in writing, within six months after the date of showing, I agree to pay agent a commission of $ _____ or _____ % of the final sale price.

This contract will become null and void if I, at any time in the future, grant an EXCLUSIVE AGENCY AND RIGHT TO SELL to a particular agent.

Sales price $ _____.

Owner _____ Date _____

Owner _____ Date _____

Appendix O

Prospect Cards

Name _____ Source _____

Address _____ Home Phone _____

City and Zip _____ Work Phone _____

Needs: Size _____ Mo. Pmt. _____ Down Pmt. _____

Location _____ Income _____

Lit. Sent _____ Liab. _____

Appt. Set _____ Where _____

Date Shown _____

Name _____ Source _____

Address _____ Home Phone _____

City and Zip _____ Work Phone _____

Needs: Size _____ Mo. Pmt. _____ Down Pmt. _____

Location _____ Income _____

Lit. Sent _____ Liab. _____

Appt. Set _____ Where _____

Date Shown _____

Glossary

abstract of title—A brief history of the previous ownership of property, including all liens or encumbrances and any claims against the property.

acceleration clause—A term of a home mortgage loan that gives the lender the right to call all sums owed immediately due upon a certain event, such as the sale of the home.

acceptance—Favorable approval of an offer or purchase contract by the seller. Acceptance of an offer means that both parties have signed a binding contract.

acre—A measure of land area which equals 43,560 square feet. An acre lot is approximately 210' × 210'.

adjustable rate mortgage—Established for federally chartered savings and loan companies, a type of mortgage in which lenders have power to vary a loan's interest rate from month to month to keep pace with current market rates.

agent—An authorized representative acting in behalf of a client and usually working under the legal responsibility of a real estate broker. Sometimes used synonymously with *broker*.

amenities—Natural or man-made attractions which increase the value of property, such as trees, nearby parks, a beautiful view, a marble tub, a swimming pool, etc.

amortization—The paying off of a loan, in installments, normally in equal monthly payments. The payments are made large enough to pay both interest and part of the principal, so the debt is gradually reduced and completely paid off at the end of the loan period.

appraisal—An estimate of the value of a property on a given date.

appreciation—An increase in the value of property caused by changes in economic conditions, improvements in the neighborhood, time, etc.

appurtenances—Property rights, privileges, or improvements. Although they are not strictly a part of the land, they go with the title to the new owner. Examples are easements, rights of way, orchards, etc.

assessed value—A value placed on property for the sake of tax collection.

assessment—A government-imposed tax for a specific purpose such as a street improvement, a sewer, etc. The assessment is levied against those who benefit the most from the improvement.

assumptions—Taking over payments of, and primary responsibility for, an existing loan under all of its terms, without the loan being renegotiated.

balloon payments—Payment of a loan in one lump sum after a predetermined period of time during which smaller, regular payments have been made.

bench mark—A permanently fixed marker in the ground, such as a metal marker, which surveyors use to establish property lines and elevation. Also called a monument.

binder—A short-term agreement by which the buyer and seller tentatively agree on the terms of a contract.

bird-dog fee—A fee given to an individual who directs a buyer to a seller, but who doesn't actually act as an agent for the seller.

breach—The act of breaking a contract.

broker—A person licensed by the state who sells real estate for a commission. A broker is usually hired by the seller. Sometimes used synonymously with *agent*.

buy-down—A creative financing method to decrease the interest rate or reduce the payment for the first three to five years on a home mortgage loan.

buyers' market—A market in which the buyer has better negotiating leverage than the seller; as a rule, when there are more houses than there are buyers.

carrying charges—The money it costs to own property, including mortgage payments, insurance, taxes, and maintenance. This is equivalent to the rent one would pay for an apartment or house.

caveat emptor—"Let the buyer beware." The buyer purchases real estate in an as-is condition and must investigate and take the risks which go with any purchase. The seller cannot be held responsible for the quality of the property unless guaranteed in a warranty.

chattel mortgage—A mortgage on personal property.

chattels—Personal property.

close of escrow (closing)—Signing of final papers and exchange of funds for the sale of a home.

closing costs—The miscellaneous charges, over and above the cost of the house, paid by the buyer and the seller at closing, when the deed to the property is transferred from the seller to the buyer.

collateral—Security such as bonds, jewelry, real estate, or other marketable items pledged for payment of a loan.

commitment—A promise made by a lender to make a specific loan to a specific person.

community property—Property acquired by a husband, a wife, or by both together which is considered to be jointly owned and equally shared. Community property laws are in effect in only a few states.

condominium—A unit within a multiple-unit dwelling. The owner of the unit has full title to the unit and has joint ownership, with the owners of the other units, in the common grounds of the complex.

contingency—In a contract, a point or condition that has not yet been accepted by both parties to the contract.

contract—A legal agreement between or among two or more parties that binds each to fulfill a specific promise or promises.

contract for deed (sale on contract)—A creative real estate transaction method that allows a buyer to purchase property without qualifying for a loan, and without receiving a deed to the property.

conventional loan—A mortgage which is not insured by the FHA nor guaranteed by the VA. The loan rates and conditions are set by the lender, subject to some controls by the government.

conveyance—The transfer of ownership of real estate by deed from one party to another.

counteroffer—An offer proposed in response to an original offer that was not completely satisfactory to the party making the counteroffer.

covenant—A promise or agreement between two parties usually applied to specific promises in a deed.

creative financing—An unconventional method of obtaining funds to purchase property.

credit unions—A cooperative association of members (usually employees of a company), formed to save money, make loans, and share profits. A cooperative bank.

deed—A document which describes property and is used to transfer ownership of that property.

deed of trust—Used in some states in place of a mortgage. The buyer deeds the property to a third party (a trustee), who holds the deed in trust to guarantee that the buyer will repay lender.

default—The failure to meet a promise on a contract, including not paying money when due, or not complying with other provisions of the contract.

deposit—A small down payment given by the buyer when the buyer makes an offer to purchase. The deposit may become the earnest money when the contract is signed, or the buyer may have to add money to the deposit to constitute the earnest money.

depreciation—The decrease in value of property caused by age, wear and tear, changing neighborhood conditions, etc.

down payment—The money a buyer must pay in cash on a house before being granted a loan.

due-on-sale clause—A clause in a mortgage or deed of trust which requires that the entire amount of a loan become due immediately because of a certain breach of the terms of the instrument by the borrower. Typically, on a conventional non-assumable loan, the breach occurs if the borrower sells the property without the consent of the lender.

earnest money—A payment made as evidence of a serious buyer's intent to go through with the purchase of real estate, usually between 1% and 2% of the purchase price. It is given by the buyer upon the signing of a contract for the sale of real estate. If the buyer defaults in carrying out the contract, the money is usually forfeited to the seller.

easement—The right, privilege, or interest which one party has in the land of another owner.

eminent domain—The right of the government to take over part or all of a person's property for public use. This may be done with or without the owner's consent. The government must pay the owner the fair price for his property.

encroachment—A trespass or invasion over the property line of another person, such as a fence, a building overhang, etc.

equity—The interest or value an owner has in real estate over and above the remaining mortgages. The equity is the difference between the selling price of the house and the unpaid mortgage(s).

escalation clause—A clause written into some loan agreements which permits the lender to raise or lower the interest rate, without the borrower's consent, as business conditions change. The right of a lender to force the borrower to prepay the entire principal balance because of conditions in the note and mortgage or deed of trust.

escrow—A third, neutral party which holds and processes documents, initiates necessary paperwork, collects money due, pays out money due, etc. Also, the amount a lender collects from the owner and uses to pay taxes and insurance on the owner's property.

escrow account—See *impound account.*

et al.—Legal doubletalk for "and others."

et ux.—Legal doubletalk for "and wife."

exclusive listing contract—A contract between the seller of a home and his real estate agent, giving that agent exclusive rights to represent him and the buyers of the home.

existing loan—A loan that is currently active.

Fannie Mae—Federal National Mortgage Association; a real estate lender that buys groups of mortgages from lenders who originate the loans.

fee simple—Ownership of real estate, free from all conditions and limitations. Complete ownership of land.

FHA—The Federal Housing Administration, an agency of the federal government.

FmHA—The Farmers Home Administration, an agency of the federal government.

first mortgage—The mortgage that is the first lien on the property; the principal mortgage. This has first claim (after delinquent taxes, if any) on the money realized in a foreclosure.

fixed interest rates—Loan interest rates that will not change during the life of the loan.

fixture—Personal property which has become real property because it is attached to the real property, or agreed by both parties to pass with the property, or because of local custom.

foreclosure—When a lender, by legal proceedings, forces the sale of a mortgaged property to recover the loan money remaining when a borrower defaults on a loan.

Freddie Mac—Federal Home Loan Mortgage Association, a real estate lender that buys groups of mortgages from lenders who originate the loans.

FSBO—For sale by owner. For sale without the services of a real estate agent.

graduated payments—Mortgage payments in which initial payments are initially less than they would be for a standard amortized loan, but in which payments increase after five to seven years to levels slightly higher (sometimes substantially higher) than they would have been for a standard amortized loan.

GI mortgage—A VA mortgage loan.

grantee—The buyer of real estate. The term often used in a deed.

grantor—The seller of real estate. The term often used in a deed.

guaranty—A promise to answer for performance of an obligation.

hard money—Cash borrowed under stringent payback terms such as high interest rates, an advance fee, and a short-term payback date.

impound account—A trust account that is established by a lender to accumulate monies to cover the cost of items such as taxes and insurance policy premiums. The money usually is collected at the time regular payments are made for the loan. Also called an escrow account.

installment sales—A real estate transaction wherein the seller carries the secondary financing on the home (becoming a lender to the buyer) and takes payments on that loan over a period of two or more tax years.

interest rate—The percentage of the principal amount of a loan that is charged per year for the use of the money.

joint tenancy—Property jointly owned by two or more persons. Each can assume full title to the property if the other dies, to avoid probate.

land lease—See *contract for deed*.

lease/purchase option—A contract under the terms of which one party (the prospective seller) gives to another party (the prospective buyer) the possession and use of property for a fixed payment and fixed time period; at the end of that time, the prospective buyer has the right to exercise an option to buy the property at a predetermined price.

lien—A hold or legal claim a person has on the property of another as security for a debt (such as a mortgage, mechanic's lien, unpaid taxes).

listing contract—A contract authorizing a real estate agent or broker to sell a home on behalf of a seller.

lock-in period—The amount of time before closing that a lender will guarantee the interest rate on a loan it expects to originate for the prospective borrower.

market value—The amount buyers will pay for a given property at a given time. The value of property on an open market.

marketable title—A title to a property, not completely clear, but with only minor objections which a court would require a buyer to accept.

mechanic's lien—A hold or claim on the property of another as security for an unpaid bill of a building contractor, material supplier or workman.

MIP—Mortgage insurance premium.

mortgage—An instrument, recognized by law, that secures payment of a debt.

mortgagee—The institution or individual which lends the money.

mortgage insurance—An insurance policy that protects the lender's loan in case of borrower default.

mortgagor—The person who borrows the money, using property as security.

note—A written agreement, sometimes secured by a mortgage or deed of trust, by which the borrower acknowledges the debt and promises to pay it in a specified time. A home buyer usually signs a note as well as a mortgage at closing. Also called a promissory note.

offer—A document signed by the buyer offering to buy certain real estate at a specific price. The signed acceptance of the seller makes it a contract if all the essential items are covered.

open end mortgage—A mortgage having a clause which permits the homeowner to refinance the mortgage in the future to raise funds without having to rewrite the mortgage and pay closing costs again.

open house—Opening a home that is for sale for public inspection without appointment.

option—The right to buy property at a specified price within a stated time. If the owner receives consideration (e.g. money), the owner is bound to honor the option.

origination and processing fees—Fees lenders charge for granting a mortgage and processing a loan. May include points if money is tight.

personal property—All types of movable, tangible items which people can own.

PI—Principal and interest.

PITI—Principal, interest, taxes, and insurance.

plat—A map showing the planned use of land, such as the layout of lots on a tract of land.

plot plan—The architectural plan showing the location of a house in relation to the lot.

PMI—Private mortgage insurance.

points—One point is 1% of the principal amount of a loan. Points are charged by lenders to compensate for loss of income due to the granting of loans at below market value rates.

prepayment penalty—A clause in a loan contract that allows the lender to charge an interest penalty if the borrower pays the loan in full prior to the end of the loan's lifetime.

principal—The seller or the buyer. Also, the base amount of money owed on a loan.

private mortgage insurance—An insurance policy issued by a private insurance company, as opposed to one by the FHA.

promissory note—See *note*.

qualify—To meet the financial requirements of a lender when applying for a loan.

quitclaim deed—A legal instrument which transfers title of property without warranties. It conveys whatever interest the owner has in the property. The buyer is responsible for any claims brought against the property.

real property (real estate)—The land and everything built or growing on it, or attached to it.

realtor—A person licensed by the state to sell real estate and who is also a member of The National Association of Realtors. A trademark of that association.

recording—Placing a transaction into the public records at the county courthouse.

refinance—Acquiring a new loan to pay in full a current loan that is due.

restrictive covenants—An agreement limiting the use of property. It is usually undertaken by land developers or neighborhood property owners to preserve open space or to prevent undesirable businesses or non-residential activities.

second mortgage—Also *second lien*. A mortgage given in addition to the first mortgage. The holder of the second mortgage has second priority on the funds realized in case of a foreclosure and sale of the property.

setback—The distance (specified by a zoning ordinance or restrictive covenant) that must be left between a building and the boundaries of the lot.

short-term loan—A loan that has a payback date sooner than is normal for most real estate loans.

simple interest—A method of computing interest rates making interest due based on the unpaid balance of the principal at the end of each pay period. Most home mortgages are of this kind.

single-family dwelling—A single structure built to house one family on a separate lot.

square footage—A measure of area. Multiply the length times the width (both in feet) to obtain the square footage or living space of a room, house, or lot. The square footage of a house is figured using the *exterior* structure dimensions.

sub-escrow—A second, nonconcurrent escrow completed on a house in order to skirt lender rules that do not allow secondary financing.

subsidized loan—A loan wherein interest rates are supplemented from a secondary source (as in buydowns).

survey—The process of determining the precise location and boundaries of a piece of land.

tax shelter—A financial investment, such as the purchase of real estate, made in order to have deductible expenses to reduce one's income taxes.

tenancy-in-common—The sharing by two or more parties (as co-buyers) in ownership of a property, without the right of survivorship. If one dies, the other does not assume full ownership of the property; each partner has the right to will his or her portion of the property to another party.

tender—An offer of money.

third mortgage—A loan that is obtained for the purchase of a home, in addition to the first and second loans acquired for its purchase.

tight-money market—A time in which loan money is scarce; commonly, this is due to inflation and high interest rates.

timesharing—Property bought in blocks of time; usually condominium units sold by the week. The buyer purchases only those weeks during which he or she intends to use the unit, thus becoming co-owner of a single unit with several other buyers.

title—A document evidencing a person's ownership rights to a particular piece of property.

title insurance—A policy written by a title company which guarantees the title to property. If the title becomes clouded because of a claim of prior ownership by someone else, the title company must make good any losses arising from these defects.

title search—An examination of public records to find out the history of ownership of property. It determines legal status of property.

transfer—A change of ownership of property.

trust deed—See *deed of trust*.

usury—Interest rates charged in excess of that permitted by law.

VA—Veterans Administration.

valuation—An estimate of a property's worth.

vendee—The buyer of real estate.

vendor—The seller of real estate.

waiver—Voluntarily giving up a claim, right, or privilege.

walk-through—A home buyer's final inspection of the property prior to the close of escrow.

warranty—A guarantee by the seller that the title is conveyed as stated in the deed.

wraparounds—A creative financing method wherein the sellers continue to make payments on their original bank loan and receive payments from the buyers for that loan and for the secondary financing that the sellers are carrying. The two loans are "wrapped" together for one monthly payment by the buyer.

zoning—Municipal laws which regulate the uses to which land can be put.

About the Author

Maurice Dubois graduated from Trinity University in San Antonio, Texas, with a major in home building. During the past twenty years he has designed and built several hundred homes, developed a half-dozen subdivisions, and designed and built countless remodeling projects. He has had building and real estate experience in Illinois, Iowa, and Texas.

He is a licensed Texas real estate broker and currently owns and manages a real estate company in the Dallas suburb of Grand Prairie, Texas. His company specializes in the sale of distressed, foreclosed, and owner-financed property throughout the Dallas/Fort Worth metropolitan area.

Dubois and his investment partners own an extensive inventory of rental homes and small multi-family units. They also purchase distressed property, rehabilitate it, and resell it through creative financing means.

Dubois has written other books, including a home building manual, a guide for home buyers, and two novels.

Index

Edited by Carl H. Silverman